A
CASEBOOK
OF
SOCIAL
CHANGE

A
CASEBOOK
OF
SOCIAL
CHANGE

EDITED BY ARTHUR H. NIEHOFF, *The University of Nigeria*

ALDINE Publishing Company/*Chicago*

First published 1966 by
Aldine Publishing Company
320 West Adams Street
Chicago, Illinois 60606

Designed by David Miller
Library of Congress Catalog Card Number 66-15206
Printed in the United States of America

Preface

Although this volume is meant to be complete in itself, it has been written as a companion to *Introducing Social Change* by Arensberg and Niehoff (Chicago: Aldine Publishing Company, 1964). In that book, an attempt was made to present in a readable fashion the characteristics of man's customs and habits, particularly those most relevant to success in bringing socioeconomic change to the people of the nonindustrialized nations. The principal influences that have bearing on the change process in those lands were discussed, as well as the primary characteristics of American culture, which can also significantly influence the change process. The book was meant to serve change agents who lacked substantial training in the social sciences as a guide to help in the solution of the social problems inherent in change efforts. We also believed the book would find some use among students of sociocultural change.

Many examples were used to illustrate the points made in *Introducing Social Change*. However, they were all short, consisting of no more than the two or three sentences necessary to exemplify our meaning graphically. The technical change adviser or social science student would be unable to visualize from those brief references the total process of change that took place in each instance. Therefore he would not be in a position to know the inter-relationships of different influences on the change process, that is, how one action on the part of a change agent could help bring about others, or help bring about certain reactions among the recipients. Moreover, he would not have been able to visualize the time element in the change process—what took place in the beginning, the middle, and the end.

Only by seeing case histories in their entirety can the full process of change be clearly understood. This is the primary purpose of the present volume. Here, instead of an analysis of the change process, the student of social change is shown that process as it actually occurred for different change agents, under varying conditions, in several parts of the world. He is thus enabled to undertake analysis and evaluation himself—and as a learning process this is always to be preferred to merely accepting the arguments of another analyst.

Contents

1. Introduction   1
2. The Process of Innovation   10
3. Land Reform and Community Development in Bolivia   42
4. Community Development in Highland Peru   58
5. Community Development in Brazil   77
6. Rural Self-Help in Costa Rica   91
7. The Prevention of Sleeping Sickness in Nigeria   107
8. Resettlement to New Lands in Nigeria   118
9. Venereal Disease Eradication in Northern Rhodesia   124
10. Urban Community Development in South Africa   135
11. Range Management in the Somali Republic   155
12. Developing a Village Co-operative in Israel   164
13. Rural Development in East Pakistan   175
14. Community Development in India   191
15. Health Education in Village India   217
16. Factionalism in Village India   225
17. Buddhism and Development in Laos   233
18. Community Development in Hong Kong   246
19. Family Planning in Taiwan   255
20. Village Improvement in the Philippines   268
21. A Literacy Campaign in Sarawak   291
    Index   307

Introduction

Man is a unique animal. Although he shares most of his physical characteristics with the other warm-blooded mammals, he has developed a different kind of ability to cope with his environment. He has developed a system of symbolic communication called language, a complicated thinking apparatus, an upright posture, and an ability to manipulate his forelimbs with great dexterity. There are some other minor differences separating man from other animals, but these are sufficient to provide an understanding of the basis for man's very singular means of dealing with his universe. As a talking biped, man has developed the ability to learn through time. He inherits vast amounts of knowledge from his predecessors, adds to this storehouse a small amount of new knowledge, and passes it on to his descendants. Basically, this is what we call culture.

Man has progressed from being a primitive hunter and food gatherer in competition with the noncultural animals to a creature who is on the verge of leaving his home base, the planet Earth, in vehicles he has developed by means of his cultural heritage. And though the achievements of great men along the way were necessary for this progressive development, their contributions would have been nothing if the new knowledge they obtained had not been infused into the social groups of which they were a part. And once it was integrated into these groups, it was transferred in each generation by parents instructing their children and teachers instructing their students. Then it became a part of the culture of that group, the total body of knowledge and customs that is passed on from one generation to the next.

It is obvious to anyone who takes a long look at man's cultural history that change is constant. If this were not so, we would not be able to transmit ideas today by means of a cultural complex called printing, nor would we be able to go aloft in aircraft weighing many tons, nor would the majority of the citizens of the more fortunate nations be able to forget about the possibility of not having enough to eat. Even the people of less fortunate nations change, though perhaps less rapidly. The Peruvian Indian herds sheep today whereas his ancient Inca ancestor had only the llama. The more fortunate East Indian villager has a bicycle or a treadle sewing machine today whereas his ancestor of only one or two generations ago went by oxcart or sewed by hand. Thus, we accept for the purpose of this book that one constant among men is that all cultures change, even though such change may take place at different rates.

What is perhaps most obvious to those interested in cultural change is this difference in rate. It can be so varying that some who have not been too familiar with the more exotic cultures of the world have been tempted to say that such people live just as their ancestors did. Such an opinion is not acceptable to a social scientist. Cultures that do not change die out. This has happened with some cultures such as many of the American Indians. However, most cultures of the non-Western world are changing today, even though at a slower rate than their leaders wish and, of course, much slower than the industrialized nations of the Western world. The basic problem is how to induce these cultures to change faster.

We believe that this process of change will become more rapid only when it is understood better than it has been in the past. There are various influences which cause cultures to change, both internal and external. A decrease or increase in population causes a repatterning of customs. Warfare brings new stresses to a culture, as well as new ideas and technical developments. Very significant new inventions, such as the motor vehicle, cause vast changes. And there is the give and take of ideas that takes place without deliberation of either donor or receiver which is called diffusion. Such change is caused by travelers whose devices or ways of doing things impress those who see them so much that they adopt them. One constant source of change is produced by the interaction of people from different cultures. The early Euro-Americans learned from the Indians just because they came in contact with them and saw the advantages of some of their practices, particularly in agriculture. Asians and Africans have been adopting new practices continuously from the Europeans they have been in contact with during the last four hundred years.

What is relatively new is that during the last two decades

a new kind of stimulus to cultural change has been set in motion. The advanced industrial nations have become involved in vast efforts to assist the less fortunate nations to speed up the process of change in their own countries. Basically, they have tried to do this in two ways: economically and technically. The economic approach has been to analyze the means of production, distribution, and consumption of wealth in the receiving nations and attempt to improve these systems by transferring considerable amounts of money or goods to develop those sectors that are deemed essential for sparking economic growth. This technique worked very well in Europe under the Marshall Plan, but it has worked considerably less efficiently in the now developing nations. The other approach has been to try to transfer technical know-how, on the reasonable assumption that technical knowledge has made the industrial nations rich and that other nations are not rich because they lack such expertise. Although this approach has undoubtedly helped the developing nations, it too has fallen short of expectations.

It is our belief that there is a third component which has too often been neglected, but which is equally necessary to induce change in the nonindustrial nations. This is the sociocultural component, which means simply that technical know-how and economic patterns are imbedded in cultural systems, elaborate patterns of customs and beliefs, which can either act as sanctions or barriers to technical or economic change. The simplest example we can give is that of cultural beliefs concerning food. From either an economic or a technical point of view, a system of pork production would be advantageous to most farming people of the earth. However, it is next to useless to consider such a possibility for people of the Islamic faith. They have a cultural belief that pork is not a proper food for man, and neither economic nor technical considerations will change this attitude. The same kind of belief affects Hindus in India in regard to beef. These examples may seem very obvious, and the reader may justifiably say that anyone with just a little familiarity with these cultures would know these facts. However, there are multitudes of beliefs of the same nature that are not so obvious.

To remain in the category of beliefs concerning food, we can mention the difficulties that have arisen because the United States has exported much surplus food familiar to North Americans but often quite strange to Latin Americans, Africans, or Asians. It has been reported that butter has frequently been used as soap. Wheat is frequently rejected by rice eaters, since they are unfamiliar with it and cannot visualize it as proper food. In one rice-eating area of South Asia, village people who were given American wheat as partial payment for working on canal construction projects sold it in order to buy rice. It is very difficult for people who have never used powdered milk to consider it as a food. It has been reported that in one Latin American country mothers gave such donated milk to their children in its powdered form and the children developed stomach-aches as a result. Also, in one Southeast Asian country, villagers who had never used milk before reportedly used donated powdered milk to make lines on their soccer fields. Since they were unfamiliar with white powder as a food, they used it for a purpose which had meaning to them. The meaning of these examples is simply that cultural differences can stand in the way of the best-intentioned efforts where only economic or technical considerations are observed. The sociocultural approach can help to correct this kind of difficulty.

Although Westerners in action capacities who are trying to assist in bringing economic improvements to the developing nations are usually aware of differences between their way of life and that of the people they are trying to help, this awareness is often of a very general nature. They are usually told that they must respect the customs of the local country and that, moreover, they need not Westernize the people in order to bring about useful economic changes. Since most such advisers lack any thorough grounding in social science, they are frequently unable to recognize the depth and intensity of local beliefs or customs; they tend to classify them as merely quaint or unusual differences that can be overlooked as far as technical or economic change is concerned. It is our belief that such cultural differences cannot be relegated to weekend photography and ignored during the workday week if economic change in the developing nations is to attain efficiency.

The foreign assistance adviser can be viewed as an engineer, but not just in regard to some new Western technique or economic practice. Whenever he is dealing with the economy or the technical practices of another people, he is really tampering with an entire social system. We believe it is more useful to regard him as a sociocultural engineer rather than merely a technical expert. He can be compared to an engineer concerned with building bridges, who certainly must know the problems of stress and the nature of steel. But an engineer must also be aware of the environment in which he constructs his bridges. He must know something about the flow of water in the river he is attempting to cross, the nature of the rocks where he is anchoring his abutments, as well as the weather conditions of the area. Intense cold will contract his steel and intense heat will expand it. In a comparable sense, though the technician or economist must know the techniques of his trade, he also must know something about the environment in which he is working. And primarily this is the cultural system of the people among whom he is working. This cannot safely be assumed to be the same as the cultural system of the adviser, any more than the physical conditions for building a bridge in a temperate climate can be assumed to be the same as in the arctic or in the tropics.

We believe the adviser must be introduced to the study of change from a sociocultural point of view. He is already committed to the necessity for change and knows how it takes place within his own culture. But he needs to understand how it can take place within other sociocultural systems. In other words, he needs to know something about the principles of cross-cultural change.

One way the techniques of change have been successfully taught within other professions in the United States has been by the case history method. In medicine, law, and business, to mention only some of the more successful fields of endeavor, the technique of studying and analyzing past efforts in order to improve current practice has been utilized thoroughly. Thus, no medical doctor believes himself qualified to undertake a serious operation until he knows well what happened during similar operations in the past. In the same sense, a practicing lawyer must depend to a very large extent on the knowledge embodied in the casebooks for each new case. Business also uses this technique in putting trainees to the task of studying and analyzing business ventures of the past in order to learn what are the factors for success. The common element in all these fields is to build knowledge progressively, to learn from the past in order to avoid the same errors in the future, and to learn what techniques bring the desired results.

We believe that if the field of international development is to become a mature, productive profession, it, too, will have to construct a body of knowledge which will be cumulative. Moreover, the individuals involved will have to assume the same role as the doctor and the lawyer, a large part of which

will be to study and analyze past efforts. Further, we believe
that the case history method is highly suitable to this field also.
This is the only way it will be possible to avert the common
difficulty of one specialist after another repeating mistakes that
have occurred many times before in other countries but in
similar circumstances.

Despite the fact that each situation encountered by an adviser in the field of international development will be unique,
there are many common principles that govern the change
process. Thus, though the type of leadership one can effectively
work through on a local village level will vary from country
to country, there are recurrent types of leadership which are
found world-wide, and from which one can expect similar
reactions.

A case in point is that of traditional religious leaders. There
are four major religions in the developing countries—Buddhism,
Christianity, Hinduism, and Islam—as well as tribal religions
in a small percentage of the world's population. Although the
leaders of these faiths have different theological beliefs, they
have a similar relationship to the rural people among whom
they work. They provide supernatural assistance to their devotees, and because of the usually high regard with which this is
received, the devotees also usually seek from them advice of a
more mundane nature. The religious leaders may also get economic advantages from their positions, and at the very least
they are concerned to safeguard such positions. Thus, when
outside forces, such as foreign assistance agencies, appear and
fail to include the religious leaders in their development plans,
these leaders are likely to talk down the new developments
and advise their devotees not to participate. It does not matter
that the innovations being brought to the villagers would really
help them; unless the advantages are very obvious, the recipients are likely to follow the advice of their religious leaders and
fail to co-operate. One general principle for including change
is, therefore: "Involve the local religious leaders in the new
developments simply because they are a powerful leadership
force."

Obviously, the characteristics of such leadership will vary
from country to country and from religion to religion, but the
variations can be analyzed on the spot by the change agent involved. At least he will have a starting point if he has some basic
principles to follow. Variations also occur for the bridge builder.
There are a number of principles that govern all bridge con-

struction problems. However, no two bridge problems are exactly alike. If the bridge is to be 2,500 feet long, the problem of stress will not be the same as if it were to be 500 feet. If it is built where there are high winds, the problem will be different than for a sheltered location. The bridge builder studies these problems on the spot and adjusts his plans accordingly. Similarly, this procedure is also necessary for the agent of social change. He can learn general principles, but he will have to learn the exact circumstances at the location of his proposed development efforts. In this book we will be concerned with the general principles.

We shall do this by combining two methods. In the next chapter we shall provide an outline for change and for the analysis of change projects. We believe that by knowing the importance of the various influences that affect such efforts, the change agent or student of change will be able to analyze his own problems and case histories in a methodical manner. This model can be considered as a guide for either analysis or action. Although it will be as comprehensive as the data studied up to this point permit, it cannot be considered final. No scientific scheme is ever final. Each is only the best that is available at the time, to be replaced or altered as more data are analyzed.

The second method is to provide actual case histories of change efforts as they have occurred and as they were described by the original analysts. We will attempt to provide an analytic guide for each case history and to point out how one or several of the influences affected the outcome.

We have selected the case histories with several criteria in mind. There are many others that are quite good but that do not fit one or more of these conditions. One such requirement was to cover the range of types of projects that have taken place within the field of international development during the last two decades. Thus, we have tried to find representative samples in the fields of agriculture, animal husbandry, co-operatives, education, health, home economics, transportation, and general community development. We have also tried to get as wide a representative sample as possible from the world areas where development efforts are taking place. We also selected the case histories according to quality, interest and length. As far as quality is concerned, we have used only those that were analyzed in a professional and complete manner, so that the reader can get a clear picture of what happened. We were concerned also that a case history be interestingly presented, on the assumption that many action people, who are normally very heavily burdened with written reports, will not take the time to read material that is dull. The length of each was significant to the extent that we selected those which contained the most information presented in the most succinct manner.

The final criterion we used for selection was success and failure of outcome. We have tried to balance the cases half and half, not because we believe that this is the normal percentage of successes and failures, but because we believe that it is equally important to know what to do and what not to do to implement the introduction of new ideas or techniques.

Two final points should be noted in regard to the selections. One is that they are on the project level, that is, the level where change agents are in interaction with the recipients. We believe that it is on this level that the final success or failure of most projects takes place, regardless of what planning has been done on a higher government level. In other words, although a country might decide in its five-year plan to increase the agricultural sector of the economy and budget a certain amount of money for this purpose, unless some effective means of transferring the knowledge of better argicultural implements or fertilizer to the rural peasants is worked out, the plans will come to naught. The same would be true of health measures. It is one thing to decide that better health would make village farmers more productive, but it is quite another to convince them to build and use latrines. It is this second part of the problem that we are concerned with here. However, we believe that this second part has strong implications for those on the planning level. There are some new ideas or techniques that can be transferred more easily than others. For instance, the idea of using fertilizer is in general easier to transfer to peasants than the idea of using latrines. If program planners were aware of this and had limited budgets, which is almost always the case, they might choose to concentrate on disseminating first the idea of fertilizer use, knowing that more food would also make villagers healthier. There would be less resistance, and thus more value gained for expenditure.

The second point is that most case histories concern the peasant farmer. This was not our choosing, but a fact that is forced on us by the nature of the developing world. Seventy to eighty per cent of the population in the developing nations lives in rural villages and consists primarily of farmers. Ultimately, these people will spell the difference between success and failure in the developing nations. Although most such nations are very interested in industrializing themselves, their basic problems stem from the fact that two-thirds of their populations are poorly fed, conservative, basically illiterate, and relatively unproductive—the village peasants. When these men become well-fed, interested in change, literate and productive, most of the overpowering problems of the developing nations will be in the past.

2

The Process of Innovation

Sociocultural change takes place through time. There is a beginning and an end of the change process. The beginning is the first presentation of any new idea to the potential recipients and the end, if the effort is successful, is the point when it is integrated into the culture of that group. From the point of view of the innovator there is a goal, some new idea or technique or more efficient means of accomplishing a traditional task that will assist in the economic improvement of the recipient group. As will be seen in the figure below, this is what we call "the plan." The line from the inception of "the plan" to the point of "integration" is broken, which signifies the possibility that the new ideas or techniques may never be integrated. Because of a variety of influences, the recipients may reject the innovation at any time after it begins. If this happens, the project ends in failure.

Throughout the change process, there are basically two forces acting on the plan-integration line: the techniques used by the innovator in his efforts to convince the local group to accept the new idea, and the behavior of the recipients toward the proposed innovation. These two forces can be characterized as the *action* and the *reaction*.

Any projected innovation will be subject to influences stemming from these two forces. Any influence or multiple of such influences, as will be described below, is theoretically sufficient to break the plan-integration line. Of course, when this happens the project has failed. When the project has succeeded and the plan achieves integration, a high percentage of the influences will have been positive. All of the influence factors can act either as barriers or stimulants to the change process. In the following model we will present a list of these influence factors, to be followed by a working description of each of them.

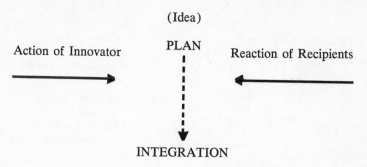

Before defining the various sets (the term we use for the larger groups) and the categories (the term for the subdivisions) of innovator characteristics, it might be well to say a few words about their general influence as compared to those of recipient reaction. Although there is a tendency for action people to place the onus for project failures on the nature of the traditional societies where they work, most unbiased analyses of such projects indicate that the failure is most often due to faulty innovation techniques. It will be noted in the case histories which follow that projects which failed almost always contained poor innovation techniques, particularly poor communication and failure to involve the potential recipients in committed participation. These occur much more frequently as negative influences than do characteristics of traditional cultures such as beliefs and practices.

It is easy enough to understand why the idea has been spread that traditional cultures are usually resistant to change, whereas little has been said about faulty innovation techniques. The vocal half of this interaction pair is the Western or Westernized change agent, whereas the potential adopter, who is often illiterate, has few opportunities to express his views. And it is well known that men of all cultures rarely accept the onus for failure in any kind of endeavor. The normal practice in psychological terms is to "externalize the blame." Thus, the "voiceless" man in the peasant village is made to accept the blame for change not happening. But there is positive evidence that lack of change is not necessarily the fault of the recipient. It will be noted that those efforts which were successful all contained good innovation techniques, particularly communication, participation of recipients, and utilization of local culture.

Innovator Characteristics

I. ROLE CHARACTERISTICS
   A. Personality
   B. Use of Local Language
   C. Technical Competence
   D. Affiliations

II. COMMUNICATION BY THE INNOVATOR
   A. Formal
   B. Personal
   C. Audio-visual
   D. Demonstration
   E. Feedback

III. PARTICIPATION OBTAINED
   A. Labor and Time
   B. Material Contributions
   C. Organizational
   D. Passive

IV. UTILIZATION OF LOCAL CULTURE

V. TIMING (*utilization of*)

VI. FLEXIBILITY (*of implementation*)

VII. CONTINUITY (*of implementation*)

VIII. MAINTENANCE (*established*)

Recipient Characteristics

IX. COMMUNICATION AMONG THE RECIPIENTS

X. MOTIVATION—FELT NEED
   A. Solicited
   B. Demonstrated
   C. Ascertained

XI. MOTIVATION—PRACTICAL BENEFIT PERCEIVED
   A. Economic
   B. Medical
   C. Educational
   D. Convenience

XII. MOTIVATION—OTHER
   A. Competition
   B. Reward and Punishment
   C. Novelty

XIII. LEADERSHIP
   A. Administrators
   B. Educators
   C. Religious Leaders
   D. Other Organizations
   E. Noninstitutional

XIV. SOCIAL STRUCTURE
   A. Kinship
   B. Caste and Class
   C. Ethnic
   D. Political
   E. Central Authority

XV. ECONOMIC PATTERN

XVI. BELIEFS
   A. Supernatural
   B. Medical
   C. Attitudinal

XVII. PRACTICES

▶   I. ROLE CHARACTERISTICS.

This set encompasses the characteristics which the innovator brings with him to the scene of the innovation, and though these are not immutable, they are probably less changeable than the other specific techniques. Basically, they are the personal characteristics of the innovator, rather than what he specifically does on the project. The reason we called the set "role" rather than "personal" characteristics is that what is really important in terms of action on the project is how the innovator appears, rather than exactly what he is. We are thus interested in the role he plays resulting from his personal characteristics as viewed by the recipients. For instance, it is less important that he be technically competent within his profession in his home country than that he be accepted by the local people as technically competent. And surprising as this may seem, men who are highly qualified in their work in Western countries often fail to take into consideration the considerably different environment where they find themselves working in the developing countries, and consequently make technically bad judgments.

A. PERSONALITY

The general characteristics of the change agent, both as a representative of his cultural system and in terms of his individual idiosyncrasies. It must be remembered that the recipients will usually know little or nothing of the innovator's culture and will consequently be unable to distinguish between actions stemming from his cultural background and those stemming from his individual peculiarities. This category is primarily responsible for the relationship known as empathy, or the establishment of rapport. The influence it exerts is that those persons who have the ability to establish empathy will be helped, whereas those who do not will be at a disadvantage in their efforts.

B. USE OF LOCAL LANGUAGE

The effect on the project outcome that is brought about through the use of the local language. It might be claimed that language use should be included in the set called "communication," since language is obviously the principal human action that produces communication. However, for understanding the change process, we have found a narrower definition of communication useful, which is the method of transferring knowledge of the new idea. Language is, of course, the basis of all kinds of communication besides merely transferring knowledge of an innovation. It is apparent that someone who can communicate in the language of the recipients will be in a better position than one who cannot. However, this facility does not appear to be a highly critical influence. People who know a local language but lack understanding of the culture in which they are working or of the strategies of sociocultural change, often find their language of little use in promoting change. Several of the other innovator characteristics appear to be more significant than merely the ability to communicate in the local language, insofar as promoting change is concerned.

C. TECHNICAL COMPETENCE

The ability of the innovator within his technical field of specialization as projected to the recipients. As we indicated above, it is less important here what kind of reputation the change agent has in his home culture than what kind of image he creates in the local community. We exclude competence in sociocultural "know-how" from this category, since this kind of expertise is covered in the other categories of innovator behavior. It is well to remember that though the outside technical adviser will initially be accepted as a wise person in his field, the local people may not be fully convinced that the improvements he talks about are really applicable to their own situation. And frequently they are right. When such misapplication of technical expertise takes place, the potential recipients will frequently assume that the "expert" is not really competent. All in all, however, this is not a frequent problem in development work as compared to other problems. This is undoubtedly because most outside change agents are selected for their technical knowledge and are therefore competent, although sociocultural "know-how" has been consistently neglected by most action agencies.

D. AFFILIATIONS

The influence projected by the image of the innovator because of his organizational affiliations. This is the role characteristic about which the individual can do least, since the organization to which he belongs is normally sponsoring his efforts in the field. If he is sponsored by a missionary group, he may labor under the stereotype of being a proselytizer even though his work is to improve the economic conditions of rural peoples; if he is from an international development agency that has provided much economic aid in the past, it may be difficult for him to convince local people that his role is anything more than to produce material goods in abundance; and if he is an officer of the national government, he may well be viewed as a power figure in a definite hierarchical relationship and local people may be afraid of him. Since the innovator cannot change his affiliations, the most that can be said is that he can try to be aware of their effect and either emphasize or de-emphasize them, as conditions may require. Fortunately, this is the least significant of the personal image variables.

▶ **II. COMMUNICATION BY THE INNOVATOR**

We have defined this set as the transference of information regarding a proposed innovation. In actuality, within the total change process two basic types of communication have been discovered: one that results from deliberate efforts by the innovator to transfer the idea of the change to the recipients, the other consisting of communication among the recipients themselves about the innovation. Here we are concerned with the first type, because it involves a definite action by the change agent in order to have his project accepted; the other type will be treated under "recipient characteristics" because it is a reaction to the action of the innovator. Communication by the innovator is probably the single most important kind of action in which he will engage, since it is a prerequisite for everything else that follows. No ideas or techniques can be transferred from one person to another unless there are channels of communication established to transfer them, and these are the patterns of communication. If no adequate patterns of communication are established, the other innovator techniques cannot take place.

A. FORMAL
The transmission of information by means of formal group meetings, usually in village or neighborhood councils, sometimes in classroom situations. The obvious advantage of formal situations is that relatively large numbers of people can be con-

tacted; the disadvantage is that the contacts are very light. An added disadvantage in the rural areas of the non-Western world is that villagers have been talked at and harangued by officials in formal situations for many decades and have developed stereotyped patterns of behavior toward such "talks." They normally appear to agree with everything the official says while actually withholding judgment. Most of what the official says will be doubted and whatever will be accepted will be decided upon by consultation with trusted leaders after the officials have left. Although international development efforts depend most heavily on formal communication, this is probably the most inefficient way to transfer knowledge in these situations. However, combined with other kinds of communication, formal techniques have their place.

B. PERSONAL
The transmission of information by means of face-to-face interaction between the change agent and the recipients, usually in paired or small group situations. This method of transferring ideas has advantages and disadvantages that are the reverse of formal communication; that is, although fewer people can be contacted through a given amount of effort, the effectiveness of contact is far greater. The peasant villager in the developing nations is accustomed to this manner of dealing with his fellows and reacts favorably to approaches by outsiders who act in the same manner. Another positive result of personal communication techniques is that feedback can most easily take place in such situations. Although it is possible for people to react to new ideas in a formal meeting, they are much less likely to do so than when they are approached individually. Moreover, because the underprivileged in the developing nations normally find themselves on a very low level of the hierarchical system, they are reluctant to respond freely to powerful outsiders in open meetings. There is little doubt, therefore, that personal communication is most effective, although it can be combined with formal techniques, thus requiring less effort in contacting each individual.

C. AUDIO-VISUAL
Methods of transmitting information regarding innovations by means of audio-visual devices such as printed material, pictures, charts, loud-speaker systems, radio, television, and other mechanical aids that have been developed for influencing public

opinion. These kinds of techniques have the same advantages and disadvantages as communication in formal meetings in accentuated form. Although even more people can be contacted with a given audio-visual effort, the situation is even more impersonal than in formal meetings. The opportunities for feedback are practically nonexistent. Also, inherent in the use of audio-visual techniques with unsophisticated populations are the numerous possibilities of misunderstanding. People who have not been subjected to exposure to the mass media throughout their lives often have great difficulties in understanding new ideas through such means. Most decisions to use audio-visual techniques in the future will probably be made on the basis of their cost effectiveness, but those who make such decisions should be aware of their distinct disadvantages for influencing opinion among unsophisticated people.

D. DEMONSTRATION

The technique of showing in a pragmatic fashion the advantages of a new idea or technique as a means of convincing the recipients to adopt it. It should be noted that there is a distinct difference between "demonstration" and "illustration." We are using the term "demonstration" in the sense that it is used by agricultural agents in the United States. A positive demonstration for them is a plot of ground where a new seed variety or agricultural technique is used which, after a growing season, produces visible proof of the advantages of the new practice. An illustration in the sense we are using it in the field of public health would be an effort to show by means of charts and pictures the relationship between the use of latrines and amoebic dysentery. There would be no immediate pragmatic proof to the potential recipients that latrine use would reduce the amount of dysentery in their families. Of course, one can show the difference in statistical tables, but to the rural villager such a "proof" has little meaning. Almost all audio-visual techniques fall in the category of illustration, since they never really "prove" anything. We are here concerned with demonstration as a pragmatic, fairly immediate "proof." It is probably the single most effective method of obtaining acceptance of a new idea among villagers, since by necessity the peasant is a very pragmatic person.

E. FEEDBACK

The response to the innovator regarding the proposed new practice. It might appear that this category would belong in the group of recipient characteristics or reactions, since it is the recipient who is acting. The reason it is not considered there is that the primary responsibility for establishing a feedback channel lies with the change agent. The underprivileged have long been accustomed to accept the pronouncements of powerful outsiders without any response other than assent, even though they may have many reservations. But because of their low position in the class hierarchy, they usually will not take the initiative to express their own opinions, particularly if they are contrary to those of the outsider. Therefore, if the outsider is going to learn their reactions, he will have to take definite steps to establish feedback channels. The establishment of such channels is accordingly an action by the change agent. Feedback channels have probably been neglected more and are probably more critical than any other aspect of communication other than personal contact. When personal communication occurs there is usually feedback also, but still the innovator must be careful that he is not doing all the talking. He can be assured that when the communication techniques of demonstration, personal contact and feedback are utilized, an innovation is well on the way toward acceptance.

▶ III. PARTICIPATION OBTAINED

This set is the basic index of commitment by the recipients. No project which will effect socioeconomic change can possibly succeed if the recipients do not participate, since ultimately it will be their responsibility to continue it. It is surprising how frequently action agents have neglected to make sure they have committed participation on their projects. It appears that the principal reason why this primary ingredient has been overlooked so often is that many technical advisers have viewed their task as simply one of providing some kind of technical solution, which from their point of view was superior to the traditional way of dealing with that kind of problem. They assumed that the technical superiority of their innovation would be immediately apparent to the recipients. Unfortunately for this kind of approach, a cultural system is a complex pattern of customs, and new ideas, even when technically superior, may conflict too much with some related beliefs or practices for the recipients to be willing to adopt them. If the potential recipients are working on the project from the beginning, these conflicts may become apparent in time, and proper measures to alter the program can be taken. It should be remembered that without initial participation by the recipients change cannot take place, although such a commitment does not absolutely ensure success, since there may be unexpected conflicts of which even the recipients are unaware at the time they begin to co-operate. And although participation in general is one of the best kinds of insurance of the continuity of any project, the types of participation obtained are even more important. Some reflect only a minimal interest whereas others indicate full commitment.

A. LABOR AND TIME

The contributions to the project's ends by the recipients of labor and/or time. This is the most common type of participation relied upon because most change projects are in communities where the people are poor; therefore, these two commodities are the easiest for them to provide. The two are often synonymous. There are some projects in which time is the major ingredient. Such would be the case in organizational change or in literacy campaigns, where the primary donation of the recipients would be the time they allot to the task.

B. MATERIAL CONTRIBUTIONS

The provision by the recipients of money or materials toward the fulfillment of the project's goals. Although this kind of contribution is probably the strongest index of commitment, it occurs less often than the provision of labor and time, since basically the communities being helped do not have many goods to provide or they would not need help. Moreover, most assistance agencies have the dual function of providing new ideas and at the same time donating material assistance toward the projects' goals. Therefore, even when local communities provide material contributions, these are often of a token nature. When local contributions are substantial, they are usually of materials that can be obtained locally, such as wood, sand, or gravel, whereas goods that must be bought are provided by the assisting agency. All in all, the provision of material contributions, even though they may be far short of what is necessary to complete a given project, are certainly desirable as an indication that the local people really want more than a simple handout from a rich development agency.

C. ORGANIZATIONAL

The incorporation of new ideas or techniques into new social groups or their incorporation into established organizations. In development jargon this phenomenon has been called "institution building." Although it is quite significant in regard to innovations depending on group action, such as community development, there are many kinds of changes that can be adopted by individuals or family units. The acceptance of new agricultural implements is an instance of the latter type. Organizational participation is not a strong index of commitment, since there are many other reasons why local communities may want to take part in group activities with outside change agents; they may view participation as a means of getting more free goods or as a means to more easily manipulate figures of power at a later time. The major importance of organizational participation and building institutions is that innovations will have a better chance of being continued if they are incorporated into a group.

D. PASSIVE

Nonactive compliance toward a projected change. Basically, this kind of participation is merely a lack of opposition and a willingness of recipients to be present when needed. As would be expected, this is the weakest type of participational base on which to build a change project. The recipients have nothing invested and lose nothing by ceasing to co-operate. Most change projects have little chance of succeeding if there is nothing more than passive participation, since the recipients will make little effort to continue them when the change agents leave. There are some projects, however, particularly in public health, where even passive participation has some value. Such is the case in inoculation programs or malaria eradication campaigns. The recipients could avoid being present for inoculations or refuse permission to have their houses sprayed with DDT. However, in other than these kinds of projects, passive participation alone is a very weak base on which to build a change project.

▶ IV. UTILIZATION OF LOCAL CULTURE

There are two basic approaches possible for introducing change: replacement and adaptation methods. The replacement method is when an outside "expert" attempts to replace inefficient practices with modern, efficient ones in a total manner. The adaptation method is when the innovator attempts to utilize old practices and graft new practices onto them, without attempting complete replacement. If sociocultural change worked in a mechanical fashion and if economic considerations were the only ones of relevance, the replacement method would be highly desirable. But a culture is an integrated whole, and however inefficient particular practices may be, the system does work and provides the members with a predictable future. People will not willingly give up their old practices until they are well convinced that the new ones really are improvements. And such considerations include more than simply economic advantages. Considerations of the relationship of the family members are often important, as are religious beliefs, and any innovation which conflicts with these may well be rejected. Consequently, as a strategy, the replacement method has much less promise than the adaptation method. If the innovations are really superior within the total way of life, they will automatically replace the older practices, but this need not be done directly by the change agent. His best strategy is to introduce the new along with the old and let the two compete on their own. Some characteristics of culture are more important than others. The most important pattern is that of local leadership. However, the local economic pattern, social structure, beliefs and practices are of some importance.

▶ V. TIMING

This strategy, along with the next two, flexibility and continuity, is of secondary importance, although it does deserve brief mention. The positive form is the introduction of a new idea or technique at an opportune time in relation to special circumstances or events, whereas the negative form is an introduction at an inopportune time. Crises or special circumstances are the usual kind of temporal events used positively, when the innovation will produce a dramatic demonstration of the advantages to be derived from the new idea or technique. An example is the introduction of drainage canals just before the potential inundation of a village area, or the inoculation of cattle just at the time an epidemic is sweeping the country.

▶ VI. FLEXIBILITY

This set is defined as the willingness of the change agent to alter his original plans to compensate for unforeseen difficulties. Although flexibility of this sort is undoubtedly important in any kind of effort to promote change, not excluding efforts within the same culture, it becomes even more important when the effort involves transfer of ideas from one culture to another. The basic reason is that even in those instances when the innovator does learn much about the local cultural patterns, this knowledge is necessarily limited. To understand the details of any culture thoroughly requires years of painstaking study even by a full-time social scientist. Therefore, it is very unlikely that action people, who devote only a small part of their time to learn about local customs, will achieve any very deep understanding. They can only compensate for this lack by being willing to alter their plans when unexpected difficulties arise. To insist that the goal remain as initially planned is to risk having the entire project rejected. However, despite the value of flexibility as a strategy, it is of secondary importance compared to such innovator techniques as communication and utilization of the local culture.

▶ VII. CONTINUITY

We define this strategy as the consistent follow-through of a plan in a general manner, even if it is altered in its details to fit local circumstances that were not foreseen at the outset. Thus, continuity fits hand-in-glove with flexibility. The most important element of this strategy is that the actions of the change agent be predictable from the point of view of the recipients. Discontinuity of projects and programs usually is a result of administrative problems the change agent has with his own sponsoring agency, or changes in policy within the agency. Although new decisions may be required on a policy level, it should always be remembered that those most directly affected, the rural villagers, will know or understand little of this, and a negative effect will be produced in getting them to co-operate the next time. Unfortunately, there is already a widespread belief among the poor of the underdeveloped nations that projects sponsored by their own governments or outside agencies are of a discontinuous nature, and more discontinuous or abandoned projects will reinforce this belief.

▶ VIII. MAINTENANCE

This set concerns the establishment of technical and organizational maintenance patterns for the continuity of the innovation within the local social group. It is obviously of great significance if a new idea or technique is to continue after the change agent has left. It is secondary in the sense that it does not become relevant unless a project is already at least partially successful. Thus, if participation is never obtained, there is no point to continue the project. But if a project does get near a successful conclusion, the single most important factor which may mean the difference between integration and abandonment is whether or not a pattern of maintenance has been established. Maintenance is both technical and organizational, the first made necessary because of the transfer of techniques which did not previously exist in the recipient groups and which often require acquisition of new skills, and the second because social groups are continuous whereas individuals are only temporary. Since an invention is classified as such only when it is accepted by a social group, so also is an idea diffused only when a social group has integrated it into its pattern of behavior.

We turn now to a consideration of the reactions of the recipients to new ideas. Although the varieties of reaction which have been discovered are considerably more numerous than the strategies and techniques of the innovators, there is no reason to believe that they are more important. In fact, to a large extent the reactions of the recipients are fairly direct results of innovator strategies. Although certain characteristics of traditional cultures are basically in opposition to certain kinds of innovations, the more common occurrence is that because of poor innovation techniques, certain aspects of traditional practices come to be in opposition. An example of the former would be an effort to introduce milk consumption to Southeast Asian villagers: milk is not classified by them as adult human food, and without extensive educational efforts as well as major shifts in their economic pattern they will not take up the practice of drinking it. However, the more common occurrence is when innovators fail to use good techniques and thus bring about opposition to their efforts even when there is no basic cultural objection to the new idea. One of the most common errors is a failure to utilize the local leadership to the fullest extent possible. When this happens, traditional leaders often oppose new ideas. Traditional religious leadership is often ignored by Western or Westernized change agents. The monks and priests then oppose the new ideas, since they see the outside influence as threatening their own position, whereas if they had been included from the first, they might have assisted the innovators.

▶   IX. COMMUNICATION AMONG THE RECIPIENTS

This set is defined as spontaneous communication among the recipients in regard to the change project. It falls basically within the normal definition of gossip and has two forms: positive gossip and rumor-mongering. As will be recognized, this type of communication is not the same as that within the innovator technique group, since it is not preplanned by the change agent. Theoretically, it could be utilized by the change agent, and it does have a potentially powerful effect. However, to understand how to use gossip in a local social group requires a fairly good understanding of that group's habits, again a depth of knowledge that most innovators of the past have lacked. Also, as would be expected, positive gossip usually occurs when the innovation techniques have been fairly good and the new idea or technique really does fulfill a need. Negative rumors are usually generated when communication by the change agent has been poor and the potential recipients do not really understand what he intends to do.

We come now to one of the two most significant groups of recipient characteristics: motivation. Basically, the motivation for accepting a new idea stems from two sources: one is how the idea is presented, which is a product of innovator techniques, and the other is whether or not the new idea really fulfills a recognized need in the local society. Thus, motivation can be considered as the adhesive that binds these two together. If the motivation is strong, the idea was well presented and a need was fulfilled. If it is weak, the technique of transferring the idea has been inefficient or no need has been fulfilled, or both.

▶ X. MOTIVATION—FELT NEED

This set refers to a need recognized by the recipients as a consequence of their own wants and values, not those of the innovator. Obviously, what the innovator wants the local people to have can be the same as what they want to have, but the two are by no means automatically the same. The poor in the developing nations, with cultural values that differ from those of Westerners or the urbanized élite, have consequently different frames of reference from which they decide what is most necessary. Innovators who think exclusively in terms of national development schemes may never understand these frames of reference. The most obvious kind of example of this difference occurs in public health projects, when Western or Westernized innovators normally decide what is needed on the basis of Western medical knowledge. Although he wants better health, the peasant villager has no means of seeing how most public health projects will really benefit him, and consequently he has no felt needs for them. Any project based on a felt need has a strong motivational base to build upon. If it is lacking, a need will have to be generated, which is usually not easy, at least not in a short period of time. There are three basic types of felt need, as indicated in the next three categories.

A. SOLICITED

A need of which the recipients are fully aware to the extent that they solicit assistance from the change agent or local authorities to fulfill it. Though this can be a good indication of the recipients' real interest and commitment to the solution of a problem, it contains one danger. The recipients may use a "problem" merely as a pretext to get goods and materials from the change agent if he fulfills both functions of providing technical advice as well as material grants.

B. DEMONSTRATED

A need of which the recipients have demonstrated their interest to the extent that they have attempted to solve the problem by their own efforts without any oustide assistance. This is obviously the most solid motivational base on which to build a project because the recipients are really committed to a solution of the problem. Their own action is a far better index of commitment than their solicitation.

C. ASCERTAINED

A need which, although already existing when the change agent arrives, is only latent within the local social group and must be ascertained by both the innovator and the recipient. In other words, a problem in the local way of life already exists, but the local people either do not know how to formulate a solution or else they do not believe they have the capacity to undertake it. It should be kept clear that this is not the same as a generated need, which before the efforts of the change agent was not even recognized as a problem. A need for boiling drinking water would be in the generated category, whereas a need for a co-operative that solves a number of economic problems would be in the ascertained category.

▶ XI. MOTIVATION—PRACTICAL BENEFIT
     PERCEIVED

This has been defined as an advantage perceived by the recipients that produces a practical benefit in this life. The key to this motivational set is that it is perceived by the recipients. In other words, what is seen as a benefit by the change agent is not necessarily seen by the recipients in the same way, again because the frame of reference of the two may be different. The recipients act because they believe a practical benefit will result from their action or fail to do so because they do not believe this will happen. When we say a practical benefit "in this life," we mean much the same as a Westerner would mean by this expression, which excludes the subsidiary benefits —such as social prestige and religious satisfaction—that accrue to the acceptance of many kinds of new ideas by the Westerner as well as the non-Westerner. Although we find that such motivations do influence the decisions of non-Western village people, they are significantly less important than the practical considerations of wealth, education and better health—though always as the villager perceives them.

A. ECONOMIC

A benefit which produces in the perception of the recipients an economic gain in the foreseeable future, usually within a few years. This is the most common type of need which inspires positive reaction to potential change by villagers and by the poor generally. This realization may be gratifying to economic aid planners, who usually assume that all peoples desire the things of life that wealth will buy, but it may be disconcerting to some technicians who have sponsored projects which they knew were profitable, but which interested the nonindustrialized village people very little. There are two basic reasons for such lack of interest. One mentioned above was that a difference may result from differing frames of reference. A peasant cannot know how a particular economic practice works in a highly industrial economy and he may therefore not be able to see how it could work in his simple economic system. The other difficulty is that most of the poor in the developing nations are living so close to the subsistence margin that they can afford to take few chances. Thus, even when a new technique that would provide real benefit is presented, but which requires that the village farmer take a chance on his meager acreage or capital resources, he may be reluctant to do so.

B. MEDICAL

A practical measure that provides a perceived improvement in health conditions, usually in the near future. Although people in the nonindustrialized countries are concerned with their health only less than with their economic improvement, the difficulties of health projects are considerably more than those which provide economic advantages. The primary cause of such difficulties is the considerable difference in points of view between a Westerner and a member of a traditional village society. The effectiveness of modern ideas of health are difficult to demonstrate; thus, the awareness of the advantages of modern sanitation practices are difficult to transmit in a short period of time, particularly through mass media communication. The idea of modern therapeutic medicine is comparatively easy to transmit, but preventive medicine is probably the most difficult kind of innovation presently being exported to the developing countries.

C. EDUCATIONAL

Benefits derived from formal education, usually perceived in terms of economic advantages, but also for improving the status positions of the recipients. In this kind of innovation there is the most comfortable fit between the wishes of the innovators and those of the recipients. People almost everywhere recognize the advantages of literacy and skills learned in schools. Moreover, school systems or even individual classes offer little threat to the traditional cultural patterns. Though the transmission of new ideas to students may in the long run change a culture more than any kind of activity, in the immediate future the threat to traditional ways is not easily apparent.

D. CONVENIENCE

A perceived benefit from the adoption of a new idea or technique that makes a necessary traditional task more convenient to accomplish. This kind of motivation stems from the very common human disinclination to value work for its own sake. No people willingly choose to do tasks the hard way, and if an easier way is presented to them they gravitate toward it. Although it is rare that modern innovators will introduce new ideas or techniques simply to make work situations more convenient for the recipients, the latter often do consider the innovations from this point of view. For instance, wells are often introduced into village societies to provide sanitary water supplies. Villagers rarely recognize the health aspects of these wells but they usually appreciate their convenience.

▶ ## XII. MOTIVATION—OTHER

The only common characteristic of the kinds of motivation that compose this set is that the benefits are indirect or subsidiary rather than directly practical. Although in the broadest sense all benefits that a recipient may perceive have an element of practicality involved, those in this set are less direct. They are, moreover, not the benefits for which the innovator usually introduces the new practice. For instance, many kinds of innovations may result in social benefits to an acceptor, but it is rare that change agents are concerned with them. Literacy campaigns are inaugurated to create reading and writing skills in a population, and though the participants may clearly see the practical benefits of acquiring these abilities, they may also be motivated by a desire to appear socially more acceptable. In this system the motivation to acquire social prestige would fall in the category of individual competition or status emulation. Finally, it should be stressed that in terms of significance for inducing chage, the types of motivation within this set are less important than those which provide direct practical benefits.

A. COMPETITION

A perceived status advantage or disadvantage to the individual or the group through the acceptance of a new idea or technique. This kind of motivation is based on the fact that individuals and groups of all sizes are in competition with one another. Although some cultures stress co-operative tendencies more than others, we do not believe there are any that do not leave some room for competition among individuals. Most commonly this is what has been called "prestige emulation," that is, individuals imitating those of higher status in the hope that they will thus improve their own prestige postion. One very common type of competition among peasants is the desire to be like urban residents. Group competition is usually that of one village with others, involving again a desire to be as good as or better than the others. Although both these kinds of competitive tendencies are less significant than perceived direct practical benefit, they are useful for innovations such as public health projects, in which practical demonstrations are very difficult.

B. REWARD AND PUNISHMENT

A reward to induce the recipients to accept a new idea or technique, or coercive pressure to induce compliance. The most common of these in modern development projects is reward, which is usually provided by outside agencies in the form of money or materials to assist in the various efforts. It is usually phrased as economic aid by the development agencies, but it is most logically viewed by the recipients as a reward for taking part in the effort. When rewards are great in the provision of large amounts of goods, the primary motivation for co-operation is often almost exclusively to get the expected reward. Sometimes small rewards are used, such as diplomas for completing literacy courses or small gifts of medical supplies for coming to clinics. This influence is much the same, though of course it is not as strong. Direct punishment is not often used by outside agencies, though some government officials do resort to this practice. In terms of actually getting local people to accept new ideas or to change their ways of doing things, neither of these motivations are very strong. Though the villager will almost always accept donations of goods and materials, if there is no perceived practical benefit involved he usually will not follow the new practices after the change agents leave.

C. NOVELTY

Interest generated for a new idea or technique because it is novel or impressive, or suspicion because it differs strongly from traditional ways. Thus many things that are imported from the West, such as new or larger varieties of domestic animals or crop plants or new mechanical devices, can attract local people who have had no experience with them before just because they are so impressive. What is more common, however, are new devices or practices that create uneasiness because they differ so much from traditional ways of doing things. Examples of these are new types of food or new kinds of medical treatment, such as taking blood samples. Village people will react sometimes positively and sometimes negatively to an innovation insofar as they perceive it in relation to their traditional ways. As a positive force this is a very weak motivation, however, and if there are no other benefits, it is not likely that the new idea will be maintained. It is fortunate that negative reactions are equally weak. Most people, even the most traditionally oriented, do not really have any objection to adopting new practices just because they are new if they bring real benefits and if the traditional patterns are not threatened too much.

The final group of reactions are those that stem from the nature of the traditional culture of the recipients. We do not mean by this any unchanging pattern of behavior that has persisted for centuries or even generations, but merely the kind of culture that exists at the time the proposed innovation is introduced to a social group. Although it is common for action people to regard the traditional ways of a people as the principal barrier to change, we believe that it need not be so. No people will willingly give up all of their time-tested ways of solving problems even when these are not very efficient by Western standards, but this does not mean that they will not change. It merely means that they will not change everything, nor will they change particular practices if these seem to threaten completely the old ways. We think that the local culture can be used in a positive manner if the change agent does not assume that his job is to break down and replace the old ways. If he utilizes as many of the old ways as possible and does not attempt openly to oppose strong vested interests, he can count on a positive reaction from the local people. In other words, he must adapt to the old ways rather than replacing them outright. This is not to say that it would not be better if he could replace many inefficient practices outright, but practically such an approach will not usually work.

▶ XIII. LEADERSHIP

There is little doubt that the single most important characteristic of the local society is its leadership. There is probably no way to ruin the chances for an innovation project more easily than to ignore the traditional leaders or to choose the wrong ones. Leaders in social groups of all cultures have strong vested interests in their positions, and if outsiders come with proposed changes and fail to work with them, these leaders tend to see potential threats to their own positions and oppose the changes. There are really only two possible ways to treat local leaders: the outsider can either work with them or he can oppose them. However, if he chooses to oppose them, he must recognize that he will need an enormous amount of skill to accomplish his task, and probably some coercive power as well. The one choice that is not possible is to ignore them, for when a potentially disruptive change agent ignores the local leaders, they almost automatically oppose him. Fortunately, Westerners usually understand the necessity for working with local leaders. The one difficulty that they sometimes have is that they do not always recognize the people who are most influential in other cultures.

A. ADMINISTRATORS
Secular officials who perform the administrative tasks of government in local societies. Basically, civil officials at all levels of governments in the developing nations come from two

sources. Middle-level officials, such as governors and district or county heads, are usually appointed by the central governments and are paid civil servants. Less frequently such officials are elected. On the village level, there are headmen, who are more usually elected and who receive little or no pay; in any event, they are practically never civil servants. Though the middle-level administrator has considerably more authority, as well as the power of the central government behind him, the village chief or headman usually has much more trust from the villagers. In many nations of the developing world the headman is filling a traditional position that existed long before any of these countries developed a central government with a civil service on Western lines. Also, it is important to note that the headman is a villager himself and is usually a farmer like his people. He knows their problems well because he shares them. Needless to say, the headman and the local officials above him are crucial people with whom to work.

B. EDUCATORS

Those government officials directly concerned with formal education in the community, usually schoolteachers. These officials have considerably more influence in the rural villages of the nonindustrialized nations than they do in the West. An educator has three characteristics that make him valuable for bringing about change. For one thing, he works and often lives in the world of the villager. Second, though he may not be well educated by Western standards, he is a comparatively well-educated man. At the very least he knows something of the trend of modernization that is taking place in the world, and he is not averse to change if it does not threaten his own position. Thus he is a man in the middle, potentially capable of helping bridge the gap between the restricted world of the rural villager and the modernizing world of the urban élite. The third characteristic in his favor is that he brings a gift to the villagers which they prize highly—literacy and education. He can, therefore, exert considerable influence, directly on the children and indirectly on their parents.

C. RELIGIOUS LEADERS

Members of the organized religious fraternities of the traditional religions. Usually, these are Hindu, Buddhist, Muslim, Christian, or tribal religious leaders. This type of leader is also more influential than many Westerners assume on the basis of their experience with similar leaders in their own cultures. The religious leader of Asia, Africa, or Latin America has considerable influence beyond purely religious affairs. The local people listen to him because he, too, brings them a gift of considerable importance—religious assistance. And when so many aspects of life cannot be controlled in a scientific manner, as is the case in practically all of the poor communities of the nonindustrialized world, religious assistance fills a vital need. Moreover, from the point of view of the innovator, it is important to remember that religious leaders are organized nationally in many countries and provide a chain of communication all the way from the capital city to the most remote villages. And again, unless their own vested interests are threatened too much, religious leaders will usually co-operate if they are fully consulted. If they are ignored, they will tend to oppose change efforts from the outside.

D. OTHER ORGANIZATIONS

All kinds of leadership derived from other types of organizations. Typical organizations are civic clubs (such as social service clubs), health committees, rural improvement clubs, various welfare institutions and co-operatives. These kinds of organizations are usually committed to promoting change and usually exert a positive influence if given an opportunity. Most are relatively new, and many have been organized by previous development groups. Obviously, it is desirable to work with them whenever they exist, though it should be mentioned that many are not fully accepted by all community members.

E. NONINSTITUTIONAL

Leadership not associated with any group membership but pertaining to individuals because of personal ability, positions of wealth or traditional prestige. Probably such types of leadership most often exist because of relative wealth. Although frequently such persons have strong vested interests in the status quo, there are some who see the need for change and will co-operate. Moreover, they can exert strong negative pressure if they are ignored.

▶ ## XIV. SOCIAL STRUCTURE

Societies everywhere are subdivided into small groups with special interests and responsibilities of their own. There are basic types that are found in all cultures, though their special characteristics may differ from society to society. For instance, there are no known societies which do not have family groups, and thus kinship relationships. However, the type of family unit found in Asia differs considerably from that found in the industrialized Western countries, as do the particular relationships of family members to one another. These differences must be dealt with if innovation is to take place, since social relations are of considerable significance, particularly in the nonindustrialized countries. In general, except for local leadership, social structure and the local pattern of economic relationships are the most significant aspects of non-Western cultures that influence the acceptance or rejection of new ideas.

A. KINSHIP

Formalized group behavior based on common ancestry, and the attitudes which stem from these relationships. The basic unit of kinship is the "nuclear" family, made up of husband, wife, and children. However, in many cultures the web of relationship, of rights and duties, extends far beyond this to include relatives many degrees removed. It can go as far as the clan, in which no direct ancestral links can be proved but where common ancestry is believed to exist, and it can include people who are dead but who are still considered part of the "great family." Local kinship patterns are like other aspects of traditional culture. If new ideas are presented that are advantageous and do not challenge the traditional relationships, the local people are likely to accept them. But if their kinship relationships will be drastically changed as a result, they will show a disinclination to co-operate.

B. CASTE AND CLASS

Social groups larger than kinship units, normally based on special status and in hierarchical order, usually with special economic interests. The basic difference between caste and class is that caste membership is completely hereditary whereas class membership is more fluid. Though it may be difficult for people to move from one class to another they may do so, but theoretically it is not possible for individuals to change their caste. Since castes and classes are composed of relatively large numbers of people, who are often relatively well organized, they can exert considerable pressure against any development that threatens their interests. This must be kept in mind by Western or Westernized change agents, who very frequently attempt to impose egalitarian ideals on groups with whom they are working. However laudatory such ideals may be, in fact most societies are not organized on an egalitarian basis, and unless the change agent has the power of enforcement, to insist on equal treatment by all as a condition for assistance may be the most efficient means to destroy all chances for successful innovation.

C. ETHNIC

Social groups larger than castes or classes and composed of people with distinctive cultural or subcultural patterns, usually speaking distinct languages, often of different racial types, and usually in hierarchical relationship with other such groups in the total culture. Examples of such groups are the mountain tribesmen of Southeast Asia or the Indians of Latin America. Although problems deriving from ethnic attitudes are less frequent than those of caste, class or kinship, they can be just as serious when they do occur. Much the same kind of attitude occurs as with caste or class subdivisions on the part of Westerners. Efforts are made to impose egalitarian ideals when the local societies are not really functioning on a basis of equality. Conflicts and friction erupt when the traditional social order is tampered with. Again it must be reiterated that though Western egalitarianism may ultimately be carried to other lands, this is not an easy task which a single change agent can hope to bring about simply by making equal treatment a precondition for assistance.

D. POLITICAL

Locally organized branches of national political or administrative groups. Power and politics are almost synonymous and political officials guard their rights jealously. If changes are proposed which threaten this power or for which they can claim no credit, their natural reaction is to oppose them. It must be remembered that the idea of economic development is at base derived from political considerations. The countries that provide assistance hope to get political advantages in so doing, and the recipient countries hope to become economically more independent so that they will be in better political bargaining positions. Unfortunately, national policies are not always reflected completely on a local level. Local officeholders are usually interested as much or more in their own positions than in the greater good of the nation of which they are a part. And since the lines of communication and discipline in most of the nonindustrialized countries are not very tight, much local independent action is possible. The local political body will, therefore, fight moves which promise it no benefit and will tend to co-operate with those changes from which it can obtain political capital.

E. CENTRAL AUTHORITY

The attitude of the local population toward the centralized control of their national goverment. This social gap between the national élite and the rural peasantry is the largest that exists in the nonindustrialized world. The role of national governments in these countries in the past has been mainly exploitative as far as the peasant is concerned. Except for schoolteachers, the government officials that the peasant is most familiar with are tax collectors, military conscription officials and land regulators. Moreover, in the past the outside representative of the national government has usually been connected with the moneylender and the landowner. In other words, when the peasant dealt with one of these officials, he usually lost something. Consequently, it is not very surprising that the rural peasant in general has a negative view of his central government. Although most such governments have embarked on positive development schemes in the past two decades, the effects have not reached most villages, and exploitation of the villagers has been continued by minor officials. The peasant will react positively if he is shown that intentions are honest, but he starts with an initial suspicion based on the experience of hundreds of years.

▶ XV. ECONOMIC PATTERN

The system of production, distribution, and consumption of goods involves in essence the utilization of material resources. Probably the most significant characteristic of the traditional economic system that should be kept in mind by any change agent is that it works within the understanding of the local people. It is easy enough to point out inefficient economic practices in the developing countries, but it is well to remember that the local people arrived at them by means of trial and error, and they will not exchange them for others unless the advantages of the new practices are very clear. Among other problems that the peasant faces is the basic one that he usually has very little capital or land. He can ill afford to experiment when a lost crop may mean famine the next year. There are several aspects of traditional economic systems that are most important to the change agent, among them patterns of work schedules, work groupings, trade, distribution of goods and ownership rights. By adapting any new idea to the local patterns, the innovator has improved the chances for his project; by ignoring them, his project may be rejected.

▶ XVI. BELIEFS

This set includes all the thought processes, beliefs and attitudes that describe the nature of man and the universe within the local frame of reference. Although the nature of such belief systems tend to make them negative toward new ideas, there are ways of using them positively, or at least of avoiding direct confrontation with them. A local belief can only explain the universe within the limits of existing knowledge. There are beliefs about health among village people that have no validity according to the principles of modern medicine. But since the local people have not been exposed to ideas emanating from modern medicine, they use the knowledge they possess in order to avoid a belief vacuum. Men require answers to the vital matters of life and death, and whether or not these are true according to modern science is not particularly relevant. After all, a superstition is only a belief of someone else not shared by the outsider. It is not easy to learn the belief system of another people, but if change is to be introduced, some minimum of understanding is necessary. There are three principal kinds of beliefs or attitudes that affect socioeconomic change projects.

A. SUPERNATURAL

Types of belief and attitudes that stem from religious and magical systems. Although in the Western world supernatural beliefs are largely derived from the dominant religions, Christianity and Judaism, this is not exclusively the case; for example, there are considerable numbers of people who believe in astrology. Outside the Western world, the proportion of beliefs not derived from the dominant religions is considerably greater. Thus, though the beliefs of Islam, Buddhism and Hinduism affect people's actions in Asia and Africa, most such people also believe in various kinds of spirits or other supernatural forces that are not derived from these religions. Since these affect their actions, it is necessary to take them into account. Perhaps the most important thing to remember regarding supernatural beliefs among non-Western people is that many things in life that are explicable to the Westerner are not explicable among non-industrialized peoples because of their relative lack of scientific concepts. Therefore, these people lean more heavily on supernatural explanations.

B. MEDICAL

Beliefs concerning the nature of the human body and physical ailments that do not stem from supernatural conceptions. It is sometimes difficult to distinguish the supernatural explanations of village people from "natural" ones. However, there are many theories that explain illness among village folk that are not related to any ideas of spirits or religious beliefs. Usually, such explanations are based on a limited knowledge of simple cause-and-effect relationships. For example, it is widely believed outside the industrialized Western countries that clear water is healthful water. This is a perfectly plausible belief if one is not aware of the existence of microbes that cannot be seen by the naked eye. Such medical beliefs among village people are not easy to change, mainly because it is difficult to demonstrate clearly the advantages of modern health practices. The benefits of therapeutic medicine, such as penicillin injections, are relatively easy to demonstrate because there are quick and obvious results, but preventive health practices, such as drinking boiled water, are difficult to transfer because the direct cause-and-effect relationship is not easy to show. In general, the most efficient strategy of medical innovation is to introduce new practices without insisting that the recipients immediately abandon their old ones.

C. ATTITUDINAL

Negative or positive attitudes toward the possibility of change. The most common attitude is that of negativism, which can be subdivided into situational and project negativism. Situational negativism is a type of realistic fatalism, based on real conditions which do make change very difficult. Some people are so poor, have so little land and resources, and have previously failed to better their own conditions so often that they simply do not believe they can improve their own circumstances. Usually such fatalism is based on a fairly realistic assessment of true conditions, but fortunately, most of the poor will usually respond again if projects which seem promising are presented to them. However, it must be recognized that when such realistic negativism exists, more effort will be required to get positive action than when it is not present.

Project negativism is a type of apathy or suspicion toward development projects that is based on previous project failures. Thus, if a rural village population has been promised assistance by their government or outside agencies and the members have invested their own time and money, and the change agency reneges on its commitment or does not follow through seriously, the villagers will be less interested in working on such a project another time. Fortunately, this kind of negativism can be most easily corrected by the change agencies, simply by seeing through to a finish any projects that are started.

The opposite attitude to negativism is, of course, positivism. This is a belief that conditions can be changed through one's own efforts, an affirmative attitude toward change based on previous project successes. It should be apparent that this kind of attitude is most rare, because if it were not, these communities would not need outside help, or at least would need no more than capital investment. There are a few places in the nonindustrialized world where development has progressed far enough that attitudes have become fairly positive, but generally such positive attitudes have not yet been developed.

▶ XVII. PRACTICES

Those patterns of behavior which do not easy fit into the previous sets are included here. Most traditional customs stem from either social structure, economic practices, or religious behavior. However, there are many practices of less over-all significance, though some may be fairly critical insofar as introducing change is concerned. The main two types are patterns of consumption and of recreation. In defining economic practices as methods of production, distribution and consumption of goods, we were referring only to the strictly utilitarian nature of consumption. That is, from an economic point of view all peoples require a minimum amount of food staples, but the kinds of food they use as staples are often arbitrarily selected or are the results of the accidents of history. For instance, there is no logical economic reason why the people of India use the milk of their water buffalo, whereas the rice farmers of Thailand and

Laos, who also have buffalo, never consume milk. The difference can only be explained on the basis of different cultural histories. Such cultural patterns of consumption, though not necessarily logical in economic terms, do nevertheless affect the reaction of people who are presented with new practices.

Other practices, such as recreation patterns, may also affect their behavior. Such customs are not extremely difficult to overcome if the change agent is aware of them and takes them into account. In general, though, since they are not closely connected with the vital necessities of life or the core of cultural beliefs, people will abandon them much more quickly than they will traditional social or economic practices.

▶ SUMMARY

Induced sociocultural change or technical innovation is a process that begins with an idea on the part of a change agent and ends in its adoption or rejection by the potential recipients. Adoption means that the new idea has been incorporated into the local society and the efforts of the change agent are no longer necessary. There are basically two forces at work once the plan of a new idea is put into effect: the action of the change agent and the reaction of the community of persons whom he expects to adopt the idea. The action is basically the body of techniques and strategies that are employed to convince the recipients to adopt the idea, whereas the reaction is the attitudes and behavior that stem from the recipients' perception of the value of the innovation and their motivations, which are products of how the idea was presented and of the ways in which the new idea will affect their traditional customs. In general, the role which the innovator plays, and particularly his techniques, are the most important ingredients in the change process. Where these techniques are poor, the innovation will almost invariably be rejected. Less often there are characteristics of traditional society which will negate the possibility of certain changes regardless of the techniques used.

Although there are at least seventeen different kinds of forces which impinge on the change process, there are six which stand out from the others. These can be regarded as the primary process variables: (1) the methods of communication used by the change agent, (2) the kind of participation he obtains from the recipients, and (3) the manner in which he utilizes and adapts his innovation to the existing cultural patterns; and as far as reaction of the recipients is concerned, the primary variables are (4) whether they have an initial felt need, (5) whether they perceive any practical benefit in adopting a change, and (6) whether their traditional leaders are brought into the planning and implementation of the process.

The first of these requirements means that the idea of the innovation has to be transferred fairly completely to the recipients, including establishing channels of feedback to get their reactions. Participation is required because it is the only true indication that the local people have any real commitment to the new idea. Active participation in the donation of labor and contribution of material, as well as organizational co-operation, is the most desirable. Utilization of the existing culture assists the change process because it presents the recipients with a change without threatening their old system completely.

The existence of a felt need is a clear indication that the local people recognize a problem themselves, and the complications of creating needs are avoided. Needs can be generated but, in general, they demand far more effort than changes based on existing needs. A practical benefit motivation is a sound basis on which to build only if it is perceived by the recipients. It must be remembered that rural peasants in the nonindustrial world have considerably different frames of reference than do technicians of the industrialized West, and their perceptions consequently will not be the same. But they are intensely practical within their limited horizons. Finally, the local leadership must be actively cultivated if change is to take place. Leaders have vested interests in their positions and if these are threatened or if they are ignored, they tend to resist outside influences.

Theoretically, if all six of these ingredients exist in a change project, the innovation will be adopted.

3

Land Reform and Community Development in Bolivia

In this first case history we find change agents attempting to deal with a problem which is widespread in Latin America, as well as in many other countries in the nonindustrialized world: gross inequality of land ownership. Although there is little doubt that exploitative land tenure systems usually prevent the efficient utilization of a country's human and natural resources, the problems in trying to correct such situations are far from simple. The most direct approach is to attempt to abolish the old system and replace it by one which provides land and opportunities for all. Unfortunately, an economic system, even an exploitative one, is a complex organization which is not easy to replace, certainly not in two or three years. Moreover, there are powerful vested interests involved in all economic systems that can exert much force against new plans, even after the old system has been abolished by law.

We find in the following account a multitude of such vested interests working against the goals of the project leaders to redistribute land and assist the new Indian landowners in achieving economic betterment. Former landowners were trying to save for themselves as much as they could, former Indian residents who had left the estate to live in the city saw the possibility of obtaining unexpected land grants, former foremen of the estate manipulated the new Indian owners by serving as interpreters to the innovators, and even schoolteachers tried to obtain elaborate living conditions through the project. Although it is difficult to know whether all these vested interests could have been satisfied, the establishment of better communication channels might have produced more project achievement than actually occurred. Not only did the foreign change agents lack ability to use the local Indian language, even most of the Bolivians involved could not speak it. The use of former foremen as interpreters created the possibility of considerable misunderstanding, since the foremen were primarily interested in maintaining their privileged position.

Another strong contributory difficulty was the failure of the change agents to learn much about the traditional economic patterns and motivations of the Indian recipients. The idea of co-operatives was not at all contrary to the values of the Indians as long as these were truly advantageous and as long as the Indians could participate fully in planning and running them. In fact, in those co-operatives where their interests were truly served, the Indians took the initiative; for example, they bought and rented out tractors on their own. Also, the Indians desired education so much that after the first school was built by the project, they began organizing and building others on their own. There were potential traditional leaders, although they were not recognized as such by the innovators.

Another common characteristic of peasant peoples of which the innovators were unaware was that preventive health practices are rarely understood by village people and, consequently, are rarely wanted. The Indians had little interest in medicine which concerned itself with the well as much as with the sick.

In sum, this effort can be viewed as having limited success primarily because of the powerful vested interests existing, the lack of good communication techniques by the innovators, and their failure to use the existing motivations for change or the potential leaders. There does not appear to be any simple solution that would have helped save this project, but perhaps the most basic principle indicated is that no change can take place through voluntary participation if no effective communication channels are established between change agents and recipients.

AN INDIAN COMMUNITY DEVELOPMENT
PROJECT IN BOLIVIA *

LORAND D. SCHWENG

For the Indians who accounted for over 60 percent of the total population of Bolivia, the Revolution of 1952 marked a turning point in history. The Revolutionary Government gave voting rights to the whole adult population of the country, "white," mixed and Indian, without any restrictions based on literacy in Spanish, which before had barred the Indians—and many of the mixed—from participation in political life. The workers of the mines, the most important export industry of Bolivia, were Indians and the nationalization of the mines brought considerable benefits to them. As far as the much larger rural Indian population was concerned, the establishment of a Ministry of Campesino Affairs and concentrating responsibility in that Ministry for social services in rural areas marked the break with the old regime. Under it the ministries which were responsible for such services as education, etc., on a functional basis, had a marked urban bias. At first the Government did not touch the land problem. It did not have a land policy spelled out, reportedly there was disagreement on the policy to be followed between the radical faction which advocated a sweeping land reform and the moderate faction which counselled caution and was against the indiscriminate wholesale redistribution of land.

When in the Cochabamba area Indians began attacking large estates and began dividing the land amongst themselves, the Government was forced to define its position and policy. A Commission was set up to study the land problem and to make recommendations within a set period. On recommendations of the Commission, on August 2, 1953, the Government promulgated the decree concerning the Land Reform.

The uncertain atmosphere prevailing in the rural areas of Bolivia after the Revolution did not permit the orderly conduct of farming operations on the larger estates. Once the Government

* Reprinted from *America Indigena*, Vol. XXII, No. 8, April, 1962, pp. 13-19, by permission of the publisher. Dr. Schweng is the former chief of the Pillapi Project of the Andean Mission in Bolivia. Since 1963 he has been with The Corporacion Venezolana de guayana, Caracas, Venezuela.

declared its intention to divide them up, ensuring the continuity of production became difficult, if not impossible. The tensions and uncertainties of the situation were increased by the extreme slowness with which the machinery set up by the Government for the carrying out of the land reform was moving. To make a bad situation worse, the Government was unable to assert its authority even in areas relatively near to and within easy reach of La Paz and could not make people respect the procedures it had laid down for the orderly implementation of the land reform.

It was estimated that only 2 percent of the total area of Bolivia was cultivated, and even before the Revolution the country relied heavily on imports of food. In the situation brought about by the land reform, on most if not all the larger estates, much of the land of the landlords was left uncultivated. The farm labourers who through the land reform or by taking the law into their own hands succeeded in enlarging the plots which they cultivated under the system of *colonato,* produced more for their own consumption, had more to eat and worked less than they had done before. But even where the *colons*-turned-*campesinos* had the desire to exert themselves and produce for the market, the lack of consumers goods and the dwindling purchasing power of money did not provide them with incentives. Nor was technical advice available. Production for the market came to a virtual standstill and the food deficit of Bolivia became even greater than it had been before the Revolution.

If the Government was concerned about improving the state of the Indian population of Bolivia, it was also concerned about restoring agricultural production to its pre-land-reform level and wanted to raise it even beyond that. The purpose of the Andean Indian Programme of ILO and the other four international organizations participating in the programme—FAO, UNTA, UNESCO and WHO—was to help the Government in both these efforts. The story of the Altiplano project of the programme is a good illustration of what happened on the divided large estates in Bolivia. Unfortunately the story has to end in the middle of 1956 because detailed information for recent years is lacking.

The Pillapi Estate on which the project was established had a total area of about 10,800 hectares and was located at the southern end of Lake Titicaca, 88 kilometers from La Paz, and was connected with La Paz both by road and railway. It comprised nine farms. The titles of five went back to colonial times, while four were acquired from Indian communities after 1900. Wedged in between the lands of the Estate there remained one small Indian community which succeeded in maintaining its independence. Some 500 Indian families lived on the lands of the Estate and supplied it with labour under the system of *colonato*. With the establishment of the Estate the original community organization of the Indians was broken up and was deprived of its functions. But the Indians living on each of the nine farms of the Estate retained a sense of community feeling which asserted itself once the Estate was broken up.

The *colons* of the Pillapi Estate were Aymara Indians. But they lived in a region which was within easy reach of La Paz and was near to a Lake Port, Guaqui, and a frontier town, Desaguadero. Also they had for decades been subjected to the discipline of a large estate which by Bolivian standards was advanced in its methods of management. They had thus been exposed to the impact of the white man's culture and passed through the early phases of acculturation long before the project was established in Pillapi. The fact that in spite of their long exposure they remained illiterate, disease-ridden and miserably poor, was proof not so much of their resistance to acculturation or the lack of desire for material improvement but rather to the lack of sympathy and interest in their welfare on the part of their former lords and masters and of the Government and, perhaps, also of the inappropriateness and lack of intensity and continuity of occasional efforts to improve their lot.

The planted acreage of the Estate was around 3,100 hectares of which nearly 2,900 hectares were the lands of the landlord and some 250 hectares were the cultivated plots of the *colons*. The rest of the land was grazed fallow, rough grazing land or was unproductive. The principal crop was barley, with potatoes a weak second; the other crops were insignificant. The Estate had a large number of pure-bred livestock: 16,000 sheep, 500 cattle and 800 pigs. The livestock of the *colons* may have added up to some 3,000 to 5,000 sheep, 1,500 to 2,000 cattle and 1,000 to 2,000 pigs of inferior quality.

The Estate was fairly well stocked with machinery and was considered advanced. But in spite of all that, yields per unit of land and per head of livestock were low not only by objective standards, but also in comparison with the averages of the region of the Lake. Nevertheless the Estate produced large quantities of potatoes, meat animals, butter, cheese and wool for the market.

In February 1954, six months after the promulgation of the Land Reform Law, the owners of the Pillapi Estate donated eight of their nine farms to a "Foundation for the Development of the Andean Peoples." The Foundation was founded in January 1954 for the purpose of promoting the cultural and economic development of the Indians, and its founders were the then Vice President of the Republic, the then Minister of Campesino Affairs who was responsible for the implementation of the Land Reform Law, and the Regional Director of the Andean Indian Programme, an international official who was a Bolivian citizen.

Having donated eight farms of the Estate to the Foundation, the owners reserved their right of ownership to the central farm of the Estate which had an area of some 2,700 hectares, and to the *casa de hacienda* on it, also to much of the equipment and the standing crops of the Estate. But they granted the Foundation the use of the house for a fixed period and stipulated that the Foundation should operate the central farm of the Estate for the mutual benefit of its owners and the Foundation for a fixed period. For this purpose they agreed to leave on the central farm some machinery and some livestock. The document made no reference to the Land Reform Law then already in force. At the invitation of the Foundation, ILO agreed to establish the Altiplano project on the Estate and the Pillapi project, as it was to be called, was started on March 1, 1954. The *colons* of the Estate were assuaged by promises of all sorts of benefits to come, e.g., a large school, a hospital, etc.

Soon after taking over, the ILO expert put in charge of the project filed a petition with the Agrarian Judge of the district and asked that the Land Reform Law be applied to the Estate. The National Land Reform Authority sent out a technical commission to prepare the plans for the repartitioning of the lands of the Estate. On three of the nine farms the *colons* denied entry to the commission and divided up the land amongst themselves. The cavalry regiment of the Guaqui which was near to that part of the Estate tried to get some land to provide it with fodder and hay for its horses but its efforts to get some lands from those of the Estate were in vain. The Government was not willing, or not able to enforce the law and make the *colons* respect the procedures laid down for the implementation of the land reform. While the plans for repartitioning the lands of the six farms were being prepared with the help of the project personnel, the owners of the Pillapi Estate sold nearly all their livestock and the standing crops to outsiders over the strong protests of the *colons*. Inevitably the *colons* had the impression that the project was working as an agent of the owners.

In May 1954 the Agrarian Judge approved the plans prepared by the commission. The total area of the farms was about 8,200 hectares. Around 4,800 hectares were divided up amongst some 450 claimants in lots of 2-50 hectares, depending on the quality of the land and the size of the family. Some 200 hectares were designated for communal use to give the *campesinos* access to the Lake and to provide land for school gardens; 1,100 hectares were declared to be for cooperative use while about 500 hectares, all on the central farm, were reserved for future distribution. With the exception of the 4,800 hectares distributed in individual holdings, the land became formally the property of the Foundation. But its use was restricted, the right of ownership was nominal and did not mean effective control even in the case of the 1,600 hectares of "forest land" which consisted of denuded hillsides and were used by the *campesinos* for grazing. The *campesinos* took possession of the 500 hectares reserved for future distribution on the central farm. The Foundation-Project remained in possession of the *casa de hacienda* and the neighbouring farm buildings although its control even over the latter was tenuous. It was left with no lands of any value for farming operations.

The Land Reform Law decreed that any adult Bolivian who could prove by simple testimony that he had been a member, or was the descendant of a member, of an Indian community which had been dispossessed after 1900—a so-called *excommunario*—could claim restitution of his former lands, irrespective of his actual residence or occupation. In the case of the Pillapi Estate several dozen such claims were filed by people who lived in La Paz and had some small businesses there. Some even took possession of sizable tracts of land on the Estate. Continuing with their business in La Paz, they took advantage of the law and let former *colons* cultivate the land so acquired. The people of Pillapi resented the intrusion of strangers even though several of the claims proved to be valid. The dispute between the *colons* and the *excomunarios* over land titles led to bitter and protracted quarrel which occasionally erupted in violence resulting in several wounded and in one case, the loss of life.

The presence of an international mission in the *casa de hacienda* and the claims it entertained on behalf of the Foundation to an undefined area of land on the central farm complicated the situation both because the claim reduced the area of land available for either *colon* or *excomunario* and because the project, by lending support to one side, could reduce the chances of the other in getting the coveted land. The *campesinos* did not distinguish between the Foundation which was a private Bolivian organization which had come to an agreement with the owners of the Pillapi Estate and the project which was a joint venture of the international agencies and the Bolivian Government and was in Pillapi as the guest of the Foundation without any direct obligations to the owners of the Estate. For the *campesinos* the project which occupied the *casa de hacienda* and was supposed to operate the central farm of the Estate for the joint benefit of the owners of Pillapi and the Foundation represented the owners. By keeping and claiming property for the owners which in the view of the *campesinos* was theirs by right, they believed that the project was protecting the interests of the owners against them. The project came under attack both from the side of the *campesinos* and the *excomunarios;* and in its predicament committed itself to defending unreservedly the position of the *campesinos* against the *excomunarios.*

The *excomunarios* appealed against the sentence of the Agrarian Judge. In September 1955, after a delay of eighteen months, on the repeated insistence of the project, the National Reform Council reviewed the sentence. It dismissed the appeal of the *excomunarios* and delimited the lands which the owners of the Pillapi Estate were allowed to retain to 80 hectares and the *casa de hacienda.*

In spite of the decision, the fight between the *campesinos* and the *excomunarios* continued and even increased in intensity. In January 1956, four months after the review of the sentence by the National Land Reform Council, the President of the Republic signed the decree which made the repartitioning of the lands of the Pillapi Estate final and recognized only five claims by *excomunarios.* At the same time the President signed another decree which expropriated the *casa de hacienda* and the 80 hectares left to the owners. Two months later, in March 1956, some of the *campesinos* were given title deeds and the distribution of the other deeds followed in due time.

The fight between the *campesinos* and the *excomunarios* interfered greatly with the work of the project and at times threatened its very existence. The terms of the agreement between the owners of the Pillapi Estate and the Foundation and its tenure in Pillapi as the guest of the Foundation put it into an ambiguous position vis a vis the *campesinos,* poisoned its relations with them, and handicapped it in its efforts to help them. Recognition of the mistake made by putting the project into Pillapi under such conditions and the correction of the mistake by the act of expropriation cleared the atmosphere but could not undo all the harm that had been done and could not make up for lost time.

One of the most important actions of the international expert who was put in charge of Pillapi when the project was started was to organize producers' cooperatives on each of the six farms of the Estate on which the project operated. The individual holdings of the *campesinos* were destined to be subsistence farms. The cooperative lands were expected to assure continuity of production for the market and provide funds for social investments. The total area of the cooperative lands was originally 1,100 hectares. When late in 1955 the sentence of the Agrarian Judge came up for review, their area was increased to some 1,500 hectares from the lands reserved for future distribution. The fact that the cooperative lands were disconnected fields, only a few of which were as large as 40-50 hectares, and that nearly all were irregular in shape and were scattered amongst the holdings of the *campesinos* detracted from their usefulness.

The cooperatives of Pillapi were rather informal organizations. They suffered from the lack of suitable leaders because most of the *campesinos* were illiterate and the few who could read and write often lacked other essential qualities of leadership. The help of the project consisted in giving advice and guidance in formalizing their procedures, in keeping their accounts, in providing them with seed, fertilizer, insecticides and pesticides, in providing tractors for the cultivation of the land and trucks for transporting the *campesinos* and their produce to La Paz. Originally no charges were made for these services because the project collected, or tried to collect, 30 percent of the crop of the cooperative lands. The *campesinos* disliked the system and it was difficult to enforce it. In 1956 it was agreed that the services required would be provided at cost and the project gave up its claim to part of the crop.

Under the scheme introduced by the Government the cooperatives of the *campesinos* were required to register. The cooperatives of Pillapi preferred independence to registration which would have put them under Government supervision and would have deprived them of control over their surpluses. As things were, in the spring of 1956, two of the larger cooperatives of Pillapi invested the proceeds from the sale of their crops in the purchase of two tractors. They made the decision on their own initiative and the role of the project was confined to helping them in negotiating the purchase and to underwriting the contract. This was the first step of the cooperatives to free themselves from the tutelage of the project.

Besides producing crops on the cooperative lands, the cooperatives kept livestock. They took possession of the livestock which the owners agreed to leave behind for the farm to be operated by the Foundation under the agreement, all told 17 head of cattle, 840 sheep and 13 pigs. By 1956 the number of livestock in the hands of the cooperatives increased to 19 head of cattle, 1,200 sheep and 38 pigs, but its quality deteriorated. The *campesinos* could not be prevailed upon to start a cooperative dairy farm using the buildings and equipment of the former Estate.

In its efforts to help the producers' cooperatives in the cultivation of their lands and in improving the crops and livestock of the *campesinos* on their individual holdings, the project was badly handicapped by lack of equipment, lack of pure-bred livestock for grading up or even the lack of buildings to house such livestock, lack of control over land for grazing and for producing fodder and roughage and lack of working capital. Most of the machinery and the buildings found on the Estate were in bad repair. For over two years the unsettled state of ownership of the central farm of the Estate and lack of funds made any serious effort to improve agriculture difficult if not impossible.

In 1954-55 the cooperatives had 142 hectares under crops. In 1955-56 the planted acreage rose to 600 hectares. If it is assumed that the odd 450 *campesino* farms had 450 hectares planted, which would have required doubling the area they had planted for themselves before the land reform, the total planted area of the six farms added up to some 1,100 hectares as against some 2,400 hectares before the land reform. As the owners succeeded in selling

most of their livestock before the Estate was divided, production of
butter and cheese stopped. The meat and wool production of the
campesino-livestock was only a fraction of what the production of
the Estate had been. The volume of production of the six farms
of the Estate was perhaps 30 percent of what it had been before
the land reform and the volume of produce sold off farms declined
even more. Even a more efficient use of the cooperative lands would
not have made up for the loss of livestock.

Other cooperatives which were set up on each of the six farms
with the help of the project were consumers' cooperatives. They
sold rice, lard, sugar, and other goods issued by the Government as
rations at reduced prices. They also started selling other goods in
demand by the *campesinos* and in 1956 began setting up small
stores.

Possibly because they were left free to run the cooperatives
themselves and no attempt was made to foist complicated rules on
illiterate *campesinos,* the cooperative idea did not meet with a hostile reception in Pillapi. Rather, the *campesinos* looked upon the
cooperatives as their concern and found in them a useful frame for
common action even in fields which were beyond the original fields
of the cooperatives. When it came to building schools, the cooperatives took upon themselves the organization of the work. The more
prosperous cooperatives began helping out the weaker ones by lending to them and later by hiring out their tractors.

Parallel with the cooperatives the Government encouraged the
formation of *sindicatos* which were political organizations, the purpose of which was to protect the rights of the *campesinos* and guard
the achievements of the social reforms of the Revolution. All adult
male and female *campesinos* were to be members of *sindicatos,*
which were knitted into a national organization and were put under
the control of district *comandos,* appointed by the ruling revolutionary party. The *campesinos* of Pillapi understood the functions and
purposes of the cooperatives which, therefore, became real and
alive organizations, but found little use for the *sindicatos* which to
them seemed to overlap or be rivals of the cooperatives. Nor were
the *sindicatos* effective instruments of control from above. When
troubles arose in Pillapi and the *campesinos* became restive and
defied the authorities, the *comandos* were just as powerless in dealing with them as were the civil authorities.

Early in 1955 ILO evolved the idea of making an industrial

vocational training center in Pillapi. It was to be equipped with power-driven machine tools donated to ILO for the Andean Programme by American and German trade unions. The region of Pillapi was singularly poor in lumber, clay and other raw materials for crafts, except wool. The only material available locally was the derelict machinery of the Estate and of the neighboring estates which had suffered a similar fate. These machines could be repaired or their material could be used for making hand implements. All other material and fuel had to be brought up from La Paz. No large market for things made in the proposed workshops existed in the area. Another difficulty was that skills acquired in the workshops would be of little value in the communities in and near Pillapi. To use these skills the *campesinos* would have to migrate to the cities and become industrial labourers. This, however, would have conflicted with the original idea of the rural rehabilitation project on the Altiplano.

In starting the vocational training center suffered delay because there were no buildings suitable for workshops, stores, dormitories nor classrooms for the trainees, etc. Lack of local funds hampered the work of reconditioning and converting existing buildings and precluded new construction. In any case, until the ownership of the *casa de hacienda* and the central farm of the Estate was settled, the wisdom of investing considerable Government funds in such work was inadvisable. Under an agreement between the owners of the Estate and the Foundation, the property was to revert to the owners after a few years without any compensation for the improvements made. In January 1956 when the property of the owners was expropriated, the situation changed and funds permitting construction could be speeded up. In the second half of 1956 some workshops could be started, but no detailed information is available about the operation of the industrial vocational training center.

The project was more successful in education and health than in its efforts to improve agriculture production or in teaching the *campesinos* crafts which they could practice in their communities. There had been a few schools on the Estate before the project was started. Little was known about them, except that they were small and must have been grossly inadequate for the large number of children of school age on the Estate. The project opened a school on each of the five larger farms of the Estate, at first using reconditioned farm buildings. Somewhat later, in 1955, a large school-house was built on one of the farms and in 1956 proper school buildings were built on the sites of school gardens to replace the temporary structures and were, in time, furnished with the necessary minimum equipment.

The interest in education the *campesinos* showed was moving. After the first school was built in 1955 at the expense of the project, the other schools were built by the *campesinos* themselves. They made the adobe bricks, levelled the ground, dug the foundations and provided all the unskilled labour. The project furnished the plans, provided supervision and the services of a mason and a carpenter, bought the material that could not be produced locally and had it transported to the building site in each instance.

In the school year 1954-55 the number of enrolled pupils was 113. In 1955-56 their number rose to 479, of whom 190 were adults attending evening literacy classes. Some 350 pupils attended school regularly and 290 completed the courses. In 1956-57 enrollment remained at about the same level. It was estimated that about 70 percent of the children of school age were attending school. The ratio was much higher for the boys than for the girls.

The schools should have been the best means for winning the confidence of the *campesinos* and for reaching the parents through the children. Unfortunately, during the first two years of the project particularly, relations between teachers and the project workers were not good. The teachers had little use for a "Gringo" project that could not provide schools greatly superior in equipment to those provided in rural areas by the Government of Bolivia and could not assure higher pay and more favorable living conditions than those prevailing in Government schools for its teachers. Instead of using their position and influence with the *campesinos* to convince them of the motives and purposes of the project, they worked against it.

In their educational effort, the schools were handicapped by the Government's insistence on using the schools as an instrument of "castellanizacion," for forcing the use of Spanish on non-Spanish speaking Indians to the exclusion of their native tongue. The mother tongue of the children of Pillapi was Aymara and no other language was spoken at home; the women spoke Aymara only and there were only a few fathers who spoke even a little Spanish. But in the schools, from the first grade, the language of instruction was Spanish and Aymara was not taught at all. The continuation of this policy after the Revolution was in strange contrast with the cult of the Indian encouraged by the Government and the freedom given for the use of Indian languages, Aymara and Quechua, in politics. Forcing Spanish made teaching very difficult and the educational effort wasteful. Without opportunity for using the language most children soon forgot the little Spanish they picked up at school in the two years they customarily attended. They learned less than would otherwise have been the case.

Health was intended to be another important field of endeavor in the project. Before the project, the *colons* of Pillapi had no health service. The landlords maintained a public bath house and periodic bathing was compulsory. The huts of the *colons* were sprayed. After the Revolution a state maternity home was built in a nearby town, Guaqui, but it was 20 kilometers by a dry weather road from the center of the Estate and the doctor and nurse who were stationed at the center had no transportation. When the project was established a doctor and a nurse, later two nurses, were stationed in Pillapi and a small dispensary was opened—one little room with two beds served as an emergency hospital. While the schools and educational efforts were welcomed, the health service encountered difficulties. The *campesinos* preferred their healers and sorcerers to the medical doctor. Some of their enmity and distrust may have been due to the insistence of the authorities on starting the work with a house to house health and family survey and to their emphasis on preventive as against curative medicine. People not accustomed to any kind of medical care or service and distrustful of "white" strangers do not understand the need for and usefulness of surveys and resent inquisitive questioning. Also for them the function of the healer is to cure sick people and they do not understand why those who appeared to be healthy should be molested. Lack of continuity caused by frequent changes of personnel and the temporary closing down of the health center were other factors which slowed down progress in this important field of activity. Until the suspension of the service in 1955, the number of inoculations and vaccinations was impressive and had, no doubt, a beneficial effect on health conditions in the area. But in health education and in improving the sanitation of the *campesino* households the success of the project was less noticeable.

In the first two years the radius of action of the project did not extend beyond the limits of the former Estate or rather the six farms of the Estate, which accepted the project. After 1956 the project began to operate in other communities near the southern end of the Lake. The original idea that Pillapi would spark off a number of little Pillapis and that Pillapi itself would develop into a training center of village leaders and rural social workers who would carry the idea of Pillapi all over the Altiplano of Bolivia failed to materialize. The large concentration of Aymara Indians near the Lake remained untouched and the project did not become the symbol of Indian advancement and integration like the school of Warisata which, incidentally, was not so very far from Pillapi.

The lessons of Pillapi were, however, of wider application. It was claimed that the project was a testing ground of the Bolivian land reform law. The test proved to be an expensive one but at least, as a result, the Government changed the provisions of the land reform law in respect to the *excomunarios*. They could still claim land if they wanted to but they were to be compensated from where land was available and not necessarily from the lands of their original communities.

Another lesson was that inability to communicate directly with the people greatly reduced the effectiveness of a community development project. International experts working on a one-year contract have little inducement to learn Aymara. But in Pillapi even the Bolivian experts could not speak the language of the Indians and the project had to rely on a few Spanish-speaking *campesinos* as intermediaries. They were former foremen of the Estate who exploited their position of vantage and added greatly to the project's difficulties. Only in the third year did the situation change when the project was given a chief who spoke Aymara.

The experience of Pillapi showed that Aymara Indians were not quite as "bad" and were not as hostile to change and improvements in their ways of life as it was often believed. But it also showed that their system of priorities was different from that of their would-be-benefactors and their wish was to live better according to their own ideas of well-being and to be left largely to themselves. They were ready to accept changes in fields where these did not conflict with and could be fitted into the pattern of their traditional beliefs and practices, but their capacity for change was limited. For success, innovations had to be sandwiched, so to speak, between things they wanted for themselves and, to carry the metaphor further, one had to be careful in not overloading the sandwich. They had a keen sense of privacy and resented the intrusion of a host of "white" strangers, especially when they could not understand and appreciate their functions.

The key to improving their life seemed to be their interest in the education of their children. Providing the right kind of education for the children held out the greatest hope of success in introducing changes in the lives of the parents as well. But the right type of education for the children would presuppose using their native language in the lowest one or two grades and introducing Spanish as a foreign language only after they acquired the rudiments of knowledge in their own language.

One important lesson of Pillapi was that without firm direction and guidance the Indian communities of the divided large estates were not able to develop and make good use of the means provided for them to improve their level of living; production tended to get stabilized at a comfortable subsistence level. The discipline of the large estate cannot be removed suddenly, without impunity; in addition to some form of organization, incentives and technical aid are necessary to maintain production at its former level and even more for raising it higher.

Once the *campesinos* learned that they had no reason to suspect the "white" strangers who came to help them, they were prepared to accept a guiding hand and even firmness as long as they were treated as human beings and felt they had a fair deal. But they were extremely suspicious, reacted quickly to wavering or a relaxation of firmness and had retentive memories. Broken promises easily destroyed confidence.

4

Community Development in Highland Peru

Wherever possible we have tried to select contrasting case histories in which the basic sociocultural situation of the recipient communities was the same although the techniques of the innovators were different. We believe that by comparing such studies the student of sociocultural change will be able clearly to see for himself what difference it makes when innovators understand the basis of change and employ techniques which bring cooperation. With this principle in mind we know of no more fitting contrast to the previous case history than that of Vicos, Peru. The recipient communities were very similar and the goal was almost identical, yet the results were completely different. The characteristic that was strikingly different was the innovation techniques. But even more than this very useful contrast, an understanding of the Vicos experiment is almost a requirement in itself for those interested in bringing about change in peasant communities.

There is frequently no clear understanding of what development consists, particularly by those who are strongly oriented toward an economic approach. It is easy to conceive of change as the development of material resources, exemplified by constructions such as bridges, roads, schools, markets or irrigation canals. If this point of view predominates, the innovator can easily forget that what makes these things possible are the people who build them, and the difference between people who do and people who don't is a matter of attitude and social organization. People who build such things do so because they are convinced they can, and have organizations that enable them to do so. From this point of view, therefore, the work of the developer in the peasant communities of the world is to build new attitudes and new organizations. Then the new schools, roads and markets will get built. The innovators at Vicos knew what their task was and went at it directly—to build confidence among the downtrodden Indians.

In contrast to the Bolivian pilot project, the Vicos innovators established efficient communication channels from the first. Although the Vicos Indians may have wondered what was happening in the beginning, since previously they had always been told what to do rather than asked what they wanted to do, they responded rapidly to the challenge of planning and working out their own lives when this became possible. This took place despite the fact that they were a hostile and disorganized people when the project began.

Because the innovators were interested in studying the local community, as well as helping it improve itself, they learned much about the recipients which the change agents in Bolivia never realized. They knew or learned at the very beginning that you do not build confidence among people who lack the very minimum of food and shelter by stressing projects that have meaning only to persons already well off. In particular, you do not emphasize latrines and sanitary improvements to people who are hungry. These things can come later, when some confidence has been built and some measure of health education has taken place. The innovators at Vicos also knew that one of the best times to get action from communities is when they are faced with a crisis for which their traditional culture gives them no solution. The potato blight described below was just that, and the solution proposed had great strategic importance.

Powerful economic vested interests occurred at Vicos, as they did in the Bolivian project, and though the resulting problems were not completely settled, Vicos went on until the *hacienda* was a self-sufficient community. Perhaps the most significant observation that can be made in this regard is that the innovators were wise enough to obtain powerful allies among government officials. Much can be done with peasants if one deals with them directly, but the facts of life in the nonindustrialized world are that no village community exists in a political vacuum. Organized changes that are instituted at a village level, but which are never built into national structures, have little chance for survival in the long run.

The final comment to be made here is in regard to the spread of new ideas beyond the point of innovation. Though we believe that a new idea is successfully transferred to another people when it is integrated into their cultural patterns, even more convincing is the process whereby it begins to spread to other communities independently of the efforts of the change agents. This has happened dramatically in the highlands of Peru, owing to the influence of Vicos.

REACHING THE HEART OF
SOUTH AMERICA *

JOHN LEAR

The Soviet revolution in Russia has captured the imagination of millions by turning an isolated and impoverished peasant people into a powerful nation in less than half a century.

It is curious that in searching for a counter to the influence of this dramatic achievement, the geopoliticians of American democracy should either overlook or ignore the presence just next door of an experiment that has lifted the human spirit across 400 years of time within one decade.

I speak of Vicos, a *hacienda* two miles up, almost unheard of in this country but fast becoming known in South America as "the cry of freedom" of the Andes.

Vicos occupies an entire mountainside in central Peru. It stretches from the lowermost edge of the glacier topping the peak to the bank of the Santa River in the valley below. A full mile up and down—from 9,000 to 14,000 feet altitude—it runs, covering 35,000 to 40,000 acres. Over one of its upper slopes a pass leads eastward into lower ranges of hills dotted with mines, and trains of pack mules daily bear silver and lead through the *hacienda* westward toward the sea.

In the year 1594, the land of Vicos and the Indians living on it were sold as a parcel by the Viceroy of Peru to Don Fernando de Colonia for 300 pesos and nine reales. From that day forward, the serfs and the rocky hills they tilled and grazed passed from owner to owner, from owner to renter, and from renter to renter, until the year 1952. Then a Minnesota-born anthropologist on the faculty of Cornell University gambled his future as a scientist on application of a psychiatric principle to anthropology.

Allan R. Holmberg, he is. He rented Vicos in hope of teaching the Indians to live as free and responsible men instead of what they had been—the animals closest to men in the evolutionary line.

"What does a psychoanalyst do?" Holmberg asked himself before undertaking his pioneer intervention at Vicos. "He starts with

* Reprinted from *Saturday Review,* Nov. 3, 1962, pp. 55-58, by permission of the publisher. Mr. Lear is Science Editor of the *Saturday Review.*

a patient who desires but is unable to function in the fullest capacity in the world in which he interacts. The fact that he cannot do so may be the fault of the society in which he lives, but if the patient is to make a satisfactory and desirable adjustment to life, he must change his behavior in various ways. The analyst cannot change his behavior for him; the patient must do it for himself. Ideally, what happens is this: through a process of self-enlightenment, with occasional strategic intervention by the analyst, the patient cures himself so that he can face up to his anxieties and shoulder his responsibilities to the best of his native abilities.

"It seems to me that the role of the participant interventionist in the process of community development is much the same. His job is to assist the community to develop itself, and to study this process while it is taking place. He cannot 'cure' the community as a surgeon cures a patient; the community must perform the operation on itself."

At the end of five years of intervening at Vicos, Professor Holmberg's lease was up. Had his experiment worked? He could only wait and wonder. A long period of excruciating uncertainty followed. The Indians, responding to his encouragements, tried to take over the place. They failed. They tried again. And on 13 July 1962 they finally signed a purchase contract and made a down payment of twenty-five percent toward buying Vicos and with it their personal liberty.

Foreign policy makers in Washington, D.C., could note with profit that the Vicos project would have collapsed if Professor Holmberg had at any time been in doubt about his true beliefs concerning the dignity of man, or timid in their pursuit, or reluctant to seize opportunities that appeared unannounced from unlikely directions.

Cornell University had no intention that any member of its faculty should become a feudal landlord when Holmberg went to Peru as an assistant professor of anthropology in 1949. Because of his prior experience among the Indians of the Amazon lowlands in Bolivia and the highlands of Peru, he had been picked by Professor Lauriston Sharp to participate in a global study of the effects of impingement of industrial civilization on agrarian peoples. The Carnegie Corporation had given Professor Sharp a grant to explore such matters in New Mexico, Canada, India, Thailand, and Peru (see SR/Research for June 1956).

Peru had been chosen for attention because a steel mill was planned on its Pacific coast at Chimbote Bay, and a hydroelectric dam to power the mill was being thrown across the top of Canyon del Pato, through which the Santa River drops precipitately westward after coursing north for miles between two mountain chains: the Black and the White Cordillera of the Andes. All along the Callajon de Huaylas, the Santa valley upstream from the dam, isolated Indian settlements had existed with little change since the days of the Spanish conquest. Holmberg's original assignment was to study what happened to these Indians after the dynamos at the dam's bottom began to generate power. But an Andean avalanche intervened, piling tons of the countryside against the dam and plugging the tunnels down which the Santa's waters were to plunge onto the power generator blades at the canyon's bottom.

Many scientists would have given up at that point and gone elsewhere. But Holmberg saw a rare chance to try something new and bold on the *hacienda* Vicos, one of the subjects of his study. Like thousands of similar properties in the Peruvian highlands (estimates range from 2,000 to 6,000; there is no official census of them), Vicos was owned by a Public Benefit Society and was rented out on a ten-year lease. The Public Benefit Societies of Peru are responsible for maintenance of local hospitals. Their purpose in renting Benefit properties is to obtain operating funds. The renters are free to gather as much profit for themselves as the traffic will bear, and these profits are customarily far in excess of the leasehold fee.

Vicos, however, hadn't brought much profit to anyone for a long time. The renter who was at the moment using the *hacienda* to grow flax and weave linen in a factory nearby had gone bankrupt halfway through his decade of tenancy.

Professor Holmberg was acquainted with Ignacio Masias, the Peruvian engineer responsible for settlement of the bankruptcy case, and could have rented the *hacienda* on his own, as a private citizen. But a "gringo" stepping into such a situation would be bound to create a sensation, which the Professor did not want. His purpose was to bring about lasting betterment in the lives of the Indians. That could be done only with the active and sustained help of farsighted Peruvians of substance who understood the explosive implications of their country's "Indian problem." Such enlightened persons were not readily available.

There did exist, on paper, in the Peruvian capital city of Lima, a Peruvian Institute of Indian Affairs. Aside from a dedicated secretary, the Institute possessed little more than an air of enthusiasm. Certainly the anthropologist from Cornell had no reason to expect material assistance from it. However, the Institute had recently acquired a new president, Dr. Carlos Monge Medrano, who was not only the most distinguished physician in Peru but also a serious student of the biology of Andean man.

An international gathering of scholarly specialists in Peruvian affairs assembled at the U.S. Embassy in Lima in August 1951. Dr. Monge was there. Professor Holmberg was there, too. They met for the first time that day and immediately formed an alliance. By the following November, Dr. Monge had managed his connections in high Peruvian society deftly enough to enlist the influence of General Armando Artola, Minister of Labor and Indigenous Affairs in the Cabinet of Peru's president of that time, Manuel Odria. As a native of the Callajon de Huaylas, General Artola knew the Vicos situation intimately and was touched by the opportunity to help a people from whose midst he had sprung. Through him, prestige came to the Peruvian Institute of Indian Affairs practically overnight, and on 30 November 1951 Dr. Monge and Professor Holmberg signed a contract making them joint landlords of Vicos.

Although he learned Quechua, the native tongue of the Vicos Indians, in order to follow the details of everything that happened, Dr. Monge remained for the most part in Lima, meshing the scientific and political aspects of the project there. Professor Holmberg, having already moved his wife and three small children from Ithaca, N. Y., to the town of Marcara near Vicos, at the beginning of the Vicos lease in January 1952 moved again into a dilapidated adobe house facing the *hacienda* plaza. There he and his family remained until September 1952—without plumbing, boiling drinking water from an irrigation ditch—while the Professor put the Indians on the road to independence.

As *patron* of the estate, the Professor held absolute power over 380 families: a total of 1,700 people. The head of every family owed him three days work a week, at any site he chose. His immediate predecessor, the flax grower, for example, had used the Indians not only for tending the flax growing on Vicos but for running the linen factory a number of miles away. The Indian women and children were also required to serve the *patron* as cooks, maids, housekeepers, grooms and shepherds.

The best fields on the *hacienda,* along the Santa river, were reserved for the *patron.* The Indians worked them free, in part payment of their three-day tax, in return for the privilege of scratching the barest living from patches of hostile soil higher on the mountainside.

Traditionally, the *patron* exercised his lordly authority from a distance, visiting Vicos on rare occasions with the right to be carried about anywhere inside the property limits on the backs of the Indians. In his absence a resident *mayordomo* ruled for him through a military hierarchy of lieutenants and sub-lieutenants in the fields and pastures. Once a week the Indians would be assembled at a central point to hear orders for the week ahead.

The attitude of the Indians toward the *patron* was one of extreme hostility, as might be expected in a situation where economic, political and judicial power were so intensely concentrated in a single pair of hands. "In fact," Professor Holmberg wrote at the time, "about the only area of culture in which his [the *patron's*] power did not seriously impinge was that of religion, which was left pretty much in local hands. Thus, while the community went through the process of annually electing an official—an indigenous mayor who appointed a number of assistants—he or they had little or nothing to say in matters of secular concern; and since positions of responsibility in public affairs were lacking, adequate leadership did not develop, almost no public services were maintained, and the community was reduced to a highly disorganized state. Beyond alliances to immediate kinship groups and a devotion to the religious *fiesta* as a relief from frustration and despair, there were almost no other values which were widely shared among the members of Vicos society. At the same time, standards of living were at a bare minimum; health and nutritional levels were extremely low; educational facilities (and consequently skills) were almost completely lacking; cooperation within the community was the exception rather than the rule; resistance to the outside world was extremely high; attitudes toward life were static and pessimistic. Nor was it in the interest of the various *patrons* to change this system, for an organized and enlightened community would have meant an end to the disproportionately favored position which they occupied."

To prevent the estate from falling apart, Professor Holmberg kept the former *mayordomo* on the job at Vicos, and allowed him a set of six lieutenants. Then, with the help of a young Peruvian anthropologist, Mario Vasquez, the Professor began gradually to change the weekly meetings of the Indians from periods of passive listening to active discussion of *hacienda* problems. To encourage a genuine exchange of opinion, the *patron's* right to personal service was abolished, and the crops from the *patron's* lands were declared community property, to be sold for the purpose of accumulating cash reserves with which ownership of Vicos might someday be acquired.

The talk of cash and freedom probably sounded insane to the Indians, for they were starving. A blight had destroyed the potatoes, their favorite food. But Professor Holmberg was not dealing in nonsense. By integrating the values he was trying to teach, he made one support another. Establishment of the old *patron* fields as common property made it possible to demonstrate that better potatoes could be grown bigger at lower cost through use of modern planting, fertilizing, spraying and harvesting methods. The example encouraged the Indians to try the new methods in cultivation of their own fields. The new methods multiplied their harvests until the Vicosinos were not only feeding themselves to satiation but were sending potatoes to market in Lima. Profits from the sales of potatoes grown on the common lands could then be used for building a school and a medical clinic. The school heightened the Indians' sense of dignity and pride, so that before Professor Holmberg's lease was up they elected a council of ten to govern themselves.

This startling evolution had been finessed on a shoestring. Having only the Carnegie Corporation's $100,000 grant to spend, the Professor had gone back to teach at Cornell in September 1952, leaving behind him at Vicos, as *patron pro tem,* first one younger American—William Mangan of Yale—and then another: William Blanchard of Cornell. Mario Vasquez, the Peruvian, stayed loyally on, continuing his researches simultaneously with subtle innovations in the Indians' affairs.

In Lima, meanwhile, Dr. Monge steadily strengthened the Peruvian Institute of Indian Affairs. Toward the end of 1956, he was ready to use its reinforced prestige to push for expropriation of Vicos by the Peruvian national government. The expropriation decree went through in 1958, but it required that a purchase price be agreed on amicably between the Public Benefit Society owner of Vicos and the Vicos Indians. Furthermore, the Indians had to pay in cash. Having learned, from the Professor's demonstration, how profitable a property Vicos could be, the Public Benefit Society declined to sell at any price the Indians could afford. The expropriation decree lapsed in 1960, for lack of compliance. At the beginning of July 1961, the Public Benefit Society brought suit to recover Vicos.

Again Dr. Monge interposed the reinforced prestige of the Peruvian Institute of Indian Affairs. He persuaded the national government to negotiate direct sale of Vicos. This removed the requirement for cash payment. In 1962 a price of 2,000,000 soles [26.8 soles: $1 US] was fixed, the Indians paid 500,000 soles down, the national government loaned them 1,000,000 soles more to add to that payment, and the Public Benefit Society agreed to accept the 500,000 sole balance over a period of three years—provided that the national government first would give the Public Benefit Society an extra 1,256,861 soles with which to build a new hospital in the city of Huaraz. Although the owners of Vicos thus collected 3,256,861 soles for what had been a rundown estate before the Cornell anthropologist's appearance, that price was only half what they demanded of the Indians before Lima cracked down.

Where does the Vicos experiment stand today?

Its people still live in adobe huts. They have no bathrooms. Their drinking water is impure. Their food is primitive. They weave their own clothes and wear them Indian style.

"But we didn't set out to change these people outside," Professor Holmberg says. "We weren't putting on a show. We wanted to change the inside, where it matters. Do you remember that the last improvement we got here in the United States was plumbing? The Indians of Vicos will have bathrooms, too, when they are ready. All sorts of changes are possible in the lives of people when they have enough to eat, shelter from the elements, and freedom to make intelligent choices.

What of the scientific implications of Vicos?

"In the natural sciences," the Professor points out, "research and development are inseparable. Scientific discovery is sooner or later inevitably put to the test of success or failure through the application of research results in engineering and technology. Research and development work in behavioral science are seldom joined as they were to some extent in Vicos, for the systematic exploitation of their reciprocal benefits. To get the feedback necessary for rapid advance in a behavioral science like anthropology, policy is needed, even if policy does not need science."

A CONTAGIOUS EXPERIMENT *

HENRY F. DOBYNS, CARLOS MONGE MEDRANO, and MARIO C. VASQUEZ

The year 1961 was the tenth year of participant intervention and follow-up research carried out by anthropologists of Cornell University in the Andean community of Vicos in Peru, in collaboration with the Peruvian Indian Institute and other governmental agencies. In discussing the progress of this community development program conceived a decade ago by what we may term "an intelligent American," we wish to consider four social structural levels of impact. These are progressively larger geographic zones of Peru: the communtty, the neighborhood, the region, and the nation.

The achievements within the Vicos community and community reactions to them have already been described, so that we need say little more about this level. However, we may inject one index of the reaction of the Vicos Indians to the total change achieved by

* Reprinted from *Saturday Review*, Nov. 3, 1962, pp. 59-62, by permission of the publisher. Dr. Dobyns, who is now lecturer in Anthropology at Cornell University and Assistant Director of the Vicos Project, was Research Coordinator of the Project from 1960 to 1962. Dr. Monge Medrano is Director of the Peruvian Institute of Indian Affairs, and is one of the foremost authorities on tropical diseases. Dr. Vasquez, who has been associated with the Vicos Project from its inception, is presently Research Coordinator of the Project and Research Associate in the Department of Anthropology at Cornell University.

their community since initiation of the project. This is the return of migrants to Vicos. A recent analysis of migratory movements in and out of Vicos found that thirty families, or seven percent of all families now living in that community, have returned to Vicos during the past seven years. The specific motivations for returning are as varied as specific reasons for emigrating from Vicos in the first place, but they may all be summed up under the rubric of taking advantage of the relatively more favorable socioeconomic environment in Vicos created by the sharing of values there set in motion by the Cornell Peru Project.

These returning migrants reinforce the dynamics of change in Vicos by bringing to the community concepts new to it which they have learned during their residence on the coast. These families are commerce-oriented, buy and sell for a quick turnover and profit instead of traditional Vicos hoarding. They are vociferously anti-*hacendado* and anti-rich. They understand the idea of the strike and have experience striking. Thus the body of returned migrants complements the group of returned army veterans with a different set of experiences outside Vicos. With the former school students, they constitute the total Vicos populace effectively exposed to modern Western civilization.

Passing to the neighborhood around Vicos (operationally defined as the administrative Province of Carhuaz), we must distinguish two types of reactions to the project. One is acceptance and the other is resistance. Within "acceptance" we can disguish at least three sub-types.

Peasant enthusiasm. First, the Indian peasants living in the immediate neighborhood of Vicos have viewed the social and economic results of project intervention with general enthusiasm. Their specific attitude is often one of jealousy of the Vicos Indians for having received special attention from the "gringos," and desire for equivalent programs for themselves. Since the direct intervention of Cornell University as administrator ceased in 1956, the community development and educational program of the Peruvian government carried on in Vicos has been extended to nine other adjacent communities, primarily through the functioning of the greatly enlarged Vicos school as a nucleus for a rural peasant school system.

Landed proprietor cooperation. The expanded rural school program involves some of the large estate owners of the neighborhood who have welcomed governmental educational efforts directed toward their serfs. These cooperating landlords have donated plots of their land for school building construction, and have even assigned obligatory peasant labor to construction projects.

Mestizo emulation. The peasant school program also reaches some mestizos [Spanish-Indian mixed bloods] farming small properties between the large estates, particularly near the towns of Marcara and Carhuaz. Residents of these towns formerly lorded their socially superior position over the Vicos Indians but now some townsmen question the Vicosinos about the details of their modern agricultural technology. The school program extends to one legally recognized "indigenous community" between Vicos and Marcara—Recuayhuanca, which actually is more mestizo than Indian. The people of Recuayhuanca joined with the people of Vicos to construct a building for a medical clinic.

Not involved in the organizational and technological progress set in motion in the local neighborhood by the project are some estate owners and managers, who manage to inhibit the participation of their Indian serfs in the benefits of general neighborhood improvement. This lack of involvement reflects the direct refusal of such landed proprietors to grant the validity of the Vicos project goals. These men are resisting the project, particularly its extension to affect the indigenous population from whose forced labor they benefit.

We may cite violent indices of this resistance. When government expropriation of Vicos was decided, four ministers of the Peruvian national government visited Vicos in January of 1957. (A visit by such dignitaries to such a community almost never occurs in Peru.) The serfs of Chancos, an adjoining estate, took advantage of this unheard of opportunity to ask the ministers to extend the Vicos program to their estate. When they returned to their homes that night, their master had them flogged for impertinence.

In 1960, the Indians on another adjoining estate, Huapra, formally included within the "zone of action" of the Vicos rural peasant school nucleus, began constructing a new school building [for their own children] and petitioned ecclesiastical authorities for permission to plant uncultivated fields of Huapra on the same community-enterprise and profit plan followed in Vicos. The hereditary renter of this church-owned property sought and obtained a fifteen-man armed detachment of national police on the plea that his life and property were endangered by invading, strange peasants. On 9 August 1960, he led this detachment to the hillside where the serfs were planting, and when the police attempted to arrest Indian leaders, police gun fire killed three peasants and seriously wounded five others. In the aftermath of this massacre, the chief executive officer of Ancash department [state], who authorized use of the police, was allowed to resign by the [national] Minister of Government.

Both landed proprietors and townsmen have a vested interest in maintaining the status quo. The mestizos of neighboring Marcara are turning more against Vicos as cultural change and economic progress in Vicos destroy or menace the hitherto privileged mestizo position.

Vicos has dried up as a fountain of free or cheap labor commanded by Marcara residents. The Vicos Indian who in the past was hired out by the renter of Vicos during the Indian's obligatory work days, or voluntarily worked by the day for a pittance, today stays at home to work his own plot. He can make more money tilling his own soil using modern methods than he could by hiring out—some families report up to 5,000 soles this season in cash realized above family food needs. The disappearance of Vicos labor from Marcara has given rise to an opposition claim that the project works the Vicos Indians harder than they were ever worked before. The mestizo, who places a negative value on manual labor, seems unable to perceive that the Indian, who places a high value on labor, is happily laboring harder than ever before *in his own interest*.

The people of Marcara can no longer casually order the Indians of Vicos to perform minor menial tasks and expect obedience. Thus when a car went off the road recently and some men from Vicos were ordered to pull it back, they left it where it sat. This makes the Vicos people "very rebellious," and the "most odious Indians" of the district in the view of the Marcara citizens.

The small merchants of Marcara are losing their traditional trade in Vicos because of consequences of project activities. The mestizo merchants who formerly supplied maize and wheat to Vicos now sell little. The Vicos community farm enterprise raises about enough wheat and maize to meet Vicos demand. Instead of selling this grain on the open market, and forcing Vicos families to purchase on that market, the community sells its own maize and wheat directly to Vicos consumers at approximately half the market price.

Freed from dependence on Marcara merchants, equipped with their new sense of self-reliance, and taking advantage of their purchase of a truck, the Vicos Indians are now by-passing Marcara, three and a half miles from their plaza, to shop in the departmental capital of Huaraz fifteen miles distant, where prices are lower, selections wider, and small city attractions lure. One Huaraz merchant also by-passes Marcara by dispatching merchandise-laden trucks directly to Vicos a couple of times a week.

An additional threat to Marcara's Vicos-exploiting economy has arisen in the last year or so. The Peruvian National Plan for Integrating the Aboriginal Population sent two sewing machines to Vicos to add to one already there, and hired a woman from Marcara to teach sewing and crocheting. Her classes have reached seventy women per week, plus a few men. As the Vicos people learn to sew, tailors and seamstresses in Marcara lose their traditional profitable market for dresses, coats, trousers, etc. As Vicos Indians learn to crochet finery for blouse collars, fronts and cuffs, another lucrative market disappears in the busy flashing of crochet hooks.

Huaraz merchants have also begun extending credit to the people of Vicos. One enterprising young Indian is purchasing his own sewing machine on time, and purchasing cloth wholesale to make up into clothing for sale. As a result, the Marcara economic parasite lashes out at the Cornell Peru Project for turning the Vicos host into a social organism too healthy to be victimized.

If we may return to the Vicos community again for a moment, it is worth pointing out that the governing council carries on its own program of "foreign aid" in favor of less fortunate indigenous enclaves. A number of communities have sent emissaries to Vicos to request technical advice, or small-scale financing, or both. The Vicos Indians have made small loans to finance communal agricultural enterprises like their own in communities unable to obtain bank financing. In general, the relatively sophisticated Vicosinos have insisted on supervising the technical agricultural operations carried out under these loans, just as their own bank-financed agricultural activities are supervised by agricultural engineers from the Interamerican Cooperative Food Production Service (changed into a purely Peruvian agency on 1 April 1961). Vicos is currently car-

rying on such a program with the Indians of the *hacienda* Ullu-
puquio, in the Province of Carhuaz. A Vicos teacher served as
innovator.

The Vicos Indians received requests for similar loans from the
people of the *haciendas* Parash, Rurish and Uchusquillo in the
Province of Huan on the eastern slope of the White Cordillera.
Vicos fowl and egg vendors carried word of the new life in their
community to these peasants.

[The case of Uchusquillo is far more dramatic than can be indicated here. The ten-year lease on that *hacienda* had expired, and
the Uchusquillo Indians decided to follow the Vicos example. With
a loan from Vicos, they rented the estate themselves and so became
free men.]

If we shift our view now from the local neighborhood immediately around Vicos to the region in which Vicos is located, we find
much the same diversity of reaction to the project as in the
neighborhood.

The region to be considered consists of the Callejon de Huaylas, a large inter-Andean valley drained by the Santa River. Nearby
Marcara is a district capital—the district [town or township] being
the minimum geographic unit of Peruvian public administration.
This fact is not very important to Vicos other than in channeling
the direction of their communications with authority. Carhuaz is
the capital of the province [county], and with its court of primary
jurisdiction, subprefect, secondary school and so on, serves somewhat more of a centralizing function than Marcara. Huaraz, however, centralizes and canalizes. It is the largest city in the valley,
and the capital of the province [state] of Ancash.

Resistance to the Vicos project at the regional level centers in
this administrative city of Huaraz. The landed proprietors of the
neighborhood are by and large absentee landlords or renters resid-
ing in Huaraz, such as the renter who set off the massacre last
August across the river from Vicos at Huapra. The proprietors have
formed the Ancash Farm Bureau (Asociacion de Agricultores de
Ancash) to consolidate their front—only landed proprietors belong
—and denounced the Vicos project before organizations such as the
Rotary Club which accurately reflect the city's social and power
structure. Inasmuch as these landed proprietors belong to the principal families of the city and department in a social sense—the long

established elite—it is easy to see why they have supporters. A re-
actionary bi-monthly newspaper owner whose job-shop occupies the
ground floor of the building where the renter of Huapra has his
law offices, has published several slanderous articles about the
project and its personnel. This gentleman expressed the point of
view every applied anthropologist is probably familiar with: "every
peasant can learn modern agricultural methods" so the fact that the
Vicos Indians have done so reflects no merit on the project. In
other words, he demonstrates no realistic perception of cultural
differences other than as topic for ridicule.

One other major source of resistance in the project exists in the
city of Huaraz—a rather healthy portion of the Communist Party,
which appears to recognize that every success of the project dimin-
ishes by that much the Communists' own chances of fomenting a
violent revolution. The Party tries to sabotage reform because it
has just as much *immediate* interest in maintaining the status quo
as the landed proprietors have.

The renter of the estate where the massacre occurred last August went so far as to visit the United States Embassy in Lima to
denounce the U. S. citizens then at Vicos as "Communists." This
epithet is believed in the region more widely than a North American
would expect, simply because the Cornell Peru Project activities
favor Indians. According to the logic of many Peruvians, anyone
who works for Indians is by definition Communist—even the Catholic priests.

Having mentioned priests, we should go on to add that the project is not opposed by one influential group one might expect to find
allied with conservative landed proprietors—the established Roman
Catholic Church. In fact, the local Marcara parish priest is a great
admirer of the "gringos." He is paid to celebrate more rites in
Vicos today than in pre-project times, as Vicos prosperity is trans-
lated into festival prestige. The Bishop of Huaraz has shown himself
to be quite friendly, visiting Vicos in January to confirm, and the
clergy in between also favors the project, which has carefully
avoided intervening in Vicos religious practice.

At the northern or lower end of the valley to which Vicos belongs, farthest from the administrative center of Huaraz, there is
little knowledge of or interest in Vicos or the project in urban
areas. The indigenous communities, however, through their contacts

with official publications of the Peruvian Institute of Indian Affairs, have generally positive although somewhat vague notions about the Vicos project.

At the rural southern or upper end of the valley, there is considerable knowledge of and interest in the project. The legally recognized indigenous communities of the Province of Bolognesi met in convention early in April of 1961 and passed a resolution of applause for the Cornell Peru Project's operations at Vicos. One indigenous community in this end of the valley, Catac, is among those that have visited Vicos to seek aid.

At the national level, the landed proprietor class has not overtly resisted the project. One very interesting phenomenon of the progress of the project has been the almost entirely favorable chorus of public pronouncements for Vicos goals. To be sure, some critical articles have appeared in the metropolitan press. One major Lima daily, *La Prensa,* published a critical article two years ago, based apparently on a reporter's twisting of the remarks of a United Nations functionary who had made a flying visit to Vicos, but this newspaper has otherwise fairly consistently supported the project. *El Comercio,* another major Lima daily, has supported the project in the past or at least reported it objectively, and has thus far discovered no basis for overt attack. *La Cronica,* the third major Lima daily newspaper, has consistently reported the project objectively to favorably. The daily organ of the APRA [land reform] party, *La Tribuna,* has never left any doubt as to its whole-hearted backing, as is to be expected from APRA's political program. The attacks against the project or its personnel which have been printed in the capital city press have appeared in a few small-circulation, more or less ephemeral, sheets published in Lima.

To what extent public opinion in Peru is molded by government action would be difficult for us to say at this point in our research. Certainly it is worth pointing out the characteristics of governmental response to the project. In the legislative sphere, reaction to the project in the Peruvian Senate and Chamber of Deputies has almost always been favorable. A bill introduced in the Chamber of Deputies in September of 1960, for example, provided for expropriation of the *hacienda* of Huapra where peasants had been slain by police the month before. The Cornell Peru Project was designated by name to take over the preparation of the peasants across the river from Vicos for effective participation in national life. [Passage of this legislation has been delayed by a dispute between the Church and a private individual over property rights in Huapra.]

The most abundant evidence of Vicos impact at the national level comes, perhaps, from the administrative branch of the government. At the Ministerial level, the project has been taken advantage of to score personal successes and obtain favorable publicity many times. This occurred under ex-President Manuel A. Odria. More recently, Prime Minister Pedro Beltran, of ex-President Manuel Prado's cabinet, based his defense of indigenous policy before the Peruvian Congress on the Vicos pilot project and an International Labor Organization project. The Prado Minister of Labor and Indigenous Affairs, Jose Luis Gonzalez Suarez, scored a personal success in the regional International Labor Organization conference at Buenos Aires during April 1961 by securing the adoption of a declaration whose philosophy is based in large part on these two pioneering integration programs. Another former Minister of Labor and Indigenous Affairs, Alvarado Garrido, used Vicos personnel to carry out exploratory investigations of crisis situations. He requested the Vicos field director, Mario Vasquez, to study the *haciendas* of Lauramarca and Q'eros in the Department of Cuzco and *haciendas* Villurcuni and Uchusquillo in the Department of Puno.

More important, the organizational structure of the Cornell Peru Project has been copied to a significant extent in setting up community development and Indian integration programs elsewhere in Peru. The Puno-Tambopata Project of the International Labor Organization operates under a government agreement much like the project's, and its chief executive in the field is a former field director at Vicos, Dr. William C. Blanchard. It differs in emphasizing vocational training, stimulating out-migration, and in having the funds to work in something like a hundred communities; and with aid from the UN Special Fund it is beginning construction of an access road into the Tambopata Valley (being spontaneously colonized) and beginning an artisan training school in Huancayo. The departmental program of Indian integration in Cuzco is operated by the anthropology faculty of the University of Cuzco under an agreement with the National Plan for Integration of the Aboriginal Population much like the agreement governing the Vicos project. The departmental program in Ayacucho is also operated by the anthropology faculty of the University of Huamanga under a similar agreement. Its action program is in the Pampa de Cangallo, where there are only scattered *rancherias*.

One of the higher level administrative innovations of the project endures with increasing force. In order to achieve the interdepartmental integration of action viewed as desirable to accomplish the aims of the pilot project in Vicos, an interministerial committee was established a number of years ago. Recently, this body has been made the governing commission of the National Plan for the Integration of the Aboriginal Population, and strengthened by adding members. This is to say that the theory of integrated governmental action in the local Indian community propounded by the Vicos project has been accepted and incorporated into the Peruvian governmental structure. Last year the NPIAP decided to foster a process of feedback into the departments [states] from the national level, and also to seek better departmental level planning by establishing similar committees in eight departments with large indigenous populations.

In conclusion, we wish to offer the view that the Vicos pilot project has become to a considerable extent the bellwether of Indian affairs and government Indian policy in Peru.

5

Community Development in Brazil

Perhaps the most important thing to learn from the following case history is the enormous latent desire for change which exists in communities of the nonindustrialized nations. Despite consistently inefficient innovation techniques, which resulted in a complete abandonment of the project, the local people had seen enough possibilities for change that they were quite critical of the council members who were responsible for the withdrawal of the change agency. They actually missed the assistance of persons who had been working on the effort, despite all the ill-will that had been created.

One consistent characteristic of "self-help" projects that fail to reach their goal is that they are top-heavy, and this effort fits the pattern. Practically all development projects today that are initiated among underprivileged people begin in the offices of government ministries or foreign assistance agencies. Elaborate plans are drawn up by specialists (usually based only on technical knowledge) and after extensive negotiations are taken to selected areas. It is here that the problems begin, since the gulf of understanding between the élite and the ultimate recipients may be enormous. And if the plans are minutely detailed before the period of interaction on the recipient level begins, there may be very serious difficulties. The idea of "self help" is valid only when it also includes planning and decision-making by the recipients. In this project, the plans were drawn in great detail before anyone in the urban slum was involved.

The fact that the various government divisions involved in this effort did not co-operate as was planned was an initial problem, but the primary difficulty throughout appears to have been an almost complete disregard of the traditional structure of the community and of the customs and values of the inhabitants. Not only was there little or no effort to learn what the nature of the community was and to adapt to it, and particularly to the traditional leaders, but the change agents deliberately attempted to bypass these critical people. Although authoritarian leaders theoretically may not be the most desirable people to work with, their power is normally too great to ignore. And in this case, as is frequent in Latin America, local power and politics were closely interrelated. By ignoring the traditional leaders and attempting to create a nonpolitical development council, powerful vested interests were unleashed that were ultimately instrumental in destroying the project.

As a result of not understanding the community and not using real local leadership, communication to the ultimate recipients was not effective. Technically good efforts of all sorts were insufficient to counterbalance the rumor campaigns that became rife. Also, although there is no indication that the change agents ever realized the necessity of learning what the local people wanted in contrast to what the change agents decided they needed, under these circumstances it is doubtful that they could have found out even had they tried.

In sum, this case should indicate that it is next to impossible to avoid local leaders. Furthermore, it must be stressed that "self help" means participation throughout, including planning. Though agencies or agents can initiate programs from the top, they need to work with local communities rather than attempting to manipulate them if meaningful change is to take place.

COMMUNITY CENTER PROJECT AT CHONIN, BRAZIL *

KALERVO OBERG

The experiment in community development to be described in the following pages took place in the District of Chonin in the Municipio of Governador Valadares in the State of Minas Gerais during the years 1951 and 1952. Before going on to discuss the origin of the project and the lessons learned in the course of its

* Reprinted from "Chonin de Cima—A Rural Community in Minas Gerais, Brazil," Government Report, May, 1956, pp. 159-170, by permission of the author. Dr. Oberg, who served in Brazil as a social science analyst for the U.S. government for twenty years, is now Chairman of the Department of Anthropology at the University of Southern California.

history, it will be necessary to describe briefly the United States-Brazilian agencies which were instrumental in its development and operation.

Since 1942, the United States Government through the Institute of Inter-American Affairs (hereafter called Institute) has carried on bilateral programs of technical assistance in most of the Latin American countries in the fields of health, education, and agriculture. To implement these programs a special administrative mechanism called the "servicio" (serviço in Portuguese) was developed within the national ministries concerned to which the United States and the host country could contribute funds and personnel. In Brazil, for instance, the Serviço Especial de Saúde Pública (hereafter called SESP) was established within the Ministry of Education and Health, the Institute's health mission forming an integral part of the organization and the American chief of field party sharing responsibility, under agreement, for the direction of the activities of the "servicio." In a similar manner a "servicio" known as the Commissão Brasileiro-Americana Industrial (hereafter called CBAI) was set up in the same ministry by means of which the Institute could further the development of industrial education and training in Brazil. Although in 1951, the Institute was not represented in Brazil by an agricultural mission, there did exist a joint American-Brazilian agricultural organization known as the Associação de Crédito e Assisténcia Rural (Rural Credit and Assistance Association) (hereafter called ACAR). These three agencies in which American technical "know how" predominated and which represented the socially strategic fields of health, education, and agriculture were to form the core of the demonstration project.

A. PROBLEM AND PLAN OF ACTION

In the course of the Institute's activities it had occurred to some Americans working in Latin America that as disease, illiteracy, and poverty are a trio that generally go together and are associated with a type of community in which they occur, greater and more rapid progress could be made if the agencies dealing with these problems selected a restricted area in which they could concentrate their efforts. To demonstrate the value of this idea, the chief of party of the Institute's health mission in Brazil approached CBAI and ACAR with a proposal for a joint Community Center Project, agreement being reached between these agencies in September 1950. At the time, administrative consideration restricted the choice of location and, as will be shown later, this restriction was highly detrimental to the operation of the project.

The underlying philosophy of the project can be summarized as follows: Through teamwork, cooperation, and supplementation of activities, the work of each agency could be made more effective than when it acts alone. By combining effort a higher standard of living could be achieved and life could become more meaningful for the rural dweller when advances are made simultaneously on all three fronts. Not just a part but the whole man would be considered in a program which would improve the welfare of the individual, the family, and the community. The objectives of the project were to demonstrate:

1. An economically feasible formula and a practical mechanism whereby official agencies on the federal, state, and local level may work together effectively in the utilization of public funds to improve both human and economic resources in a specific rural area.

2. The importance of a cooperative and coordinated approach in such fields as agriculture, education, health, and transportation.

3. The value and the methods of securing community participation or "helping the people to help themselves" in improving their own welfare.

4. The combination of a community center with a nuclear system for providing services in a rural area.

Even before the project was fully under way, administrative restrictions again intervened and it was discovered that CBAI, which was to work in the highly important field of rural education, was not able to cooperate. This was a severe blow to the balanced program of the project. To strengthen the program various Brazilian federal and state agencies were asked for help, the final roster of cooperating agencies shaping up as follows:

1. Serviço Especial de Saúde Pública (SESP)
2. Associação de Crédito e Assisténcia (ACAR)
3. The federal Campanha Nacional de Educação Rural (CNER)
4. The following secretariats of the State of Minas Gerais:
    a. Secretary of Health and Assistance
    b. Secretary of Agriculture
    c. Secretary of Education

d. Secretary of Roads and Public Works
5. The Prefeitura of the Municipio of Governador Valadares

The plan further proposed that there be established a Joint Committee with representation from all agencies involved to decide overall policy, program, budget, and personnel; and an Executive Committee to act for the larger group between meetings and actually to decide many of the details connected with the operation of the project.

The Joint Committee selected a Federal Coordinator to serve in a liaison capacity between the agencies involved, to act as chairman of the Executive Committee, and to coordinate the plans made by the Joint Committee with the work in the field.

It also appointed a Local Coordinator who was responsible locally for supervision of the entire demonstration. He presided at regular staff meetings of the service personnel called for the purpose of planning the execution of the program, correlating activities, and developing cooperation. He also had charge of receiving and expending such funds as were authorized by the Joint Committee. He was not to decide technical or professional matters outside his own field, employ separate personnel, commit any of the agencies financially except as authorized by the Joint Committee, nor take action in regard to the personnel or program of the demonstration which was contrary to the administrative policies of the agencies involved.

There was established in a strategic location a community center building housing the personnel of all agencies, and at suitable locations in the surrounding area there were to be smaller community centers, thus establishing a nuclear system. Personnel of the main center were to visit the smaller units on a regular schedule which was to be known to the residents of the entire area.

In addition, there was formed a Community Council through which active participation of the people themselves in improving their own welfare was to be achieved.

B. ORGANIZATION OF SERVICES

The proposed community centers were designed to serve as effective focal points for reaching the rural residents with the three principal services of agriculture, education, and health. In agriculture the center was to be the focal point for giving information about financial credit available, about technical assistance in phases of agronomy, and about advances in home economics. Home making classes were to be held for adults in cooperation with the expert in adult education and the nurse or health educator.

The program in adult education was to consist of two phases: general and vocational. The former was to include those aspects of the rural campaign as were indicated, while the latter was to be mainly in the field of agriculture. Developments in the field of general education were dependent upon the interests of the State Secretary of Education. Both ACAR and SESP, which normally have contacts with schools, were to continue this practice.

The health personnel were to provide medical examination and treatment, nursing services and health education at the community center clinic, as well as demonstrations and information in the field of sanitation such as the building of privies and well construction. It was recognized that health work would be of primary importance, particularly in the opening phases of the project. Sick farmers were not fit subjects to carry out an intensive agricultural program. Children suffering from intestinal parasites made poor students. The community had first to be cleared of infectious diseases.

To carry out these services each agency was to contribute funds and personnel. ACAR was to appoint one full-time agronomist and one full-time home economist. For the use of this staff a jeep, office furniture, home demonstration center, and educational films and literature were to be made available. SESP was to provide one part-time doctor, one full-time nurse, one full-time sanitary assistant, and one part-time health educator. The medical staff was to be provided with a jeep, office furniture, medicines and clinical supplies, a motion picture projector and educational films and materials.

It was expected that the Prefeitura of Governador Valadares would support the program by providing office space in the city of Governador Valadares for the project personnel, by assisting in the transportation of materials, and by making workmen available when necessary to carry out construction activities. The Secretary of Education was expected to endorse the educational program and to provide consultation, equipment, and materials. The Secretary of Agriculture was expected to provide technical consultation and the loan of heavy agricultural machinery. The Secretary of Roads and Public Works was expected to maintain and improve road communication to and within the District. The Community Council was expected to act in a non-political advisory capacity, expressing the wishes of the local population.

Each cooperating agency was to provide funds for two purposes: one, for the payment of personnel and materials in its own sector of cooperative work; the other, to cover expenses of a general nature such as the salary of the local coordinator, rent for the Nucleo buildings, a servant, a secretary, demonstration equipment, and certain supplies and materials. The decision concerning the allocation of expenses was to be made by the Executive Committee of the project. The local staff was to be composed entirely of Brazilians.

C. HISTORY OF THE PROJECT

The first step in the implementation of the program consisted in the acquisition and preparation of a satisfactory building to serve as the Nucleo headquarters in the village of Chonin de Cima. For this purpose the project was fortunate in being able to rent a large house belonging to the local church organization. Under the direction of the ACAR agronomist, who served as an acting local coordinator, this building was repaired and offices for the various agencies' representatives were established. A demonstration kitchen, sewing room, and a model bedroom were established for the use of the home supervisor. A small outbuilding was outfitted as a carpenter shop. A water tank was built at the back of the house which was connected to a well equipped with a pump. The basement of the building was fitted out as a clinic for the use of SESP, including a kerosene refrigerator for the storage of medicines. Sufficient beds, dishes, and furniture were provided for the members of the Nucleo staff who had not yet found accommodations in the village. These preparations began in January 1951 but it was not until April that the clinic was ready for the activities of the SESP doctor and nurse.

1. *The Activities of ACAR.* This organization, as has been mentioned, was charged with the development of improved agricultural practices, largely through supervised credit. Although the Brazilian agronomist was occupied with the task of supervising the repair of the Nucleo building, he had time to begin his professional activities. Under supervised credit a farmer is given a loan for the purpose of buying equipment, seeds, insecticides, and for payment of necessary labor. With the endorsement of a loan, ACAR also provides the technical assistance of an agronomist to see that the equipment, seeds, and labor are used to the best advantage.

2. *Activities of the State Secretariat of Agriculture.* The activities of this agency were of minor significance to the agricultural development of the district although they would have been important if combined with a supervised loan program. Although some of the farmers took advantage of these services they were not highly valued by the farm population as a whole.

3. *The Activities of SESP.* After establishing a sub-post in Chonin de Cima, SESP inaugurated its health and sanitation program under the administrative supervision of the staff of the SESP Health Center in Governador Valadares. The program consisted in the following activities: (1) medical assistance, (2) environmental sanitation, and (3) health education. The medical assistance activities were carried out by a doctor and a nurse who came from Governador Valadares once a week, receiving and treating patients at the sub-post from 8 a.m. to 5 p.m. During the remainder of the week the resident sanitary assistant gave injections and treated minor injuries. During the two-year period, 6,519 visits for treatment were made to the sub-post. In the same period, 2,175 individuals received medical treatment for the first time in their lives.

The principal activity in environmental sanitation was the construction of pit privies. This was a cooperative program in which SESP provided the concrete basement slab to be placed over the pit while the house owner was responsible for the digging of the pit and the construction of the building over the slab. The sanitary assistant, however, provided technical assistance in choosing the location of the pit and in the construction of the privy building. The privy construction program proceeded rapidly, at first, but during the second year difficulties began to appear. The wealthier families were able to pay for the excavation and for the construction and responded readily. However, when the poorer levels of the village were reached the families claimed that they did not have the money to build a privy. These families can be broken down into two groups: those in which the father had died, had left the family, or was too ill to work; and those in which the father was a drifting agricultural laborer. These families lived in rented houses, neither the tenant nor the owner being interested in the installation of a privy. To meet this problem, SESP built privies for those who were willing to make small monthly payments until the privy was paid for. This still left a number of absentee-owned, rented houses for which privies could not be provided. In the course of the two years

SESP installed 90 pit privies in the village. Out of 125 families this left 35 without privies, a situation about which, under the circumstances, nothing could be done. In addition to the privy construction program, the resident sanitary assistant inspected backyards and instructed the people in proper methods of garbage disposal, advised them about well construction, and warned them against the use of the water in the stream unless it was first boiled.

SESP carries on health education in two ways, indirectly through its doctors, nurses, engineers, and auxiliary personnel; and directly by means of public film showing, talks, home visits by nurses aides, and by posters and pamphlets. In Chonin de Cima 688 pamphlets were passed on to the people, 172 posters were put up, 54 public talks were given, and 35 still and movie projections were used.

4. *Activities of the State Secretariat of Health.* During the last year of the project this agency brought in a full-time doctor to supplement the activities of SESP in the field of health.

Thus it can be said that the medical assistance, environmental sanitation, and health education services were well organized and performed their duties in an exemplary manner. Much of this success, no doubt, was due to the fact that the health program had much to offer free and demanded less in the way of active cooperation than the agricultural program.

5. *Activities of the State Secretariat of Education.* This agency equipped the village school with desks, maps, books, and other materials, provided an extra schoolteacher, and conducted two teachers' training courses in Chonin de Cima during the holiday seasons. In spite of these improvements the educational phase of the project never really got under way. The three local teachers were ill trained, neglected to carry out the school regulations as to hours and curriculum, and were resentful to suggested improvements in school management. Some of this difficulty rose from the fact that teachers think of themselves as political appointees which makes strict supervision difficult.

6. *The Activities of the State Secretariat of Roads and Public Works.* This agency made no contribution to the project.

7. *The Activities of the Prefeitura of the Municipio.* This agency fell down badly in its support of the project.

8. *The Activities of the Local Coordinator.* The local coordinator was to serve as the link between the various activities of the agencies and the people represented by their community council.

This council included from 8 to 10 leading members of the community selected so as to represent farmers, shopkeepers, craftsmen, and housewives, and was to be non-political in character. The coordinator called weekly meetings in the Nucleo building attended by the community council and the representatives of the participating agencies who worked in the District. At these meetings he explained to the council the nature of the activities and solicited the wishes and advice of the council in planning activities for the future.

The coordinator was also responsible for organizing the villagers to carry out certain activities that would further the project as a whole. Among the organizations created by the coordinator in the two-year period were: a health club, an agriculture club, a football club, parents and teachers association, a local school board, and a cash fund for the purpose of inaugurating a school lunch program, the money to be collected by voluntary contributors, entrance charges to public functions, and from the sale of produce from the agricultural demonstration plots.

In addition, the coordinator was to organize educational meetings in the school building or in the Nucleo building, at which the agency representatives could give talks about the activities in their respective fields, answer questions, and generally to get the message across to the people. He was also responsible for the showing of films, and for the distribution of educational material to the people. Finally he was responsible for the maintenance of the Nucleo building, the payment of rent, and in making monthly over-all reports to the Executive Committee informing this Committee of the progress made and suggesting lines of action.

From the organizational standpoint it was local coordination which created the greatest difficulties and which ultimately was responsible for the withdrawal of the project from Chonin. Quite aside from the very real difficulties presented by the conditions in Chonin de Cima itself and the lack of full support of the project by the participating agencies, the project was never successful in getting the right man for this position. The ACAR agronomist who was acting coordinator during the initial phases of the project might very well have made a successful coordinator if he had remained. His successor was an ex-schoolteacher who lacked essential qualities of leadership and never quite grasped the purposes of the project. After six months he was replaced by an agricultural technician who had initiative but lacked tact and understanding of the various phases of the project. One reason for the failure to get a successful coordinator was due to the low salary rating given to the position. Neither the ex-schoolteacher nor the agricultural technician were university trained men. Among a people where a university education is an outstanding symbol of status this had a tendency on the one hand to make the agency technicians to underrate the coordinator, and on the other, to make the coordinator aggressive in order to compensate for his feeling of inferiority. The job of coordinator was a delicate one and called for a mature person with status, a knowledge of human relations and considerable experience in community leadership.

As one would expect, differences of opinion appeared in the community council. These differences were heightened by political cleavages. Instead of stressing the non-political and community nature of the council, the coordinator entered into the disputes and played one part of the council against the other. This irritated about one half of the members of the community council who began a whispering campaign against the project as a whole. Although most of the criticism was levelled at the coordinator, some of it was shed on the other personnel and to some extent affected the morale of the technical staff of the project as a whole. These irritations came to a head during the spring festival in October 1952. Although a committee consisting of some of the members of the community council were to organize the festival, the coordinator kept taking unilateral action in the preparatory proceedings. While the festival was in progress in the school building the coordinator took steps to bar people improperly dressed from entering the building. This caused an open quarrel in which the committee worsted the coordinator. The following day the coordinator left the project and although SESP continued providing medical services as usual and the state-appointed doctor acted as a coordinator until the end of the year, it became apparent that it would be difficult to operate the project along originally planned lines with the full cooperation and good will of the local population. At the end of the year the project was withdrawn from Chonin de Cima and transferred to another municipio in the State of Minas Gerais. Although the incident which brought about the collapse of the project appears trivial it, however, indicates a weak point in the organizational setup of the project.

The Institute of Social Anthropology of the Smithsonian Institution contributed to the project by maintaining a social anthro-

pologist on the project for a period of five months. By contributing
two graduate students in the social sciences to assist the anthropologist, the Escola de Sociologia e Politica de São Paulo also participated in the research aspect of the project.

D. ANALYSIS OF THE PROJECT IN CHONIN DE CIMA

The following factors and conditions appear to have been important in obstructing the Community Center Project from successfully demonstrating the value of a cooperative and coordinated
approach in the fields of agriculture, education, health, and transportation to improve the living standards of the people in the District of Chonin.

1. *Physical Difficulties.* Within half a century, improper land
use methods had depleted the limited areas of once good soil. The
task of rehabilitating the soil through the use of fertilizers and crop
rotation would have taken a number of years and would have
proved costly to the owners. The absence of farm roads prevented
the entry of tractors into the cultivable areas.

2. *Service Difficulties.* The value of the entire rural education
program was immeasurably lowered by the withdrawal of CBAI
which was equipped to introduce modern educational methods into
the area. The inability of ACAR to establish a supervised loan program in agriculture reduced ACAR activity to home supervision
alone. The limited activities of the State Secretariat of Agriculture
in no way compensated for the loss. Similarly the loss of CBAI to
the project was not counterbalanced by the contributions which the
State Secretariat of Education made. The difficulties over communications were in large measure due to the failure of the Prefeitura
and the State Secretariat of Roads and Public Works to repair the
roads and bridges. SESP alone carried out its commitments according to plan.

3. *Inadequate Basic Information.* Although, at the time, the
choice of location was limited to the Chonin District, a more complete knowledge of the facts relating to soils, communications, land
tenure, and the large percentage of itinerant farm laborers and
sharecroppers would have caused the Joint Committee to hesitate
in going ahead with the project in Chonin.

4. *Difficulties of Communication.* Throughout the demonstration
period considerable difficulty was experienced in articulating the
program with the local community organization and in getting the

message across to the people. Brazilian rural communities, as a rule, are organized along paternalistic, authoritarian lines, leadership being vested in the hands of family heads, priests, landowning patrons, and political chiefs. Informal leadership tends to follow the same pattern. The Community Council constituted a break in the traditional lines of authority. Through it the local coordinator was able to dictate and to undermine the customary pattern of individual leadership. Greater success could have been achieved by first using the traditional form of leadership and by forming the Community Council only after concrete community interests had appeared demanding permanent community action.

E. IMPACT OF PROJECT UPON THE COMMUNITY

Although the project remained in Chonin for only two years it can justifiably be said that in spite of all the difficulties a number of lasting effects were achieved.

When the project arrived in Chonin de Cima the school building was in need of repairs, there were not enough benches, books, maps, and other materials for the needs of the pupils and teachers. And there was no water. When the project was withdrawn, the school was partitioned so that the four classes were separated from one another thus facilitating the teaching in each class. A sufficient number of school benches, books, and other materials were provided. A well equipped with a pump was installed. Four sanitary privies were built. The school premises were fenced. A cement walk from the gate to the front door was put in. The front yard was planted with flowers and a vegetable garden was made in the back yard, both being maintained by the students.

In the village, the main street was widened and a number of drainage ditches were put in. Two of the bridges leading to the village were repaired. The building used by the project staff was left repaired, with a stove, with piped water, and a sanitary privy. The great majority of the living houses in the village were left with privies constructed with the help and guidance of SESP.

Many of the houses have and continue to make the simple but useful furniture introduced into the village by the home supervisor. Small wall racks with tooth brushes were seen in numerous houses. Some people continue to boil their drinking water. The use of hybrid corn seed, vegetable gardens, and improved breeds of chickens have come in, apparently to stay. The people continue to buy medicine for the treatment of malaria, dysentery, and other common ailments to the treatment of which they have become accustomed.

Perhaps the greatest and most lasting effect of the project was the awakening of the minds of the people to the realization that a fuller and richer life was possible. This was shown by the repeated statements of the people as to how they missed the project with its assistance and guidance, and their criticism of those members of the community who were responsible for its withdrawal. This creation of a felt need for better health, better education, and an improved level of living is essentially the foundation and prerequisite for the improvement of rural life in Brazil. Moreover, the experience gained by those who participated in the service side of the project has led them to believe that under more favorable conditions community development in rural Brazil is a distinct possibility.

Rural Self-Help in
Costa Rica

6

The problems of initiating change in the rural communities of the world vary considerably in proportion to the degree of advancement of specific countries and the communities in them. In countries where the illiteracy rate is from 80 to 90 per cent, the standard of living is just above the starvation level and government services are practically nonexistent, the difficulties are much greater than in the more advanced nations. The case history that follows is from one of the more progressive nations of the nonindustrialized world. Although Costa Rica is generally classified as a "developing" nation, it is well ahead of most of its neighbors in Latin America, as well as most developing nations in other parts of the world. The education level and the standard of living of the population are relatively high, and viable government organizations exist that are active in promoting the advancement of the rural people. Thus, comparatively, the problems are of small magnitude. However, this is not to say that no knowledge of the social change process is necessary, for even in the most advanced nations of the world communities react negatively to ill-conceived and badly managed projects. It is, therefore, most significant that the innovators in this instance were very careful both in selecting the community and in handling the social problems that always exist when change is being introduced.

One of the principles of change that is dramatically illustrated here is the matter of selection of communities. The philosophy of this agency was to select a community which had the necessary social prequisites and, moreover, was made up of inhabitants who were interested in improving their own conditions. Such selection can only be based on a fairly careful study of local communities, and in this instance the change agents were willing to undertake such a study. This is the only sure way of avoiding the social difficulties that arose and caused the failure in the Brazilian self-help project.

The Costa Rican effort was classified as a pilot project, from which ideas learned could be extended to communities which were less ready for self-help efforts. Of course, the communities that need help most are those that are least ready for change, but it must be admitted that they present the most difficult problems. That they can be changed initially is well demonstrated by the Vicos experiment, which also can be viewed as a pilot project, but it must be recognized that the change agents in Vicos had a depth of understanding of their community that is not often found.

Although the community of San José had the desired preconditions of good leadership, good land tenure practices, a homogeneous population and a desire for improvement, the innovators still employed a strategy that is always a solid basis for change. They began on a type of project that was already desired by the community. By basing the effort on an existing felt need, they had a solid motivational base from which to work. They did not need to generate interest. Furthermore, they developed very complete methods of communication to inform everyone about the project. The next and always essential step was to get the local people involved in all ways: to get their active participation in developing their own organizations, to help plan, and to provide the material assistance and labor needed. There could be little doubt among the Costa Ricans involved that the co-operative was their own relatively early in the project history.

A final comparison can be made with the Vicos experiment in that the village level project was closely tied to a national organization. The Vicos project was supported by the Institute of Indian Affairs, and the San José effort was backed by the National Bank of Costa Rica. Through these ties, powerful governmental interests could help safeguard and support the local gains.

PROJECT FOR
A RURAL COOPERATIVE IN COSTA RICA *

A. BACKGROUND

On May 26, 1955, the National Bank of Costa Rica and the Pan American Union signed an agreement to establish in Costa Rica a Pilot Project for Rural Cooperatives, setting forth the respective responsibilities of the two parties in this undertaking.

The principal circumstances which were taken into account in signing the above-mentioned agreement were the following:

a. That the Pan American Union had offered to help the Governments of the Member States of the Organization of American States (OAS) so that pilot projects for rural cooperatives might be developed in their respective territories.

b. That the National Bank of Costa Rica believed that these projects would provide a technical and practical way of demonstrating, on an experimental basis, how a rural cooperative might be organized.

c. That the National Bank of Costa Rica believed that a pilot rural cooperative would be of great benefit in stimulating the cooperative movement in Costa Rica and thus contribute in part to the discharge of the functions which, in this connection, had been assigned to it by the Organic Law of the National Banking System.

d. That the Inter-American Economic and Social Council had stated that a pilot project for a rural cooperative should be organized by an autonomous agency whose interest and experience in the cooperative field, and whose financial resources would assure its success.

e. That the National Bank of Costa Rica, through its Department for the Promotion of Cooperatives, was technically and financially able to meet the above requirements.

f. That mutual collaboration between the National Bank of Costa Rica and the Pan American Union in successfully carrying out the project in question, is obviously desirable.

On the basis of the above-mentioned considerations, the two agencies resolved to plan and carry out a cooperative pilot project in a rural community of Costa Rica, and their respective responsibilities were specified. The National Bank of Costa Rica pledged an initial sum of not less than 30,000 colones (US$4,524.88) to

* Excerpts reprinted from "Summary Report on the First Pilot Project for a Rural Co-operative—San José Naranjo, Costa Rica," Pan America Union, pp. 4-16, by permission of the publisher.

finance the Project; agreed to assume responsibility for the technical organization and direction of the same; to provide the necessary technical and administrative staff which it would be necessary to hire in Costa Rica, and to evaluate the project in cooperation with the Pan American Union.

The latter organization on its part agreed to offer the necessary technical advice and to send to Costa Rica an expert on cooperatives who within the period between July 1955 and June 1957 would make two different trips to that country and remain for a period not to exceed sixty days on each occasion.

In addition to this agreement between the National Bank of Costa Rica and the Pan American Union, collateral agreements were signed between the Bank and "Project 39 of Technical Cooperation" (OAS), and between the Bank and the Inter-American Technical Service for Agricultural Cooperation (STICA), thus providing for coordination between various national and international organizations and all the benefits deriving therefrom.

B. PRINCIPAL OBJECTIVES

It was decided that the principal objectives of the Project, in accordance with the general objectives already mentioned, would be the following:

a. To experiment with techniques which would demonstrate an efficient way of organizing rural cooperatives.

b. To demonstrate that rural cooperatives are dynamic agencies through which it is possible to carry out programs of a social and cultural, as well as of an economic nature.

C. INITIAL ACTIVITIES

1. Designation of Authorities

The first step was the appointment of a Project Director, an official of the National Bank of Costa Rica, being designated for this purpose.

At the same time, an Advisory Committee was appointed, including two representatives of the National Bank of Costa Rica, one of the Inter-American Technical Service for Agricultural Cooperation (STICA), one from Project 39 of the Technical Cooperation Program of the OAS, and one from the National Institute of Housing and City Planning ((INVU) of Costa Rica.

Whenever the expert designated by the Pan American Union would visit Costa Rica to work on the Pilot Project, he would automatically be incorporated as a member of this Committee. Later, a representative of the Costa Rican Electrical Institute (ICE) was also incorporated.

The functions of the Advisory Committee were, in general terms, as follows:

a. To set the standards to be followed in selecting the community, making the necessary recommendations and suggestions, to the end that the Department for Promotion of Cooperatives of the National Bank of Costa Rica might have a solid basis for the selection of the most appropriate community.

b. To indicate the type of cooperative that should be recommended in accordance with the results of a socio-economic survey.

c. To suggest guidelines for the educational campaign in the community finally selected.

d. To serve as an Advisory Committee without directive or executive functions since these functions belong to the Department for Promotion of Cooperatives of the National Bank of Costa Rica.

e. To offer whatever advice might be deemed advisable to assure the success of the activities and work of the Pilot Project for a Rural Cooperative.

2. Selection of the Community

In accordance with the recommendations formulated in the appropriate documents, the first undertaking was the selection of the most suitable community for the development of the Pilot Project.

Among the factors taken into account in making this selection the following are worthy of mention:

The community should be one whose area would enable the Project to receive the necessary attention and supervision;

Stability of population;

A certain degree of demographic homogeneity;

Spirit of progress and desire for achievement;

Good means of communication within the community and the principal centers of population and within the region in which the community is located;

A cultural level sufficiently high to permit easy grasp of the basic concepts of cooperativism;

More or less stable leaders or directors, in order to avoid frequent changes;

A favorable situation with respect to land tenure and use;

Increasing economic development;

National or provincial governmental agents fully identified with the community and preferably natives thereof;

Previous experience in joint undertakings in the community;

The experience of the National Bank of Costa Rica in the handling of credit for members of the community, especially in relation to needs and the percentage of repayment;

One or more felt needs which could be met through the Project, thereby contributing to the economic, social and cultural improvement of the community and the raising of its standard of living.

The selection of a community involved three stages: a) Observation of various rural communities which apparently met the required conditions, with a first process of elimination; b) socioeconomic survey of those communities with the greatest possibility of selection; and c) final selection of community.

A. OBSERVATION OF RURAL COMMUNITIES AS SITES OF THE PILOT PROJECT

The Project Director, accompanied by officials of the Department of Cooperatives of the National Bank of Costa Rica, and various members of the Advisory Committee, visited a total of 12 rural communities which, in accordance with information supplied especially by the Inter-American Technical Service for Agricultural Cooperation and the Department of Rural Credit Boards of the National Bank of Costa Rica, were considered as possible sites of the pilot project. Abundant information was obtained from all of them with respect to their principal economic and social problems.

B. SOCIO-ECONOMIC SURVEY OF THREE COMMUNITIES
SELECTED AS POSSIBLE SITES

The Project Director and the Advisory Committee, with the cooperation of a rural sociologist and an agricultural economist, reached the conclusion that Palmares de San Isidro del General;

Santa Eulalia de Atenas; and San José de Naranjo were the three communities which, of the 12 studied superficially, met the conditions for a socio-economic survey, which was made later by the Technical Experts mentioned.

In general, in all three communities this survey analyzed the factors previously mentioned with special emphasis on the following: condition of the means of communication and transportation; stability and homogeneity of the population; attitudes towards progress and improvement, cultural development, stability of leadership, land tenure and use, experience in community work and problems of an economic character.

As a final stage of their work, the Experts in question, taking into consideration all the factors studied, reported to the Advisory Committee that the community of San José de Naranjo offered the most favorable conditions for the Pilot Project.

In addition to this conclusion—which was the principal objective of the study made—the survey also served to establish a precedent derived from the following recommendation: "The preliminary study has demonstrated that even in a society as homogeneous as that of Costa Rica, it is almost impossible to know clearly the conditions operating in a locality sufficiently well to make a selection independently of intuition, prejudices, etc., except by means of a scientific study in the locality itself. The questionnaire used in this study might have been much shorter or much longer, depending upon the objective of the project; but in any case a questionnaire is very valuable."

C. FINAL SELECTION OF THE COMMUNITY

At a meeting of the Advisory Committee on January 2, 1956, which was attended by the Expert from the Pan American Union as a full member with voice and vote, there was a final discussion of the site of the project.

Following a careful analysis, and taking into account the suggestions of the technicians who participated in the socio-economic survey—which were judged to be well-founded—and the special characteristics of San José de Naranjo, which had been noted by members of the Advisory Committee in person, this community was selected as the site of the Pilot Project.

San José de Naranjo is a small rural settlement located 65

kilometers from the Capital of Costa Rica. More than three-quarters of its inhabitants are owners of small farms devoted to the cultivation of coffee.

This community is characterized by the stability of its population, the existence of outstanding community leaders, and its great spirit of progress. Notwithstanding all of this, it still had at that time serious problems resulting from a lack of conduits for running water and lack of electric power; a dearth of recreational facilities; the absence of a library; commercial establishments with a limited assortment of merchandise; and lack of adequate service of transportation to the two nearest towns of greater size. (Zarcero, located 14 kilometers to the West and Naranjo, located 10 kilometers to the East.)

D. ORGANIZATION OF THE COOPERATIVE

1. First Steps

First of all, the Project Director and the Technical Expert designated by the Pan American Union paid an informal visit to the Community of San José de Naranjo.

During this visit it was possible to exchange impressions with various leaders who expressed the desire of the people to set up an electric light plant—a project which they had had for several years—and also the desire to organize a cooperative which had not yet been done because they lacked knowledge of the basic principles of cooperativism and the necessary technical principles.

These two spontaneously expressed desires facilitated the task, with the result that by common accord it was resolved that officials from the National Bank of Costa Rica and the technician from the Pan American Union would give some informal talks for the purpose of explaining various aspects of cooperative societies.

2. Selection and Training of Leaders

The selection of leaders was one of the results of the preliminary socio-economic survey in which two questions were asked: Are there any persons in this locality in conditions similar to yours who know well the problems affecting them? Can you give their names? Who are the persons who can best represent the people of this locality in discussing these economic and social problems with the various governmental agencies?

In this way it was really the people themselves who, in a completely democratic way, selected the group and community leaders who in turn collaborated effectively in the development of the project first of all and, later, as members of the Board of Directors, the Supervision Committee, and the Board of Arbitration and management, once the people had renewed their expression of confidence and recognition by entrusting these responsibilities to them.

The training began with a first talk (addressed to the total population in order to stimulate their interest) in which it was suggested that the first phase of the educational program be restricted to the Directors and extended later to the rest of the community. It was explained that it would be desirable for the program to be developed by stages and for instruction to be given to small groups, not only because of space limitations but also for pedagogical reasons.

The suggestion was accepted without objection.

In reality, in obtaining consent that this first stage be limited to the community leaders, action was prompted not only by the need to follow an orderly educational process, but to make sure that the instruction given would lead to the best possible results, it being felt that if the leaders accepted and assimilated the instruction given during this first period of the educational program they would be better prepared to influence the rest of the people in the community, to the end that they, in turn, would support the remaining educational stages of the program, thus reaching progressively a greater number of individuals.

In this way the valuable cooperation of the local leaders was obtained in line with recommendations made in the documents relating to development of Pilot Projects—while at the same time strengthening their position in the community.

3. Educational Campaign

Having carried out the first phase of the preliminary educational campaign planned for the community leaders—through informal visits and talks by the Pan American Union Technician and staff of the Cooperatives Department of the National Bank of Costa Rica—the next step was the development of a special, simple, attractive, and varied program for the rest of the community, with a view to stimulating among them a spirit of cooperation and mutual assistance, as well as understanding, through simple and graphic media, of the fundamentals of cooperativism.

The final stage of this campaign was an evaluation of the knowledge acquired by the members of the community—and all persons interested in cooperatives who were working in the community—with respect to the nature, objectives, and principles of cooperation.

The educational program mentioned above included the following stages:

A. INFORMAL VISITS

Taking advantage of every favorable opportunity that presented itself, the promoters made numerous visits to the community. During these visits, information was made widely available concerning the objectives of the Pilot Project and the procedures to be followed in its development, in an effort to interest and obtain the cooperation of the greatest possible number of people in the locality.

B. TALKS ON COOPERATIVES

Much emphasis was given to this matter at the beginning with the help of the Technician from the Pan American Union and, later through weekly visits by the Project Director and, occasionally, by other officials of the Cooperatives Department of the National Bank of Costa Rica.

Representatives of the other agencies concerned with the development of the project; staff members of the Victoria Industrial Cooperative; and representatives of educational agencies also participated in these talks.

The number of the talks given totaled 54, with an average attendance of 14 people. During this stage an effort was made to introduce the "Study Club" technique with optimum results. In addition, interest was added in some instances through the advance distribution of informational material relating to the topics to be dealt with.

C. VISITS TO OTHER COOPERATIVES AND AGENCIES

Arrangements were made for a group of those interested in the Pilot Project to visit San Pedro Poas—a small village also located in the Province of Alajuela—where a consumer cooperative had been organized by the rural people of the area.

As a result of the exchange of impressions between the visitors and the Manager and Administrative Council of this Cooperative, the former arrived at valuable conclusions which they later passed on to the other members of their community.

Similar visits were paid to the Institute Costarricense de Electricidad with a view to enabling the inhabitants of San José de Naranjo to inform themselves with respect to various aspects of the production and distribution of electric power, a problem of great concern to the community.

D. FILM SHOWINGS

It is a well-known fact that, among the various audio-visual techniques, film showings occupy a prominent place for recreational as well as pedagogical purposes, a matter of special significance in the rural areas of Latin America.

Because of this, films were used, selected not merely because of their educational nature, but also for their recreational impact, and these awakened general interest in the population.

This educational activity was made possible through the cooperation of the United States Embassy in Costa Rica which, in due course, made available not only films with Spanish sound track but operators and equipment as well.

The large attendance from all sectors of the population, and the continued general interest were eloquent testimony to the success of this system.

During the development of this particular Pilot Project, the National Bank of Costa Rica made a color film which will unquestionably serve as a valuable documentary record and an excellent means of publicizing the work done.

E. POSTERS

In dealing with rural people, the most simple and attractive methods are usually the most useful, since they communicate ideas without requiring too much effort on the part of the individual.

Well designed and illustrated posters can do much to make an educational program of a popular character more effective.

Consequently, the walls of the 4-S Club of San José de Naranjo were hung with posters, with the cooperative symbol and others illustrating the seven classical principles of the cooperative movement.

F. COURSES ON COOPERATIVISM

As the most advanced stage of the educational program, an expert was contracted to give weekly classes on cooperativism.

More than 40 people registered for this course, financed through the National Bank of Costa Rica. The number of lessons given was 27, with an average attendance of 22 persons. In addition, the local school gave valuable cooperation, giving 62 classes on cooperatives to the pupils of the V and VI grades.

G. MISCELLANEOUS

A Recording Secretary was designated so that he might later serve in the same capacity in the Cooperative itself, or at least serve to orient whoever might be charged with this responsibility at a later date.

As requested, the outstanding members of San José de Naranjo published a weekly Information Bulletin that besides its training value was designed to stimulate the townspeople to cooperate in the project, to express and write their opinions on community problems, to clear up doubts and misunderstandings concerning different aspects of the project, and, finally, to try to attract all those people who, for one reason or another, had not participated actively, as was needed.

4. Appointment of Committees

In due course various "working committees" were appointed, each with three members, and which, in accordance with the wishes of the members, were identified as follows: "Education Committee," "Committee on Membership and Publicity"; "Committee on Finances and Economic Matters"; and "Legal Committee."

In addition, these committees as a group, with a "Work Coordinator" appointed for the purpose, established the "Central Organizing Committee."

Some idea of the activities of these Committees may be derived from the fact that in a few months the preliminary educational stage was completed; the Cooperative Society was constituted as planned; it received its by-laws; the necessary capital was collected; the pertinent credit negotiations were transacted; necessary purchases were made; and, lastly, the members themselves contributed their personal labor for the installation of the machinery, distribution lines, etc., for the undertaking. These activities are dealt with under the following heading.

E. ESTABLISHMENT OF THE ELECTRICAL COOPERATIVE

1. Preliminary Technical Study

One of the principal factors responsible for previous efforts made by the people of San José de Naranjo to get electric power had been the existence of technical problems which the inhabitants were naturally unable to focus on and cope with in the necessary way.

In view of this background, the promoters of the Pilot Project recommended, as a first measure a thorough technical study which would analyze causes and recommend solutions.

To this end, the disinterested collaboration of the Costa Rican Electrical Institute was obtained. After a study of various nearby waterfalls, the representatives of this Institute presented a full report.

This document proposed two alternatives: a) Construction of a hydro-electric plant; b) installation of a thermic or Diesel plant.

From the analysis made by the technicians of the two alternatives, it was concluded that a very important advantage of the hydro-electric plant would be the lesser cost of the kilowatt hour; and the principal problem would be the higher investment which would be required for its installation. On the other hand, the Diesel plant offered the advantage of a lower initial investment; possibility of being located in the center of population; greater facility of operation; and more rapid installation. Among its disadvantages were the higher cost of the kilowatt hour and the possibility of having to limit its operation to an average of eight hours per day in order to avoid excessive operation costs.

After careful study of all factors involved and taking into account the fact that the Instituto Costarricense de Electricidad was planning to supply the San José de Naranjo area with electricity in 1965, the final decision was in favor of a Diesel plant.

Immediately, and with the joint activity of technicians, organizations, and inhabitants of the locality interested in the project, estimates were made of possible consumption, operating costs, necessary machinery and equipment, type of such machinery, etc.

2. Financing the Project

The work of the Committee appointed to this effect, the activity of the officials of the National Bank of Costa Rica, together with the intensive campaign of education and publicity which had been carried on, made it possible within a few months to raise the capital needed to acquire the Diesel plant that had been recommended and to construct the necessary installations for the distribution of electric power.

The cost was financed as follows: 43.21% by the members of the Cooperative directly, and 56.79% by credit .by the National Bank of Costa Rica, with the Diesel plant as security and the installation as an extra guarantee.

The amortization of the credit was strictly related to the amortization of the work as a whole, which had, logically, been considered as part of the production costs.

3. Legal and Administration Organization of the Entity

From the legal point of view, the organization of the entity presented no difficulties. The Cooperatives Department of the National Bank of Costa Rica drafted the by-laws which were studied and approved by the community leaders first and then by the Constitutional Assembly of the Cooperative. The Pan American Union helped with the drafting.

The Cooperatives Section of the Pan American Union gave technical advice in connection with the accounting procedures, in an effort to develop the simplest possible pattern within existing legal requirements and the technical standards adopted by similar agencies within the country.

On these bases it was possible for the new entity to be administered by its Council of Administration—represented by a Manager—the accounts being kept by a member of the community, with advice from the Cooperatives Department of the National Bank of Costa Rica.

4. Execution of the Work

Under the direction of the technical staff of the Instituto Costarricense de Electricidad, the members of the Electrical Cooperative of San José de Naranjo themselves did the work necessary to install a plant and to produce and distribute electric power in the locality.

Thanks to this effort and to the decisive collaboration of all contributing agencies, on January 19, 1957, the community of San José de Naranjo was able for the first time in its history to enjcy a regular supply of electric power.

The service was officially inaugurated April 28, 1957, in a simple but significant ceremony attended by governmental authorities, high officials of the National Bank of Costa Rica, representatives of the Instituto Costarricense de Electricidad, delegates from STICA, members of the 4-S Clubs, the local school teachers, and the public.

F. CONCLUSIONS

The official inauguration of the Plant of the Electric Cooperative of San José de Naranjo brought to a successful conclusion the Pilot Project for Rural Cooperatives, organized by the Cooperatives Department of the National Bank of Costa Rica, with technical advice from the Pan American Union and with the collaboration of the Inter-American Institute of Agricultural Sciences (STICA), and the National Institute of Housing and City Planning. This experiment, first of its kind in Latin America, has demonstrated that a Cooperative organized along technical lines is a conquest of incalculable value in the progress of a community.

The two basic aspects, association and enterprise, were perfectly balanced: the former by means of an educational campaign which developed awareness of the need for joint action for the common good, and the latter through the conviction that the maximum contribution compatible with the possibilities of each individual would be needed to insure the economic and financial solidity of the organization. In short, the need for a total moral and material contribution in solving the problems which concern them, was emphasized.

This Project demonstrated that when communities are stimulated and guided to achieve something through their own efforts, the response is fully forthcoming. The publicizing of results and the repetition of such projects, not on a trial basis but as a general policy, represent steps for the future since what has been done is only a first step.

In conclusion, special mention should be made of the efficiency and responsibility with which the Cooperatives Department of the National Bank of Costa Rica accepted the task of organizing the project and the valuable cooperation received from the collaborating agencies mentioned above.

The valuable experience acquired will no doubt be most useful both for Costa Rica and other countries which may wish to take advantage of it. This alone would justify the participation of the Pan American Union, which is always eager, insofar as it is able, to assist in stimulating the social and economic progress of the Member States.

7

The Prevention of
Sleeping Sickness in Nigeria

Although most of these case studies were made after the colonial period of history was over, we have found some excellent analyses that were done in the terminal stages of the colonial era, particularly in British Africa. In fact, one can easily take the position that much of the groundwork for present village development techniques was laid by British administrators in the thirties and forties, when their colonial empire was phasing out. Although much of their work was very good, particularly considering their lack of knowledge of how change takes place, certain aspects of colonial administrative techniques were incorporated into change projects, sometimes to their detriment. However, since the developing world at the village level has changed little since the independence of these countries, with mainly a change in administrative leaders, lessons learned from British colonial days are still valuable today.

We find in the following account some very important lessons change agents still need to learn. One of the prime values of this analysis is that it was made ten years after the commencement of the project. Consequently, the reader is able to see more clearly the difficulties of integrating a strange, new idea into another cultural system, no matter how beneficial it is in technical terms. Perhaps the chief observation that should be made is the necessity of having more than technical knowledge and traditional administrative techniques. Indeed, it is very ironic that the humanitarian goal of this project, based on a unique medical discovery that brought benefits to a large population, was still not appreciated by its recipients.

Here again we encounter the problems that are created when administrators draw up elaborate blueprints and then try to get the recipients to carry them out. Westerners, even those who have some familiarity with the peoples of Asia and Africa, are often prone to underestimate the resistant powers of the rural peasant. Also, Westerners and members of the ruling élite in the nonindustrialized countries tend to equate power with strength. There is one kind of strength, however, which does not require overt power. This is passive resistance, a technique which the underprivileged have relied upon since time immemorial and in the use of which the peasant of the non-Western world is a past master. For hundreds of years he has not been able overtly to resist those in power because the punishment was too severe. So he has developed the technique of never disagreeing openly, but of disassociating himself in the overseer's absence. When the overseer returns and sees that work is not done, he demands answers, but these the peasant can provide in abundance. He has had much practice. In fact, his very survival often depends on his ability to provide satisfactory explanations, whether true or not. Coercion and punishment for not co-operating can be applied, as in this instance, but unless the innovators or administrators are willing to apply it for a long time, it will probably be of no avail. The person who adopts a new practice without being convinced of its utility, or only because he will be punished if he does not do so, will almost invariably abandon it the moment the pressure is taken away.

We find in this case history some common characteristics of peasant societies that inhibit open communication and the acceptance of new practices, particularly the hierarchical social order and supernatural beliefs as to the nature of disease. Such beliefs are very frequently used by non-Western people to explain diseases. They lack knowledge of the germ theory, and being unwilling to leave unexplained such important problems as sickness, they rely on religious or magical ideas. These people had been perceptive enough within their own knowledge system, and realized that sickness was connected with the brushy areas on the edge of rivers. However, they thought the sickness was caused by spirits, not by the tsetse fly. There was a possibility for an educational campaign to bring them the new knowledge—the innovators might have tried to inculcate the idea that the spirits were in the flies, thus adapting a new idea to the old belief—but the approach of the innovators was "rational" and authoritarian, and thus resistance was created.

Perhaps the final point worthy of note here is the lack of integration of this innovation into the customs and thoughts of the people. Though they were cutting the brush because of the threat of punishment, they had not adopted the practice as their own after ten years. They had not integrated it into their cultural patterns, and they might well abandon it when the authority was relaxed.

CULTURE CHANGE UNDER PRESSURE: A HAUSA CASE

HORACE MINER *

Programs of technical assistance and community development create culture contact conditions which are particularly well suited to the study of change. The contact situation is narrowly delimited and it is easier to identify the agents of change, the pressures for change and the results of the contact. The study here reported in preliminary fashion is an attempt to capitalize on such a research situation in northern Nigeria. Here, among the Hausa, the British Colonial government instituted a program of resettlement, health improvement and economic development. The Anchau Scheme, as it was known, was initiated in 1937 and continued with diminishing intensity for the next decade. Since 1948 the area has received no special attention. These facts about the scheme contributed to the decision to study it, for they provided one condition frequently lacking in previous case studies. The assistance program was old enough that its ultimate effects, rather than just its immediate effects, should be evident. The price paid for the advantage of studying the end results of the contact was, of course, the necessity of reconstructing the operational phase of the program.

The disadvantages of such an approach were mitigated by two things: extensive files of the day-to-day working papers of the Scheme personnel were still available, along with all the related reports and publications. In addition, both the British and Hausa who had been most involved in the Scheme were still available as informants. While memories are notoriously selective, this fact proved to be a methodological asset. When the records and the recollections of the two groups corresponded, the facts of the case were obvious. But when they diverged, in every case the divergences were traceable to specific differences in the cultural perspectives with which the same events were viewed. Once the bases of the distortion were understood, the true nature of the events became perfectly clear.

* Reprinted from *Human Organization,* Fall, 1960, pp. 164-167, by permission of the publisher. Dr. Miner, who is a specialist on Africa, is Professor of Anthropology and Sociology at the University of Michigan.

The Anchau Scheme was originally developed to meet a specific problem—the widsepread occurrence of sleeping sickness among the Hausa. Although the Scheme was ultimately expanded to include other goals, we shall limit our discussion to the measures used to control this disease.

The British instituted a special investigation of sleeping sickness in 1921, but it was not until 1928 that they discovered that the disease had reached epidemic proportions and was rapidly decimating the population. Interestingly, the epidemic was an indirect result of the advent of *Pax Britannica*. Before the conquest of northern Nigeria in 1903, the area was in a state of turbulence as a result of incessant slave raids. Towns were heavily walled and the working of fields at any distance from the towns involved considerable risk. Large areas of the countryside were uninhabited and communication was limited. Although there was an area of endemic sleeping sickness to the south and tsetse flies were prevalent all over the North at this time, the disease remained localized. With the establishment of peace, farmers moved out into the bush and mobility increased generally. The increased fly-man contact soon produced the epidemic.

Field surveys showed that in some areas up to forty percent of the people had the disease. The basic problem was that, although there were effective curative drugs, they did little good as long as reinfection from tsetse fly bites was inevitable. The government established a research station to attack the problem and Dr. T. A. M. Nash, the staff entomologist, discovered that the tsetse fly could only live in a microclimate distinctly cooler than the generally prevailing temperatures in sunlight. The fly was therefore confined to the shaded banks of streams, the rest of the country being generally open. It was at fords and water holes that fly-man contact occurred.

Tests revealed that if the brush were cut down along the streams, the fly could not persist in the area. On the basis of these findings the Anchau Scheme was drawn up to initiate control measures in the worst affected region. The proposal was to keep the stream banks clear in an area of 700 square miles within which lived some 50,000 people. In order to accomplish this end, part of the population had to be resettled to create sufficient density to provide the manpower to keep the streams cleared. We shall limit ourselves simply to that part of the plan which involved convincing the

Hausa to keep the brush cut along the streams. In order to understand the Hausa reactions to the program, we must describe those elements of Hausa culture which are immediately relevant.

Important in this regard is their political organization. The Fulani conquest of the ancient Hausa, or Habe, States at the beginning of the nineteenth century resulted in the establishment of a series of feudally organized emirates. Each was autonomous and headed by an emir descended from the Fulani conquerors. The emirates were divided into fiefs, each allocated to a Fulani, commonly a relative of the emir. The fiefs in turns were divided into village areas, each under the control of a Hausa headman, resident in the principal settlement in his area. Even the headmen held their appointments subject to the approval of the emir. The functions of this hierarchy were the maintenance of order, the organization of defensive and offensive forces, and the collection of taxes.

The emirs were all-powerful, even to the extent of interfering with the administration of Moslem justice by the cadis. The emir's position could only be jeopardized by alienating powerful groups of fiefholders. The latter were supreme within their domains as long as they kept the emir satisfied. The village headmen had the support of the fiefholder and his forces but, in the regulation of mundane affairs within the village areas, the headman's power derived directly from the support accorded him by his villagers. Being a Hausa, his traditional role depended upon his understanding and manipulation of the local culture.

Even with peers the Hausa peasant adheres to elaborate forms of politeness. The deference shown to superiors is almost oriental in flavor. In the presence of the *hakimi,* or lord of the fief, a peasant removes his sandals, prostrates himself and remains bowed to the ground, keeps his eyes lowered, speaks only when addressed, and employs highly formalized deferential phrases when he does speak. He would never think of expressing a point of view contrary to that of the *hakimi.* Village headmen, although they are peasants themselves, are treated with extreme politeness but the system permits greater freedom of expression with these arbiters of village problems. In summary we may say that Hausa society, including its overlords, is very hierarchically organized. The advent of the British did little to change this except to limit some of the excesses of the emirs and fiefholders. Indirect rule was studiously adhered to. Although British district officers were appointed to oversee colonial administration at the local level, all administrative acts were promulgated by British authorities through the emirs. If problems arose at the local level, recommendations were made upward through the Colonial channels, the emir was persuaded to act, and the directives came down the indigenous lines of power. Because of the powerful position of the British vis-à-vis the emir and because the district officer had access to top colonial officials, a district officer could, if so inclined, wield a considerable amount of derived power in his relation to a *hakimi*.

Another aspect of the Hausa power system involves the cultural devices for holding the power of the overlords within reasonable bounds. One method which the peasants employ in limiting the nominal omnipotence of their rulers is passive resistance. When a headman transmits orders from the *hakimi* which the peasants do not want to follow, they simply fail to comply. The headman can exert his influence to try to secure compliance, but his power is only as strong as his local support. General resistance to repeated orders may be continued until sanctions are applied by the *hakimi*. Such sanctions consist of fines or jail terms and the headman may be replaced if he has been sufficiently noncooperative.

In addition to the political structure, the other aspect of Hausa culture most relevant to the Anchau plan for sleeping sickness control is the native belief concerning the nature and cause of the disease. These ideas are best understood in relation to Western concepts. In its most characteristic Nigerian form, sleeping sickness produces sporadic fever, headache, edema of the face and limbs, accompanied by swelling of the cervical glands and persistent weakness. The condition may continue for years but the associated lowered resistance to disease frequently results in death from other causes. Death may even result from a flareup of the toxic effects of sleeping sickness itself, without the central nervous system becoming involved so as to produce the classic condition of continued somnolence and mental disorder. The proportion of patients who show these latter symptoms is always small. This form of the disease is normally fatal and even with treatment the patient may not recover. If he does, he will still show damage to the nervous system. The more prevalent form of sleeping sickness is not easily recognized, even by doctors, unless they have had experience with the disease. On a number of occasions medical officers sent out to investigate epidemics of what later proved to be sleeping sickness failed to diagnose the underlying sickness and reported that the people were dying of pneumonia.

The Hausa recognized only the rarely occurring sleeping and mania symptoms as characterizing the disease *ciwon barci,* a literal translation of "sleeping sickness." They did not recognize the other more prevalent symptoms as characterizing any single disease and, in fact, most of the symptoms occur separately in connection with other maladies. *Ciwon barci* was greatly feared for it was fatal and believed to be highly contagious. Any Hausa so afflicted was completely isolated, even from his family. Although he might be driven from the community, he was more usually fed by a relative who avoided any contact with the patient or his utensils. Not infrequently the mentally deranged invalid would wander off and starve before he died of his disease. When treatment was attempted, it consisted of herbal remedies or written Koranic charms.

Some of the other terms employed to identify sleeping sickness are indicative of Hausa beliefs as to its cause. The disease was also known as *kunturu,* a word which also designates a region which has a reputation of being under evil supernatural influence. *Dudduru* refers to the disease and also means a small stream with wooded banks. Both words refer to the fundamental belief that sleeping sickness is caused by *iska,* or spirits, who live in natural features such as clumps of brush along the streams. The *iska* are pre-Islamic supernaturals who have survived the conversion of the Hausa and are still actively propitiated by the Maguzawa, who are probably pagan remnants of the early Hausa still scattered through the area. Spirit possession in the form of *bori* dancing is still common to Maguzawa and Moslem Hausa alike. The Galma River, which flows to the south of Anchau, is considered to be infested with malevolent spirits and the area is actually still dangerous for sleeping sickness. Because spirits are local, the only way to escape their effects is to leave the region. Whole villages have moved when threatened with epidemic disease. Although such action might remove a population from an area badly infested with tsetse, the insects were ubiquitous and complete escape was impossible. While the Hausa thus recognized the relation between the habitat of the tsetse fly and sleeping sickness, the role of the fly in the transmission of the disease was unknown—the *iska* were the vector.

Against the background just sketched, we are in a position to consider Hausa reactions to the methods of sleeping sickness control instituted by the British. Even before the Anchau Scheme went into operation, medical officers had made an intensive survey of the population to determine the extent of sleeping sickness and to provide treatment. Clinical diagnosis followed by microscopic verification revealed large numbers of cases who showed none of the classic symptoms. Even when tests proved the presence of the infection, the Hausa were very loath to admit that they had the awful disease which previously made them outcasts. Still today, a headman may deny that there is any sleeping sickness in his village, although he knows of cases under treatment. The British interpret these facts as representing a feeling of shame concerning the disease. On the other hand, there is considerable doubt that the Hausa ever accepted the idea that what they and the British called sleeping sickness were really the same thing. None of the old fear of the disease was felt toward medically diagnosed cases which did not fit the Hausa concept of sleeping sickness. The conflicting conceptions need not be resolved now, for advanced cases have disappeared entirely.

When the Anchau Scheme went into operation, the system of indirect rule was adhered to and the necessary orders were issued through the Emir. To strengthen the native authority channel and to reinforce on-the-spot interpretations of the Emir's orders, the Emir was persuaded to send a personal representative to remain in Anchau. Through him the British personnel could put immediate pressure on the *Hakimi,* whose residence was permanently transferred to Anchau. These changes resulted in a concentration of authority previously unknown in the area. The resettlement phase of the Scheme brought together the scattered peasants so that they were under administrative scrutiny of a sort they dearly loved to avoid. The *Hakimi* found he was no longer the highest local official and even the Emir ultimately complained that, as a result of the intense British activity around Anchau, he had been deprived of part of his emirate. In short, while native channels of power were used, everyone along the line felt under unusual administrative pressure. This method of administration of the Scheme did have one very important implication for the success of the plan. The specific methods of implementation of many of its aspects were left up to the native authorities and the acculturative adjustments to the changes were as little disruptive to the local culture as they could be.

Before stream clearance was begun, the reasons for it were explained to the Hausa from the Emir to the village elders. They were told that sleeping sickness was common among them, that it was caused by little "fish-like animals" in the blood, that these animals got into the blood when a person was bitten by a tsetse fly, and that the way to get rid of the flies was to cut down the brush along the streams. As we have seen, these statements were in conflict with native beliefs and the explanation of the idea of microörganisms was entirely beyond their experience and comprehension. It is also clear that the Hausa patterns of respect toward superiors made it impossible for them to question openly what they were told. As a result, the British were effectively isolated from any knowledge of their failure to convey to the Hausa any real understanding of what was being done.

Initial stream clearance was carried out with hired native labor. In at least two instances local Hausa refused to cut certain patches of brush because these were sacred and inhabited by spirits. Finally non-Hausa natives from the French Sudan were used to cut the sacred brush. Once the streams were cleared, a plan was drawn up to provide for annual slashing thereafter. Each headman was impressed with his responsibility and the benefits which his village would derive from the elimination of the flies. On a rough average, some two weeks of part-time communal labor would be involved during a period of agricultural inactivity. Orders for the first reslashing went out from the Emir, through the *Hakimi*. The British supervisors and native foremen appeared at the villages to oversee the work but the communal laborers failed to appear. Subsequent attempts to secure cooperation produced only a handful of men and they arrived hours late. Exasperated, the British forced the Emir to stringent action. Headmen were removed from office and fines imposed on the peasants. These methods ultimately produced results. By checking the operations year after year, the pattern of annual stream clearance was finally established.

The result of the disease treatment and the eradication of the fly was the virtual elimination of sleeping sickness. The population began to increase and even migrants came to fill up the land now free from disease. For the past ten years there have been no Scheme personnel at Anchau but a thorough check of the streams showed that the annual orders of the Emir have been carried out in almost all instances and that the area is still virtually free of fly and sleeping sickness. One may well conclude that this, the major phase of the scheme, has been a success. In terms of culture change, the

Hausa have for twenty years carried out a new pattern of behavior which is essential for the biological preservation of the group.

It comes as something of a shock, therefore, to discover that stream clearance cannot be said to have been adopted into the culture of the Hausa around Anchau. The basis for such a statement is an exhaustive study of the present attitudes and conceptions of village headmen regarding sleeping sickness and its control. The village leaders were asked why they cleared the streams every year. The common denominator of the responses was that the slashing was carried out because they were forced to do it. A quarter of the headmen literally had no idea why the work was done. All of the others, however, stated that clearing the brush eliminated tsetse fly, although sometimes this response was added as an afterthought to an initial statement of ignorance of any reason for the task.

Half of those who mentioned flies also stated that they transmitted sleeping sickness. But when one pursued the subject, it became clear that this was a simple repetition of what they had been told. They saw this as the British explanation, but held firmly to their old belief that sleeping sickness was caused by spirits. Elimination of the flies was rationalized by others as desirable because the bite was painful. Still others saw the clearing as a means of driving out crop-destroying monkeys or of improving pasturage for Fulani cattle. Finally, the interviews produced that rarity in social science data, unanimous concurrence. When asked if they would continue to clear the streams if they were not forced to do so, every headman replied, "No."

What we find, therefore, is that the now long-standing practice of clearance has not been integrated into local culture at all. The foregoing material points to a clear answer as to why this vital practice would be abandoned tomorrow if administrative pressure were not maintained from outside the area. We have long known that the adoption of a new culture trait involves its ability to meet some functional need in the culture. Expressed in psychological phraseology, action agencies now commonly refer to the necessity of operating in terms of a people's "felt needs." But what can be done if a people feel no need for the innovation the agency wishes to introduce? Faced with the necessity of making people accept things for which they perceive no need, the concept of "induced needs" has arisen. The Anchau evidence fully supports the role of perceived need in culture change and constitutes a warning with regard to methods of inducing change regardless of local perceptions of the innovation.

To recapitulate what happened at Anchau, it is clear that the Hausa experienced no particular need to eliminate sleeping sickness as they knew it. The new culture pattern of stream clearance was adopted and continued solely because of the need to escape administrative sanctions applied in traditional ways. The fact that the new trait was never effectively related to local problems and beliefs produced the anomaly of the adoption of an innovation without its integration into the culture. We find that coercion can produce compliance without any fundamental cultural alteration.

8

Resettlement to New Lands in Nigeria

The account that follows is particularly valuable because of the very useful comparison that can be made with the previous case history. Like the Bolivian and Peruvian community development efforts, both of these had many of the same characteristics, though they ended quite differently. They occurred in the same country, the innovators were British administrators in both instances, and the people were Nigerian farmers in both projects. Also, both were begun only after elaborate plans were drawn up by the innovators.

However, there was one initial difference of significance in this resettlement effort—the administrators decided that they would not apply coercion to get compliance. Although one could say this was to their credit, this project also would probably have been a failure if this had been the only important decision or event to take place. The new houses being offered were not satisfactory to the local people, primarily because their needs were not the same as those of the designers. Designers often go ahead with their plans for housing projects for the underprivileged without ever bothering to consult the people who will use their buildings. Most house designers would probably prefer never to listen to clients, but they must when the clients pay for the work. However, on housing projects for the poor, in the United States as well as in Africa, where the clients do not pay, the designers tend not to consult them. But even the poor have certain felt needs in house design and when they are not met, they attempt either to alter the buildings to fit these needs or reject them altogether. In the Nigerian case they rejected them.

The resettlement effort was saved by an accident, coupled with a positive action by the administrators. If either had been missing, there would probably be little more than bush in this part of Nigeria today. The accident, as far as the project was concerned, was a change in administration which put local leaders into political positions where they could carry the objections of their clients to the administrators, and which enabled them to transmit information from the administrators to their constituents. For the first time meaningful communication channels were established. Of most significance, the objections of the recipients were heard by the innovators.

The positive action was flexibility on the part of the innovators. After they learned of the objections, they decided to let the local people alter the houses to a limited extent. Primarily because communication was well-established, and because of the flexibility of the innovators, the interest of the recipients was kindled for the first time. Participation grew. There was an added incentive, however, in that the government provided considerable support in goods and other assistance. Thus, a reward motivation was provided. This was in contrast to the sleeping sickness campaign where instead of being rewarded for cooperating, the people were punished if they did not.

Perhaps the final note of importance that should be made here is in regard to integration. As we have indicated previously, no new idea can be considered as successfully transferred to a community until it has been incorporated into their body of customs and the efforts of outside stimulators are no longer needed. It was patently indicated that this did not happen in the case of the sleeping sickness eradication campaign. Only through continuous application of pressure was it possible to get the local people to continue cutting the brush. Here we have the opposite and more desirable reaction—not only did the local people accept the new idea, but they began applying social pressure on new community members to keep up standards. Moreover, they went a step farther, which is the most that can ever be expected of any newly planted idea: they began spreading the news to other communities of their own volition. They even went back to improve their old community.

NEW ERUWA*

B. K. COOPER

This is the story of an attempt to give a village community in Nigeria an opportunity to live in more healthy and pleasant conditions by the establishment of a model planned village near their existing homes. Eruwa, a group of some eight thousand people, is situated in the Ibadan Division of Oyo Province, one of the Western Provinces of Nigeria. The surrounding country is rolling savannah but the village lies in a hollow surrounded by steep granite hills. This location was determined for reasons of defence, as right up to the beginning of the present century the country was ravaged by inter-tribal wars. The inhabitants are Yorubas and owe allegiance to the senior Chiefs of Ibadan, fifty miles to the east, since it was the Ibadan warriors who came to their aid in the inter-tribal wars. The people are poor and secure their livelihood by farming the surrounding ample yet rather indifferent land, growing subsistence crops of yams, egusi, cassava, maize and guinea corn. The soil does not support cocoa, oil-palms or ground-nuts. Following the establishment of the *pax britannica* at the beginning of this century, the population and prosperity of the village grew. As a result more and larger houses were built, but expansion was restricted by the surrounding hills. The picture a few years ago was of an overcrowded village badly eroded by the run-off of rain water from the heights above.

Several years ago the Administration conceived the idea of establishing a model village in this area. The local Chiefs were persuaded by the District Officer to make available an area of flat unoccupied land by the side of the motor road three miles away. The Government Health Department then drew up a blueprint plan for a village layout on this site. Each house was to occupy a plot of land eighty feet by sixty feet, the plots being arranged in straight rows at fixed intervals apart. Provision was also made in the plan for a market, wells, lorry park, church, and playing ground. In addition to avoiding the overcrowding of houses in the new village, it

* Reprinted from *Corona,* June, 1952, pp. 225-227, by permission of the Controller of Her Britannic Majesty's Stationery Office. Mr. Cooper served as an administrative officer in the British Overseas Service of Western Nigeria for 15 years.

was envisaged that the houses themselves should follow an approved design. The Health Authorities recommended a type of model house and, under their supervision, the first householder to move to the new site erected his house. The design of the house did not appear to be popular and even the first house to be erected did not conform entirely to the plan. A few more families moved in and built houses conforming in their main details to the original "model" house. Apart from this little row of new houses the new site remained vacant for the next two years.

The people were clearly not convinced of the benefit of moving to the new site—in any case they were reluctant to leave their family homes, under whose floors lay the bones of their ancestors. In addition they did not consider that the design of the model house was suitable. Since there was never any question of compelling people to move to the new site, deadlock had apparently been reached.

The traditional council of Chiefs in this area, drawn from Eruwa and the nearby town of Lanlate, had been long recognised as the organ of Local Government being constituted as a Native Authority subordinate to that at Ibadan. In practice, apart from continuing to exercise their individual and important functions as local Chiefs, the Council had little opportunity to interest itself in such matters as health, education and forestry. These aspects of their District were largely planned and controlled from the centre, Ibadan, and it was to Ibadan that their annual taxes were paid. In the past few years radical changes have been made in the structure of the Local Government body in this area which among many other things have greatly contributed to the ultimate success of the resettlement plan. To inculcate local interest and responsibility in financial affairs a separate Treasury building was erected at Eruwa and a separate set of annual estimates of revenue and expenditure prepared for this District. The Council was reorganised to include literate Councillors from the two main towns, Eruwa and Lanlate. A subsequent reorganisation of membership occurred to include a larger proportion of elected Councillors and, as the new settlement grew, a Chief and Councillor from there were given seats on the District Council.

These changes led to a great awakening of interest in local affairs. Visiting Administrative Officers could now more easily convey their ideas and suggestions to the local people. The local people in turn could more readily express their views and difficulties. Gradually a medium and stimulus were created for resolving the deadlock concerning the resettlement scheme. Local interest had been reawakened.

The principal objection to the model house design was of excess ventilation. Compared with local houses the increase of window space was very large and the idea of inside verandahs in place of walls an innovation. The village site was very exposed to winds which blow cold at night during the harmattan months. Furthermore the customary heating of living quarters provided by the cooking fire was absent since this fire in the model house was situated in an exterior kitchen. It appeared that the model house was suitable for a considerably warmer climate and that modification was necessary. It was decided in consequence that, provided an honest attempt was made on the part of the householder to follow the design of the existing model house, individual modifications of detail such as the substitution of a wall with large double windows in place of a verandah, would be permitted. No deviation was allowed from the village layout, each house occupying its allotted plot. This concession in the question of design was followed up by vigorous and repeated propaganda on the part of the Administrative Officer at local Council meetings. As interest grew in local affairs so did the attendance of the general public at these meetings.

Relaxation of the rigidity of the model house plan called for leadership and supervision of all house building in the new village if the standards aimed at were to be achieved. Control in this matter could not effectively be maintained by Government Officers. In any case this was not desirable. The more responsibility that could be undertaken by the people themselves the more would the village grow as a true development of a community. The earlier standards set by the first row of houses fostered the growth of a strong village pride. These owners became jealous of their village's reputation and standards and, as a result, they wished them to be retained by newcomers. Through their Chief, the locally paid Sanitary Inspector, and regular visits from an Administration Officer effective direction and restraint were given to new settlers with the result that house standards have improved rather than detracted from the original design.

In the past three years the population has increased from less than a hundred to upwards of a thousand. Judicious priming has been given by the Government in the form of financial assistance as the scheme progressed. The surveying and pegging out of the first housing plots were done by Government Officers. An excellent well was provided from Government Development funds at the same time as the building of the first houses. Later, when the population was about half its present size, stimulus was given to village pride by the erection of a block of stone market stalls, the first in the district, from funds provided by the Government. A further well was provided. Last year by communal labour a Community Centre was completed, Government funds paying for the roofing materials.

New difficulties were created as the village grew. The Chiefs of old Eruwa were apt to be suspicious of the growing prestige of the new village and its leaders. The common structure of the Native Authority Council on which sat representatives from the two large villages, Eruwa and Lanlate, and latterly from New Eruwa, the common interests in aspects of the Native Authority such as the Treasury, Dispensary and Postal Agency, as well as the common use of the Mission schools in the area all assisted to promote unity. The energies of the Chiefs and people of old Eruwa were directed to an improvement of their town and a successful programme of town improvement has been completed there recently. The removal of a part of the population to the New Site made easier the widening and straightening of the existing town road and the building of a further road through the town. A fine Community Centre has been built. Teak plantations are being established in the area by the Native Authority financed by a £4,000 loan from the Western Regional Production Development Board. Envy of the New Settlement has given place to renewed pride in their old town. A real awakening has resulted. The people of Lanlate have drawn up and started on a plan for improvement in their town. A second programme is under way at old Eruwa.

The resettlement scheme has not only resulted in better living conditions for a community. It has acted as a spur to the whole District to seek better conditions of living through their own efforts.

9

Venereal Disease Eradication in Northern Rhodesia

There is little doubt that the most difficult area of behavior to change is that in which the advantages of new practices are most difficult to demonstrate. Furthermore, there is little doubt that among the ideas being carried from the Western world, those concerning health are the most difficult to demonstrate. The passage of a microbe from one person to another as a cause for illness is a relatively subtle idea, one which has only existed in Western medical knowledge for approximately 100 years. Westerners rarely stop to consider that despite the general acceptance of this idea within their own cultures, it still takes from fourteen to fifteen years of constant indoctrination to inculcate it into the minds of their own children. For the first dozen or more years of their lives, Western children wash their hands before eating only because there are penalties for not doing so, and it is probable that even when they do start washing on their own, it is as much a matter of habit and acceptance on faith as an understanding of the germ theory of disease. Thus, it should be apparent that health campaigns based on such Western medical concepts will have great difficulties if the changes are expected to take place rapidly.

The difficulties of transmitting new health practices are not caused by a lack of interest in health; to the contrary, peasant people everywhere are quite concerned about their physical well-being. But their recognition of an ailment may differ considerably from its Western definition. Thus, we find that an ailment which occurs in stages that are not apparently related will not necessarily be taken for a single disease, and as a result will not necessarily be taken seriously. This is frequently the case with venereal disease, where the initial infection is not considered to be part of the terminal stage, as is indicated in the following example.

There are two possible approaches to lack of awareness of this kind—education and compulsion. Westerners use a combination of both techniques in training their own children. In this well-meaning attempt to save an African tribe, the change agents relied almost exclusively on compulsion. Unfortunately, a system based on legislation, fines and general coercion is unlikely to change any attitudes, as was indicated in the case of tsetse eradication. Peasant or tribal people will either avoid the imposed rules or abandon them the moment the pressure is released.

An added complication with many diseases is that they are as much social as physical. Though it is the body that is infected, it is the interaction of bodies that keeps the diseases rampant. This can be no more clearly demonstrated than with venereal disease. Merely to treat the infected bodies without making any effort to alter the social conditions that brought about the infections is largely wasted effort. In this case, the customs of casual sexual relations kept the disease rate almost as high after treatment as before. This was not immorality by the standards of these people, but it undoubtedly was the major cause of the continued high incidence of infection.

Some recommendations of what might have been done do suggest themselves. Above all else, more efficient communication in the form of health education was required. It was not enough to get the agreement of chiefs. Another peoples' moral code is not easy to change, but their interest in personal health is ever-present and concentration on prophylactic measures might have brought about better results. All this would take considerable time and effort, which is the required price for transferring a new health idea. For more immediate results there might have been the possibility of utilizing individual competition, or status emulation, to establish a standard which local people would want to emulate. Once the idea is disseminated that a certain health practice makes a person more proper, there is some chance that others will adopt it for the status they hope to achieve in so doing.

THE ILA V.D. CAMPAIGN *

A. J. EVANS

The Ba-Ila are a small tribe living on the bank of the Kafue River. They are a backward people and have always been noted for their ability as fighters and for their wealth in cattle. They also have a reputation, a less savoury one, for the high incidence of venereal disease among them and for the fact that with a falling birth-rate they are slowly dying out. This latter has been a cause of anxiety for 10 years or more, and plans were in hand for investigating this unhappy state of affairs in 1939 but had to be shelved on the outbreak of war. It had always been assumed that the falling birth-rate was the result of the frequency of venereal disease, but the assumption remained to be proved.

Certain it is that the birth-rate is dropping. Almost every visitor to the district commented on the absence of the usual crowds of children in every village and the infrequency with which a woman with a baby on her back was seen. The District Commissioner in 1944 showed among the Ila that for 5,426 women (of all ages over 16 years) there were 2,809 children or about one child for every two women. No figures are readily available for comparison say twenty years previously, but Smith & Dale (*The Ila Speaking People of Northern Rhodesia,* published in 1920) make mention of a shortage of children and they also describe venereal diseases as being extremely common.

In 1945 the problem of the falling birth-rate and high venereal disease incidence again came to the fore and was the subject of a lively debate in Legislative Council. Plans were put into operation to obtain staff and equipment to undertake a V.D. campaign among the Ba-Ila, and this campaign began its work in September 1946.

Long before September 1946, the District Commissioner had been discussing the possibilities of such a campaign with the Native Authority chiefs. It was indeed fortunate that the District Commissioner was a man who not only had a very wide knowledge of the

---

* Reprinted from *The Rhodes-Livingstone Journal,* No. 9, 1950, pp. 40-47, by permission of the publisher. Mr. Evans was a colonial civil servant stationed in Northern Rhodesia for about 15 years and subsequently transferred to another territory; for about half of his Rhodesian term he worked as a venereal disease specialist.

Ba-Ila but also took a very great interest in their welfare and believed whole-heartedly in the necessity of such a campaign. So successful had he been in 'selling' the idea to the Ila chiefs that they accepted it to a man, promised their co-operation and, in 1946, made it compulsory for all Africans under their authority to attend for examination and treatment as directed.

It has been no easy problem to find the best method of examining and taking treatment to the people of this tribe. On either side of the Kafue River lie areas of flat country, always known as 'the flats,' which flood during the rains each year. Most of the villages are grouped on the strips of high ground between the flood level and the forest edge. During the rains the cattle are kept around the villages where they can graze without going into the forest, in which tsetse-fly usually abound, and in the dry months the cattle are sent down to graze on 'the flats' and along the river bank. Thus, generally speaking, the villages are in groups on the higher ground, and by taking each chief's area in turn, and going to each group of villages it has been found possible to examine the people and take treatment to them without making any of them walk more than five miles from their village.

Rough but serviceable grass shelters are built in each group of villages. They are a poor substitute for the amenities of an up-to-date clinic, but with a little ingenuity can be made serviceable. An Army Mobile Canteen which has been converted as a Mobile Laboratory is also available and proves very useful though it is not the ideal vehicle to drive along bush tracks, and there are certain parts of the area where it is just impossible to take it.

When work is to begin in a new chief's area, the chief is notified some time before and arrangements are made to see the people from each vilage at their nearest centre on one definite day. The village headmen are responsible for seeing that all the people belonging to his village do attend at the appointed time and place. After each village has been examined the headman is interrogated as to any absentees. A certain number of people are always away working in the industrial areas or elsewhere and nothing can be done about them. Others will be away visiting within the district and the headman is instructed to send them to be examined as soon as they return to their village (such visits rarely last more than 2-3 weeks), while others will be away at the gardens or with the cattle on 'the flats,' and arrangements are made to send reliefs for them.

That a certain number of people can and do slip through the net is certain but comparison with the tax register shows this number to be small.

Very early on it became obvious that, of the two common venereal diseases, syphilis was very common, whereas gonorrhoea was relatively rare. This is a complete reversal of the usual finding in European countries and a reversal of the finding among some other African tribes. There is some evidence that this relative immunity from gonorrhoea is a new development among the Ba-Ila in the last twenty years. Whether this is due to the building up of an acquired immunity to the disease or to some other factor not yet ascertained must remain a matter for conjecture.

Also, from the examination of the villages it was obvious that the birth-rate was dangerously low. Of 267 adult women from 21 villages in one chief's area, only 3 (1.1 per cent) were pregnant at the time of examination. It is difficult to diagnose pregnancy without special tests before the third month. This means therefore that 267 women would produce 6 children a year, and therefore, assuming the total number of Ba-Ila women to be about 5,400, only 120 babies would be born to the Ba-Ila each year, even if there were no still-births or miscarriages among them. When allowance is made for the high-neo-natal and infant mortality which is present among all African tribes it can readily be understood why the population statistics for each five year period show a steady drop.

The ordinary routine of treatment for syphilis consists of two courses of injections, each course consisting of weekly injections of an arsenic and of a bismuth compound for 10 weeks with a rest period of 3 weeks between each course. This is the routine, but it sometimes has to be modified slightly for various reasons. Periodical re-examination throughout treatment is undertaken of course. On the whole, contrary to the usual opinion that Africans do not stand up well to the standard methods of treatment, it has been found that untoward effects of treatment are rare among the Ba-Ila. The drugs in use are potent ones and untoward results do occur but they have been much rarer than are commonly found in European clinics. This is the more surprising when it is remembered that treatment is not being given under ideal conditions. The water used for boiling instruments is the village water supply and, though boiling will kill the bacteria in it, it will not destroy chemical contaminants. Then again after instruments have been sterilized it is difficult to keep them uncontaminated in a grass-shelter. One puff of wind and dust, grass, pollen, etc., are flying everywhere to leave a thin layer on syringes and needles.

Recently small supplies of penicillin have become available for use in treating syphilis. Treatment with this drug is very much shorter than with the older methods, a course of injections night and morning largely replacing the routine twenty week course of the older method. It is a most popular method of treatment with the Africans, and the only difficulty encountered has been to explain why it is not possible for every patient to have penicillin treatment. The actual cost of the drug is greater with penicillin than with the arsenic and bismuth routine, but the saving in time probably more than balances the additional cost of the penicillin. The use of penicillin in the treatment of syphilis is still *sub judice*. The immediate results are excellent, but it is as yet too early to tell what the long term results will be.

Venereal diseases other than syphilis are of course treated as they are encountered. While the emphasis of this work is on venereal disease, a good deal of general medicine is undertaken too and it is rare to visit a village without receiving a request to see some sick.

There are a good many difficulties to the smooth working of such routine as that outlined above. Not the least of these is the geography of the district. Where large areas of the countryside are under either Kafue flood water or rain water for 4-7 months in the year travelling can never be of the easiest. It has been found by bitter experience that unless treatment is given at the same place on the same day of the week and at approximately the same time of day, then the number of patients who become irregular in their attendance mounts at once. Similarly it has been found that if patients have to walk more than 2 or 3 miles for their treatment the default rate again rises. Persistent defaulters are dealt with by the chief's court, the usual penalty being a fine of £1, but occasional defaulters are merely cautioned, this usually being sufficient to prevent a further lapse. The number of cases taken to the chief's courts each year is very small.

Another difficulty which is constantly encountered is the problem of stragglers. Always when an area is first examined a certain number of people are away visiting or working in other parts of the territory. Most of those away visiting and a certain number of those away working will return to their homes during the time the campaign is working in that area and inevitably some of them will require treatment, which they will commence later than all the others. Thus when say 95 per cent of all the patients have completed their treatment there will be a residual 5 per cent who still require several or many weeks treatment.

Not the least interesting feature in the work of this Campaign has been the Africans' reactions. On the whole they have accepted it amazingly well. Of course there are those who regard the whole thing as a piece of nastiness on the part of Government, but their number is extremely small. The original publicity campaign undertaken by the District Commissioner in 1945-6 was amazingly successful. It is difficult to imagine what would be the results of an attempt at compulsory universal medical examination and treatment for venereal disease in any more civilized community. Certain it is that strong methods are the only ones that have any hope of succeeding in this particular case, and as mentioned above the number of times when powers of compulsion have had to be used is extremely small.

The attitude of the Ba-Ila to venereal diseases, in particular to syphilis, is interesting. They certainly feel no sense of disgrace or shame at having a venereal disease. Their attitude used to be similar to that which most Europeans have to a disease such as German measles, a nuisance at the time, but a fairly inevitable nuisance which it is best to have over and done with while young. As syphilis is a disease which the patient rarely or never gets a second time until the first attack is completely cured, there is some justification for this attitude of theirs. Frequently the sores of early syphilis heal easily, often with only scanty treatment, and then the patient is free of the nuisance of the disease, and the persistence of the disease internally does not worry him unduly. Whatever the reason, this nonchalant attitude certainly exists. When a headman is told to bring the people of his village for treatment, they all come along quite happily, and at first it was a constant source of amusement to see patients come out of the grass shelter after examination and announce that they were 'on treatment,' each such announcement being greeted with cheers and laughter from their assembled friends awaiting their own turn for examination. Similarly cards giving name, village and serial number are issued to each patient receiving treatment, and these are very popular as a form of personal adornment, being tied round the forehead or worn on a string round the neck.

While the Ba-Ila seem to have accepted the workings of the V.D. campaign, there are few if any signs that they have accepted the implications of such a campaign, to wit a readiness to change their sexual customs. There has been a certain amount of argument in the past as to whether the Ba-Ila are more immoral (by European standards) than certain other tribes, but this can only be a matter of opinion. No doubt can however exist that the Ba-Ila as a whole are very immoral. True, certain of their less pleasing customs such as sharing of wives and some of the practises during the initiation period at puberty have of recent years died out or at least gone underground, but adultery still remains very common. The man with cattle is the important man among the Ba-Ila and love of cattle and respect for ownership of cattle are deeply ingrained in their nature. Too often a man will regard his wife as a means of gaining cattle for him, and there is a phrase 'catching cattle' which is synonymous with adultery. A woman who by her adulteries gained many cattle for her husband as compensation was, and still is to some extent, considered an admirable wife. The Native Authority have tried to stamp out this practice by increasing the court fines for both parties for adultery and reducing the compensation to the injured husband, but very many of these cases are settled out of court (illegally) to the mutual benefit of husband and co-respondent who thus both save court fines.

The Ba-Ila are in some ways a painfully logical people. Now that there is a potent drug available for the treatment of 'fly-struck' cattle their attitude is that they can now reasonably graze their cattle at the edge of forest country where the danger of fly is great. Their assumption is that the Veterinary Department have a remedy for 'fly-struck' animals and so it doesn't matter much if their animals do become infected. So, with similar logic, what little fears they had of getting venereal infection have been allayed by the knowledge that there is an adequate and reasonably painless form of treatment available.

It will be 5 or 10 years before it is possible to give a full assessment of the result of this campaign. There are so many variable factors to be taken into consideration. One thing has however already been accomplished. The Ba-Ila are getting the idea of using

what medical facilities are available. At first it was a constant surprise to find Africans sitting in their villages only a mile or two
from a Government Dispensary or Mission Hospital knowing that
they were suffering from a venereal disease, or for that matter from
any other disease, and making no effort at all to go and get treatment. Now slowly they are getting the idea that if they are sick
they should go and get treatment right away. They still usually give
their own native medicines a trial first but they are resorting to the
Government Dispensary and the Mission Hospital much earlier than
they did.

Their is some evidence that the birth-rate is being favourably
influenced. We usually return to each chief's area 6-12 months after
the completion of treatment there and re-examine as many of the
old patients as can be found in their villages. No attempt is made
to round up patients who are away visiting, working in their gardens, etc., as it is considered that this re-examination is for the
good of the campaign rather than for the good of individual patients and that no unnecessary hardships should be enforced. Incidentally this re-examining is the thing to which the Ba-Ila most
persistently object and about which they complain bitterly that it is
pointless and unnecessary. In all, nine chiefs' areas have been so
re-examined and in all of them from 8-16 per cent of the women
treated 6-15 months previously were either pregnant or had healthy
babies since treatment. One chief's area (the first one treated) has
been further re-examined 2 years after the commencement of treatment. Here, to 67 women of all ages who received treatment 15
children had been born in the last 2 years and 3 of them were pregnant at the time of examination. That is to say that of women who
had received treatment 2 years ago the pregnancy rate was 4.5 per
cent, as against the figure of 1.1 per cent among women before
treatment, an increase in the pregnancy rate of 400 per cent. It will
be interesting to see what the birth-rate and pregnancy rate will be
in, say, 5 and 10 years.

Regrettably, though hardly surprisingly, at re-examination a
certain number of cases of re-infection have been seen at each
re-examination, particularly among those seen at the end of 2 years.
It may well be asked how re-infection occurs if everybody who is
infected is examined and treated at the same time. There are at
least four ways by which infection is re-introduced. Firstly there are
a certain number who 'dodge the column' by leaving their village

when they know that the campaign is coming, and staying away until after it has gone. Their number is believed to be very small but they are a potential source of danger. Then too the incubation period of syphilis is 10 days to 6 weeks during which time the patient shows no signs of disease but is infectious. Thus it must happen in a certain number of cases that a patient attends for examination during the incubation period, is passed as being free from infection and later develops the disease. From time to time such patients have returned and reported their condition 2 or 3 weeks after examination but others must thus be missed. Probably neither of these two factors play a large part in the occurrence of reinfected cases.

What does, it is believed, play a very large part is the return of workers from the industrial areas to their villages. The Ba-Ila do not go away to work very much as compared with some other tribes. The percentage who do go from each chief's area is, interestingly enough, in inverse proportion to the wealth in cattle of the area. Thus from the two chiefs' areas richest in cattle 15 per cent and 16 per cent respectively of the taxable males are away at work, while from a chief poor in cattle 40 per cent of the taxable males are away. These workers when they return to their villages, whether on holiday or permanently, are frequently found to be suffering from venereal disease. Workers often leave their wives behind when they go away to work and the wife very often acquires one or more lovers during her husband's absence. If the husband returns to his village on holiday with a venereal infection he will then infect his wife who will in turn pass on the infection to her lovers when her husband goes back to work again. The Native Authority made an order originally that any person returning to his village after the campaign had been there must be sent for medical examination. This is a good idea but unfortunately an impracticable one and one which it is manifestly impossible to carry out. There seems to be no certain method of preventing the re-introduction of infection in this way.

Another potent factor in the re-introduction of infections is the widespread visiting that goes on between chiefs' areas. These visits are often made to attend a beer-drink or a funeral. A funeral is always the occasion for a beer drink, though by no means the only one, and beer drinks are fruitful occasions for the acquisition of venereal disease. Thus it often happens that after treatment has been given in chief A's area, a funeral will occur in chief B's area, where treatment has not yet been given, and a large number of chief A's people will go to chief B's village to attend the funeral and subsequent beer drink and on their return some of them well may bring back a fresh venereal infection. Where a chief or an important headman dies, whole villages will come from other chiefs' areas to attend the funeral. Attendance at these funerals is obligatory on close friends and relations, and it is doubtful if any legislation could stop this custom.

Also on the debit side must be placed the fact that there is as yet little or no sign that the Ba-Ila are changing their sexual customs. There are certain sources of re-infection, as mentioned above, which cannot reasonably be controlled by any form of legislation. Probably an intensive V.D. campaign could keep the incidence of venereal disease among them to within reasonable limits, but it is obvious that once the campaign ceases the incidence will start to rise again, though not necessarily to its previous high level. The Ba-Ila have however a great love of children, perhaps their most likeable feature, and herein possibly lies their hope in the future. If the birth-rate remains at its present higher level, and if people can point to women in their own villages who were sterile until their venereal infection was treated and have since had healthy children then they may begin to realise that a venereal infection is a serious matter. From that point onwards it should not be difficult to convince them that it is impossible to eradicate venereal disease completely while they persist in their present sexual habits. It will then remain to be seen whether their love of children will prove stronger than their age-old promiscuous customs.

10

Urban Community Development in South Africa

A world-wide phenomenon in this era of rapid change is the movement of peasant and tribal peoples to large urban centers. They are attracted by the glitter of the city and the hope that they will escape the economic bondage of their rural environment. Unfortunately, the economic realities are usually harsh for such untrained people, and many of the city's advantages are kept from them even when they live in it. Added to this is the fact that they have been uprooted from the familiar social environment of the village which they understood and where they had a place. In the urban slum they find what place they can alongside strangers who have come from villages or tribes or other parts of the country, who have different customs, and who may speak different languages. The old familiarity is gone, and often there is little to serve as a replacement. In a sense, such people live without any culture, having lost the means to follow village ways without learning or being permitted by circumstance to engage fully in the ways of the city. They live in a state of "anomie," where there are no generally accepted norms of behavior. Such a social environment is a difficult one in which to promote organized change. But it must be dealt with because migration to the city, rather than diminishing, is likely to increase in the next few decades.

The problems of uprooted peasant populations are probably no more serious anywhere in the world than in Africa, mainly because Africans have to make one of the longest cultural jumps of any people to become full participants in the twentieth century. They have to move from the personal realm of tribal loyalties to the impersonal world of the state and its cities. These problems are illustrated well in the following case history, but with an added complication—racism. Since it took place in South Africa, one of the last of the avowedly racial states of the world, race feeling entered into all considerations. In fact, it will be noted that despite considerable success in the project, it was

135

finally terminated by the state because of racial policies. Moreover, the change agent could not escape her own racial affiliations. Her actions were judged as much or more on the basis of her skin color and national origin than on her actual behavior.

The change agent from outside is usually a figure of power to the underprivileged, whether in an urban slum or a rural village, and if his skin color is white, the power is believed to be even greater. Such role characteristics are part of the personality of the change agent that cannot be eliminated even if their effects can be minimized. Perhaps this case is best considered in terms of the effect of personal characteristics, which besides race included age, sex and marital status, all of which had a negative effect.

Despite these disabilities, meaningful change took place, perhaps mainly because of the change agent's dependence on educated Africans to actually carry out the program. These were her cultural translators. She worked hard to create meaningful communication with them and they carried it to the ultimate recipients. The distinction made by the author of "innovator-activator" is a useful one to remember.

Perhaps the final lesson of importance to learn from this experience was the reaction of the recipients toward traditional crafts and ways. Although urban migrants display a more marked lack of interest in traditional crafts than do village folk, even the latter in most parts of the world hold their own handicraft goods in relatively low esteem. To the outsider, such goods often have high artistic merit, but the villager and the urban slum dweller desire the factory-produced goods that come from outside. What they want is the kerosene lantern or flashlight, not the oil lamp or torch; and aluminum cookware, not locally made pottery. Thus, beadwork meant little to these Africans, who desired the things of the city, not those which they had left behind. Their consent to produce such goods was forthcoming only when they learned that there was money in their manufacture. This motivation almost always outweighs all others, even among African slum dwellers recently emerged from tribal life.

ENTOKOZWENI:
MANAGING A COMMUNITY SERVICE IN AN
URBAN AFRICAN AREA

VIOLAINE JUNOD *

What is the role of a social scientist in an African health service? What stability can be provided for Africans undergoing rapid
changes through urbanization?

In August 1946, several years after I had left college, I was
asked to serve as Director of a Family Welfare Center (subse-
quently referred to as the Center) in Alexandra Township, South
Africa. I had recently completed my B.A. Social Studies at the
Witerwatersrand University and subsequently worked at the John
Gray Community Health Center in a "poor white" area in
Johannesburg.

The new task involved supervising the completion of the Center
building, planning the services the Center would provide, and ap-
pointing staff. Establishing and running the Center were to pose
many personal and professional problems for me in the following
three years. These problems are case examples of factors in social
change in a community setting.

The project itself was a pilot venture—the first of its kind in
the country. Our original objectives were limited, but community
pressures and growing needs created conflicts of goals and realities
and forced us to lower our standards and embark on extensive program activities. In addition, we operated within a racial and cultural setting which posed innumerable problems to both myself, as
Director, and to the Center as a whole.

REASONS FOR ESTABLISHING THE PROJECT

Alexandra Township is an African location one mile square,
situated on the northeastern border of Johannesburg. Its population
is estimated variously at between 60,000 and 80,000. Its unique
feature lies in the fact that Africans may own land within its borders, in contrast to the policy laid down under the Natives (Urban)

* Reprinted from *Human Organization,* Spring, 1964, Vol. 3, No.
1, pp. 28-35, by permission of the publisher. Miss Junod was at the
time of this study a member of the Social Science Faculty at Makerere
University, Uganda.

Areas Amendment Act of 1937, which prohibits African ownership of land in urban areas. As a result Alexandra Township quickly became one of the country's most overcrowded urban African areas. African landlords, quick to grasp the opportunity of making ready and easy money, erected as many rooms to rent as their small holdings would allow. Africans, notwithstanding this exploitation, flocked into the area in uncontrolled thousands. Consequently this township suffers from all the social, economic, and psychological malaise of an overcrowded slum.

Alexandra is laid out in a uniform grid pattern. It is governed by a Health Committee of appointed and elected white and African members working with a very limited budget. It can barely meet the basic minimum requirements: the streets—if they can be so called—are not regularly maintained and, apart from two main tarred arteries, are a series of rough, pot-holed country roads, frequently intersected by large, gaping 'dongas,' safely negotiated only with a Landrover; the only electricity supply is along the two main tarred roads, leaving most domestic lighting to kerosene lamps or burning brasiers, a frequent cause of fatal burns; there is no waterborne sewerage; residents obtain their drinking and cooking water from "stand pipes" situated at most street intersections; most shanties are built of corrugated iron or wood, and houses of brick. A lot may have as many as 15-20 rooms running in two or three dismal rows, or else one 3-4 room house with a row of 6-10 rooms. Because trading by non-Africans inside the township is prohibited by law, a variety of trading stores are to be found strung along its boundaries operated mostly by Chinese and Indian traders. The only white-controlled store was opened in 1949 by the local transport company, a huge department store employing an all-African sales staff. Entertainment consists of one cinema whose standard of showing seldom reaches above third grade thrillers or cowboy films.

The township has no trees nor parks. Three squares were set aside to act as "air lungs," but were never developed: one acts as the bus terminus and at the top end of another our Center was built. The paucity of social and educational facilities is a feature of the township. There is no compulsory educational system for Africans throughout the country, and it is estimated that only between 30 to 40 percent of children of school-going age attend school. In the 1940's there were some 8-10 primary schools and one secondary school conducted by the government and mission societies. There was one nursery school run by a voluntary organization. The Alexandra Health Center and University Clinic (subsequently referred to as the Clinic) provided the only health services available to the community.

The needs of the community were great. A small pilot survey conducted in 1945-1946 by a social scientist in the area had revealed extreme poverty, overcrowded living conditions, an average family size of 5, general poor health conditions and food habits. It was impossible to tackle all the problems pointed out by this survey. At the outset we had to select a major but manageable field of operation, and so we decided to limit our objectives to health promotion services. Our decision was largely determined by the fact that the Clinic already provided a wide range of curative medical services, and a small Health Center attached to it provided a limited number of preventive medical services.

The Center worked in close cooperation with the Clinic, concentrating on the provision of social and educational services to complement the strictly medical services of the Clinic. It was further agreed that as a pilot project, the Center should concentrate on providing social and health services for family units. Of necessity this required keeping numbers down to manageable proportions and membership in the Center was restricted. The family was to be the unit of membership, not individuals, and in the initial stages these were to be drawn from only two streets on either side of the "square" on which the Center was situated. The only condition of membership was a thorough health examination of all members of the family prior to joining, followed by annual health checkups. This service was to be provided by Clinic staff.

Because of its family membership basis the Center had to gear its services to meet the needs of all age groups and even then to assign strict priorities. The following functions were chosen: a day nursery; children's group activities both outdoor and indoor; women's clubs, including sewing, cooking, and pre- and post-natal care classes; and a night school for adult illiterates. These activities were considered "in services." In addition a basic field work program was instituted involving regular home visiting by all members of the staff.

The Center was also to be used for training purposes. African students in social work were assigned to it from Johannesburg's Jan Hofmeyer School of Social Work for term and vacation work;

white and non-white (including Indian) students came from all the English speaking universities for vacation work.

At first five (later eight) African members of the staff were appointed. These included three nursery school teachers (Miss Sithole, Mrs. Mkize, and Mrs. Jabavu), three social workers (Messrs. N'Tsie, Kotsi, and Sibanda), one nutritionist cookery demonstrator (Mrs. Mvabaza), and one assistant director (Mrs. Twala).

The Center received the bulk of its financial aid from two private sources: The Witwatersrand University Student Rag Benefit Fund and the Union of Jewish Women. In addition, state subsidies were received from the Social Welfare Department for staff salaries and for the nursery school and from the Education Department for the night school. Our first annual budget showed an expenditure of roughly £1,000 which was to increase to over £3,000 by 1949.

At first the Center fell under the control of the Clinic Board of Management. As staff and services increased it became necessary to create a separate controlling and policy-making body. A new Board of Management was appointed, consisting of representatives from the Clinic, the Center (myself and later Mrs. Twala), the Clinic's Board of Management, the local community and Health Committee, and the various organisations giving financial assistance.

THE ROLE OF CENTER AND STAFF

The Center was essentially an agent of social change. It functioned in an urban community in which many pressures for change were operating. It presented problems of a complex order and its individuals were caught up in a complex web of conflicting pushes and pulls. The innovator is less able to control the situation in which he finds himself than he would be in a rural community, and less able to assess his own specific contributions.

The Center had to cope with two types of change: those which the project itself aimed at bringing about—a greater awareness of the value of healthy living (put at its simplest and most generalised level)—and those created by a variety of Westernising pressures. Apart from pursuing its own specific role of introducing changes in attitudes toward health with the necessary concomitant changes in living, the Center had a more diffuse and general role, viz: as a stabilising agent attempting to assist its members in their adjustment to the new world of urban Western living. It was both initiator and stabilizer.

The roles of the staff including myself, have to be seen against this general context. Our main task was to translate *into meaningful terms* the new values the Center was trying to introduce, and then to cope with the resistances which this created. In addition we had to help members adjust to the problems created by urban-Western living.

In order to translate into meaningful terms our objectives and goals, I used my African staff who had the great advantage of being Western-educated. Belong as they did to both worlds—the white Western world by virtue of their training, the black African world by virtue of their birth and upbringing—I came to rely considerably on their cultural insights, their judgments, and their opinions. I looked to them to be the active and direct agents of change as contrasted with my essential job as Director and member of the culture initiating the change. If I was innovator, they were the activators, the ones responsible for actually putting ideas into practice and thus starting the change.

ORGANISATIONAL PROBLEMS

Staff

Although responsible to the Board for general policy-making, I was directly responsible for the Center's program and for the allocation of responsibilities and duties among the staff members.

Mrs. Regina Twala, a Zulu, was appointed assistant director at the end of 1947. She was the first Union African woman to receive a degree in Social Studies. She was in her forties and married to a well-known African sports personality. Her only child, Mvusi, attended our nursery school. She lived in Orlando, another African location, and I picked her up from and took her back to town everyday. Our relationship was a friendly one. When difficulties arose between other staff members and myself I would frequently ask her to act as go-between. In this way many interpersonal tensions were eased without open conflict. Apart from substituting in my absence, she supervised specific activities for women and young girls.

Messrs. Kotsi, N'Tsie and later Sibanda had all obtained their diplomas at the Jan Hofmeyer School of Social Work. The only married male staff member was Mr. N'Tsie. Throughout my service I was conscious of ambivalence in their attitude toward me, especially that of Mr. Kotsi, a Zulu, who seemed rather distant and cold. He was the least adjusted, the most inwardly disturbed member of the group and appeared to be living in two worlds. The other two men seemed much less restrained, more fluid and balanced in their behaviour. All three were responsible for children's group activities, home-visiting, and alternate night school duties.

Mrs. Mvabaza, a fat, extroverted and jovial human being, had received her training at a mission school in Zululand. She was the oldest member of the staff. As a Zulu she considered herself a slight cut above the others, a factor she would jokingly make use of when wishing to assert herself. Her attitude toward me was that of a warm, affectionate mother. She was responsible for family services in the field of nutrition; and of her own accord she instituted our daily staff luncheon.

The most difficult staff group was that of the nursery school teachers. They were somewhat isolated from the rest of Center personnel by virtue of their full day's program in a single limited activity. They were constantly in each other's presence. Miss Sithole, as senior member, was appointed supervisor causing resentment by the other two. Their training, although similar, had been received at different institutions.

Staff Meetings

At least once a week the entire staff, sometimes joined by student trainees, would meet in my office to discuss group activities, problems of member families, and special projects. Staff meetings thoroughly aired and discussed the introduction of a new activity, advisability of terminating an activity, problem members and their participation in groups, student training and other problems. Staff members also presented written reports on their home visits and individual contacts with members of families. The reports were discussed in full at staff meetings and decisions were taken regarding action based on the general or specific problems which had emerged. Family records were kept in a central family files system so that at any time a full progress record was at hand including records of home visits, medical findings, and group activities on both an individual and family basis. The discussions of special projects, included "the family budget survey," the sample social survey of four streets (part of the student training program), a Center celebration day, and other items.

Each week I would meet separately with each member of the staff to deal with personal and intra-staff problems. We also held monthly Group Activities meetings at which specific Center activities would be discussed by those responsible.

Activities

The day started with the opening of the nursery school at 7 a.m. This service continued throughout the day to 5 p.m. At first we had an enrolment of a dozen children. The numbers grew so rapidly that we stopped further enrolments after a year at a total of 75. As in many other activities of the Center, the nursery continually created new demands which our own resources could not meet. The children were taken to the Clinic for a monthly checkup. Cases of ill health were dealt with immediately.

In the mornings the social workers and the nutritionist would either be busy home visiting, writing up reports, or conducting group activities. Normally the women's activities continued from ten to noon. Attendances varied because most women were engaged in part time employment, generally washing for white homes.

The afternoon from 2 to 6 p.m. were the Center's busiest hours. Children's activities attracted the greatest following, with attendances varying between 50-250. An attempt was made to introduce morning activities for non-school children. These were soon discontinued when it was found that these children were otherwise regularly employed replacing a parent or else working on their own. The afternoon groups were divided into indoor and outdoor activities, either for boys and girls separately or in combined groups. All of the Center's staff resources were occupied with the rapidly growing children's section. Increasing pressure from churches, teachers, and other community groups was put upon us to extend this section of the Center's program. Attempts were first made to draw in various welfare organisations centered in Johannesburg, but with little success. Unable to cater for additional numbers at the Center, we set up a number of "street groups" all over the township. Equipped with a ball, an old cricket bat and ideas, a student trainee would set out to organise such a group basing it wherever he felt the need.

A slight lull would follow between 6 and 7:30 p.m. when evening activities would start. Most rooms were occupied by night school classes held under the dim light of kerosene lamps. Every now and then evenings of films and games would be offered. African teachers were drawn into the night school section and at first were put under the supervision of one of the social workers. By the time I left three more schools had been established in township school buildings, and the entire program had been put under the supervision of the teaching profession.

The only other regular evening activity was a Boxing Club for adolescent boys. A local champion, staff member of the Clinic, was put in charge. This group proved the most popular of all. Within a year it had produced its own national champion. Membership grew rapidly and included non-Center family members.

The only regular week-end activity was the Saturday morning "Vegetable Club." Foodstuffs and vegetables were distributed at cost to the members of the Club. For a nominal amount, families were able to balance up their otherwise monotonous diet. Of all our failures this was the worst. Membership was very slow in coming forward and we were forced to extend the service to non-Center families in order to keep it going. The reason for this lack of support is to be found in the fact that we were introducing a new item of expenditure in family budgets.

Membership

Initially membership in the Center was limited to families from a selected area of two streets (subsequently increased to four). The pressures to adopt an open policy in regard to many services were such that we were repeatedly forced to drop our membership conditions. No single problem could better illustrate the conflict between goals and realities than this one. The social and educational needs of an urban African community are of such magnitude that any attempt to introduce a restrictive intensive scheme produces problems of its own. It creates a small privileged group within a large underprivileged community giving rise to tensions and constant criticisms. During my three years' service, our family membership never exceeded 120-130, i.e., about 700 individuals, out of a total population of 60-80,000. We were not touching the basic problems and could only consider ourselves a palliative service in a situation which ought to be altered at the national level. We reluctantly lowered our standards and introduced extensive services in an effort to adjust to the pressing realities which surrounded us. It is estimated that in this way the Center's program must have reached between 1,000 to 2,000 people.

Notwithstanding this problem, the nucleus of the Center's activities continued to be the family membership. Our families averaged six persons and had an extremely low income. None belonged to the professional class. A few were families of traders operating within the township and consequently a little better off. They represented all tribal groups, with a slight preponderance of Suthos. The heads of families for the most part were employed in unskilled work as delivery boys, manual workers, and similar jobs. Most of the women were employed part-time. A few were beer brewers, a very lucrative illicit trade but subject to great vicissitudes including frequent jailing. One or two were factory hands. Many of the nonschool children were peddlers, selling diluted milk (at the price of pure milk), vegetables procured from nearby Portuguese gardeners, and old clothes. A few were newspaper vendors. The membership represented a true cross section of any urban African community situated on the fringes of a fast-growing white-controlled, industrial metropolis.

Toward the end of my service, the staff initiated the idea of creating a Members' Committee with advisory powers. The committee was established on the basis of group representation (Night school, boys' club etc.). The idea of committee participation was new to them and at the time of my departure the committee was going through extremely difficult times.

The Race Barrier

The problem of crossing the race barrier was essentially mine. The Africans were never conscious that they too might have racial prejudices of their own to combat and overcome. Setting this aside, my very authority placed upon me the responsibility of taking the first steps. I was the only white, except for an occasional voluntary worker or student trainee, in a sea of black.

In South Africa the white person who has little racial prejudice is faced with the formidable task of breaking down the stereotype Africans have of him, a stereotype which finds much basis in fact. The racial resistances to me of staff and members were rooted in this stereotype, and in order to achieve success in my relationship with them I had to break down its various elements consciously: whites personify authority; whites' desire to help the blacks is never altruistic but is motivated by ulterior motives of self-advancement or power; whites wish to "keep the African down"; whites do not wish to help the African progress; the white man is essentially an exploiter.

It was with some surprise that I found that personally directed reactions to my race came from my own staff colleagues. Their very advancement, their acquisition of Western skills through education, their ability to earn more and therefore live better than the average African, made my position—as reflecting that of the whites generally in the South African context—all the more untenable. To them my authority was rooted not in better qualifications, but in my membership of the white race. Yet they had to concede grudgingly that as a white person I was better equipped and knew more than they did about the white-Western culture. Their ambivalence was difficult to handle. I attempted to lessen the tensions by giving each one a large measure of responsibility and authority in his or her own field of activity. If I felt some new idea should be introduced, I tried to persuade rather than impose.

The question of this close relationship between white and authority in African thinking was dramatically illustrated when the question of my successor came up. The post was advertised and I encouraged Mrs. Twala to apply. Out of a number of white and African applicants a short list of three was drawn up including Mrs. Twala. The choice was difficult on the grounds of both experience and qualifications. Mrs. Twala's two years with us weighed in her favour. On the other hand one of the other applicants, a white woman, had much higher academic qualifications and many more years of practical experience. The issue was finally settled on a discussion of the Center's liaison with the wider community: such problems as negotiations with government departments, dealing with white-controlled firms in Johannesburg, and in short administrative problems vital to the Center's efficient functioning. I personally felt that Mrs. Twala with time would be able to establish efficient channels of communication, but in the meantime the Center's development would be affected. The issue of efficient administration within the South African racial context was the very serious consideration that led the Board to appoint the white applicant. I was told to advise Mrs. Twala of the decision before she received official confirmation. Her immediate reaction was highly emotional and she burst out saying:

You have stabbed me in the back.

All of my efforts to calm her were of no avail. I told her of the grounds on which the final selection was made, emphasizing our desire to select on the basis of merit alone but being forced to recognise the problems raised by the racial context in which the Center had to work. All these efforts failed and Mrs. Twala accused both the Board and me of outright racism.

A point in this story helps illustrate some of the additional burdens which a white person has to carry in such situations. I could not delegate certain routine administrative tasks to the staff, because such delegation would simply have made for inefficiency and subjected African staff members to numerous indignities and humiliations. Going into town to purchase equipment for the Center, and dealing with a local Portuguese gardener for Vegetable Club supplies, were tasks which only I could undertake. In each case whites had to be negotiated with, and given the South African racial complex, Africans would not have received the courteous and prompt service I received.

Repeatedly, all attempts I made to break down their resentment to my whiteness were counterfoiled by my very whiteness. Because of it I lived better, could afford a car, leave the sordid environment of an African location, and bask in the privileges which my whiteness entitled me to in South African society. Had I chosen to live like them and be of them—had it been at all possible—would simply have aroused their contempt. "Going African" is counter to their very image of the white man, reflecting once more their ambivalence. It was a dilemma I simply had to learn to live with, accepting its insolubility, the resolution of which lay in forces far beyond my control.

The reactions of the members of the Center to my race were far more diffuse and generalised. They would express it in these terms:

How can you feel it. You're white, you don't have to live in a location.

Yes, you could do it because you're white, I can't, I'm black!

What's the use of your advice? I can't do it. I haven't the money. You can because you're white.

In both instances my race was used by them in their dealings with other white authority, e.g., acting as their spokesman with the local police, taking a sick child to the hospital in my car, providing legal defense and in any other situation.

The Cultural Barriers

Two distinctions must be drawn here: breaking my own personal cultural resistances; and breaking cultural resistances to the Center's program.

PERSONAL

I had expected that my lack of speaking knowledge of a Bantu language would create numerous problems. This was not so. It was a slight handicap in person-to-person contact with older members, but not a barrier. Urban African communities are mixed tribally, and their *lingua franca* is that of the white controlling group. The position would be very different in an African rural community, where experience has shown that knowledge of the local language is very important.

One of the most irritating African habits any white has to adjust to, unless prepared to live in a constant state of irritation, is the African's sense of time. The African has not yet adjusted to the white man's clock-controlled and driven routine. So much is this a feature of his way of life that in South Africa at least it is jokingly referred to as "African time," meaning about an hour late. For major events we adjusted to this problem by simply advertising our starting times an hour earlier than scheduled.

Another cultural feature which prevails mostly among uneducated Africans is one I referred to as "the art of circumlocution." It is rooted in the old customary etiquette and rule by unanimity and *not* majority. This was particularly evident in person-to-person contacts and group discussions among members. There appeared to be an inherent inability to come straight to the point. I would be called upon by an old woman for a purpose which would not be known until we had gone through all the graces required of a social visit. At first this irritated me profoundly, and I regarded it as so much waste of valuable time. I soon recognized that this art of circumlocution provided me with a wide range of information giving me valuable insights into that individual and his family and frequently throwing light on certain problems.

My youth, sex, and single status considerably weakened my authority in the eyes of older members. They had not yet come to value the acquisition of skills or expertise as giving authority. To them age and married status were still deeply rooted symbols of authority. Each of these—youth, female, single status—meant lack of experience. This attitude would be expressed in the following terms:

> *How can you possibly know, you're so young . . . or you're not married.*

A number of small cross-cultural experiences had to be adjusted to. One example will suffice: the fondling case. Early in my work I noted that each time I paid a visit to the nursery school, the children would rush up to me and unconcernedly fondle and stroke my breasts. I was a little taken aback and curious, but I made no immediate comment to the staff, waiting for the propitious occasion to arise. One day driving home from work with Mrs. Twala we came across a young couple in one of the township's streets. The girl was standing, talking to the young man who held his bicycle with the one hand and was gently fondling her breasts with the other. I made a passing comment to which Mrs. Twala exclaimed:

> *Didn't you know? If we think a person has a nice body we express this by either stroking their breasts or else patting their buttocks.*

Happily for me this custom remained restricted to the young ones who were still completely uninhibited in their dealings with whites.

THE CENTER

Cultural resistances to the Center's program emerged from two different, but related areas. Those arising out of a desire to be associated with "modernisation-Westernisation," and those arising out of the still deeply rooted traditional values and customs. Two examples will help illustrate the first type:

a) We had decided to introduce a beadwork group for the women, and because I was unable to find a member of the group who was familiar with this customary art form, I had to learn it myself in order to teach them. At first the African women resented this attempt to *push them back to their tribal ways [when our task was] to help them become modern*—a resentment freely and vigorously voiced. We felt this a worthwhile venture that should be continued. It fitted into one of our specific aims to make the Africans more "whole" by helping them appreciate the values of their own cultural art forms, giving a dignity to their own cultural elements which the white man in his haste had often trampled upon and contemptuously declared barbarous and savage. My African staff, more educated and beginning themselves to seek worth in their own cultural traditions were keen to push ahead with the project. The problem was to keep the women at it by providing an alternate goal of more direct and practical bearing to them. This was done by playing up the economic benefit to them: whites, especially, tourists, love African beadwork. There is a big market for it. Group members found they could earn money by selling their goods and thus benefit economically. The beadwork group flourished. Later the women began to express satisfaction in the art form itself for its worth in purely African culture terms.

b) A somewhat similar incident occurred with our children's dance and drama group. All attempts to introduce a traditional African Dance group met with an active resistance, once again voiced in terms of our wish to push them back. The problem was raised at a staff meeting and we agreed on a new approach. It was decided to call it a Folk Dance group and introduce members to the folk dance of different lands. We would start with the music of Sir Roger de Coverley, some Scottish folk dances, square dances, and Eastern European folk dances, as well as African dances. Here we would start with the local Afrikaans Volkspeletjies and lead on to Bantu dances. From the day we first returned to African dances, we never looked back. The group became strictly an African dance group. They were delighted to find that their dances compared most favorably with those of other nations and even admitted that being "theirs" they were far more at home doing them.

Three examples will help illustrate traditionally rooted cultural resistances:

a) Resort to witchcraft and magic in cases of illness was frequent. The cases are far too numerous to list. One even involved a member of the staff. Mrs. Mvabaza's baby daughter fell desperately ill. At the Clinic an illness was diagnosed and a prolonged treatment prescribed. Shortly afterwards the baby died. I was asked to make the necessary funeral arrangements and was present when the small child's body was placed in her coffin. I noticed numerous festering sores on the child's body and an amulet strung round her neck. I later asked Mrs. Mvabaza about it, and she admitted that she had been dissatisfied with slow progress of Clinic treatment and had gone to a local witchdoctor. He had given the child emetics, made cuts in her body and inserted various powders.

The casting of curses was another frequent occurrence. Once again the staff were involved in such a case. I had sensed a growing tension between Mrs. Mvabaza and Miss Sithole. It all came out one day in one of my weekly meetings with Mrs. Mvazaba. It appeared Miss Sithole had cast a curse on her because I had shown Mrs. Mvabaza favored treatment.

I found these cases extremely difficult to handle. In the first case there was nothing I could do. Realising that the child's death had been hastened, if not caused, by the witchdoctor's treatment, I spoke to Mrs. Mvabaza in the hope that a similar occurrence would never take place. In the second case I called the two women together and tried to get them to talk it out rationally. This proved of no avail. Miss Sithole bluntly rejected the charge. To bring matters to a head, I suggested calling in a diviner, whereupon Miss Sithole broke down, admitting her "guilt." We returned to rational discussion: had I shown favoritism? When? How? Finally by removing misunderstanding and misinterpretations of my actions we resolved the conflict.

b) The establishment of the Members' Committee did not raise a problem of traditionally rooted cultural resistance so much as simple lack of knowledge of Western skills and techniques. Few, if any, of the members were used to conducting a democratically elected committee meeting. Fewer yet knew what a committee was for, and consequently the staff had to participate more than we had anticipated. Members had to be trained in the art of democratic rule and procedures. Unknowingly we had embarked on one of our most difficult educational projects and by the time I left the Committee was making very slow and tedious headway.

c) The problem of introducing new food habits and methods of cooking was not so much caused by traditional taboos concerning food as (1) a paucity of experience concerning foods beyond maize and meat and (2) poor cooking facilities in the homes. One could argue that this was due more to poverty than cultural factors. But the resistance by the people was phrased in cultural terms:

Our ancestors lived well on meat and maize . . . they didn't have different cooking pans and pots for foods.

Once again we had embarked on a very long educational project. We started by holding cooking demonstrations at the Center, using our own equipment. But on returning home the women did not follow the advice given, for lack of suitable facilities. We resolved this technical problem by subsequently holding the demonstrations in their homes, using their equipment. In addition classes were given on food values and nutrition.

Assessment

It is impossible to assess either the success or failure of the project except in the widest possible terms. I left it only three years after its inception. It continued to function and grow for 11 more years when the Nationalist Government closed it for being conducted in a manner contrary to government policy. In the three years I was there it had grown so rapidly that in terms of numbers alone our resources were being taxed to the hilt. On the positive side we had stimulated needs vital to more healthy living. The response to all our activities illustrates this point clearly. On the negative side it might be said that the very needs we stimulated created administrative and financial problems of such magnitude that they remained largely unresolved.

An assessment of the resistances and responses to the project might prove a more useful measuring rod of success or failure.

Resistances were divided into two broad categories: racial and cultural. Each in turn was divided into personal and Center level.

Racial Resistances and Responses

I suggested that I regarded the responsibility of breaking down racial resistances as primarily my own. Nevertheless I did attempt to get staff and members to recognise some of their own prejudices. The responses can be broken down into three types:

1) Where problems were not due to factors of race but racial dimensions were unnecessarily used or superimposed, I tried to get them discussed outside of the racial dimension. The response could be of two kinds:

a. either this was accepted—i.e., the response was one which resolved the problem.

b. or else it was not, and the racial dimension persisted (e.g., Mrs. Twala's reaction to the appointment of the new Director. I was faced with an inverted racial prejudice which no reason could dissuade). In such instances the response did not resolve the problem, and the conflict persisted.

2) Where problems were racial, i.e., rooted in the realities of the South African situation, there was little I could do. The whole problem of the Center's liaison with the outside world illustrates this problem well. Staff and members generally accepted such facts and seldom begrudged me the role I was compelled to play. In such cases the response was one of accommodation.

CULTURAL RESISTANCES AND RESPONSES

The cultural resistances were of a different order and the responses depended upon a number of factors: the techniques used to break down the resistance, how deeply rooted the resistances were, and whether resistance was due to complete lack of similar cultural experience.

I would say that the techniques used to break down deeply rooted resistances (e.g., to new foods), or resistances due to lack of cultural experience (e.g., to the introduction of democratic rule and procedures) involved long term action. On the other hand techniques used to break down superficially rooted resistances (e.g., to the introduction of African folk dancing or beadwork) did not involve long term action. These were broken down in a matter of a few months.

But whether to be used over a long or short term period, the techniques always had to be indirect. No direct frontal attack on any cultural resistance could be successful. By trial and error, by pragmatic methods we had to devise ways and means of handling each resistance as it became known.

Cuultural resistances were of three kinds:

1. those rooted in traditional culture and closely associated with the traditional world of values;
2. those rooted in the traditional material culture; and
3. those rooted in the changing culture of the present.

Those easiest to break down were the resistances to material changes, such as new clothing, new artifacts, or domestic utensils.

Next in order of difficulty were those resistances rooted in the present-day changing culture. Finally deeply rooted traditional values were those most difficult to break down.

CONCLUSIONS

The agent of social change in a situation such as ours faces two kinds of problems: those arising out of the national social, political, and economic situation, and those which he creates himself by stimulating new needs and consequently new demands.

In the first instance there is little he can do but accommodate himself to living with them. In the case of the Center, for example, we could not alter the economic status of our members. We could only hope to assist them make better use of their limited financial resources. We tried improvement within a given framework.

Awakening members to a new sense of direction, or to a new conception of what healthy living involves, was an essential part of our function. But the inevitable consequence was the creating of needs we were subsequently unable to meet because of our own limited resources. It brought us once more to the level of societal problems which could only be tackled by factors and forces beyond our immediate control. Nevertheless where needs arose which our resources enabled us to meet, we would embark on a new program or activity such as the street groups.

This pressure to meet new needs led us away from our initial objective which was to run an intensive pilot project. The community had created conflicts between our goals and realities forcing us to lower our standards and embark on extensive project activities.

11

Range Management
in the Somali Republic

A constantly recurring theme in development projects that have not met their goals has been that the given problems have been treated as purely technical. It should not come as a surprise that highly trained technical specialists would regard problems of underdevelopment principally as technical, for much the same reason that orthodox economists regard these problems as principally matters of capital investment. After all, technical specialists have produced marvels of productivity in the United States and Europe. Unfortunately, it has not often been recognized that the technical expert who is working in his own culture automatically uses its values and concepts. He does so because he shares them. Such a principle as exclusive proprietary rights over land is considered a normal part of existence in the United States. It is an attitude accepted by all, and supported by the national legal structure. That this attitude is not shared by all peoples of the world is not usually a part of the Western technical expert's professional knowledge, but it should be apparent that it could have a grave effect on certain development efforts he might undertake. What is pointed out very vividly in the following case history is that the economic practices, as well as other kinds of behavior of a people, are imbedded in a sociocultural system. By acting on the assumption that the solution is merely to change specific technical or economic practices is to take a considerable chance that the solution will be rejected.

In our system of the primary variables in cross-cultural change (discussed in Chapter 1), we emphasized the importance of utilizing the local culture when introducing innovations. This technique can be also called "adaptation to local culture," which means attempting to graft new practices onto old ones. The other alternative, which is normally found to occur in efforts that are dominated by a purely technical outlook, can be referred to as the "replacement" technique. In simplest terms it is the replacement of inefficient practices by efficient ones. Unfortunately, it does not work nearly as well as the adaptation technique, principally because it threatens the sociocultural system too much. People will accept minor changes that do not seem to threaten the basis of their way of life, but major changes that challenge their whole cultural system are usually viewed with suspicion and are often rejected. We find this phenomenon in the following account, where the innovators made practically no attempt to adapt to the existing culture. Their idea was to improve conditions as they would have done in their own country. The fact that land ownership patterns, local rules governing water resources, and the attitude toward range animals were not the same as those at home was given no consideration. Despite the advantages of improved water resources, which the people clearly recognized, they did not cooperate toward the goal of the change agents.

A last note regarding efforts that are primarily technically oriented is that the necessity for efficient communication channels is rarely recognized. If the change agent does not clearly understand that transferring his idea to the recipients is more important than the idea itself, it is likely that he will neglect to establish efficient communication. Thus, as we find in the following case, the potential recipients never really learn what the technician is trying to do and he never learns what their reaction is until the effort is faltering.

The author himself has made the best suggestions of what might have been done and we will only recapitulate them: communications should have been established by using Somalis to learn the felt needs of the local people, as well as to educate them in the principles of range management and to promote this kind of change gradually.

THE PILOT PROJECT
IN RANGE MANAGEMENT NEAR AFMADU *

FRANK MAHONY

In an area near Afmadu (Somali Republic), in a 30 by 32 kilometer square, several *uars* † out of a contemplated total of eleven have already been completed for this pilot project in range management. The plan is that approximately three thousand cattle be run within this area, the exact number being adjusted from time to time by sales or purchases to maintain a technically correct balance between numbers of cattle and the amount of food and water available. It is also being planned to have the people involved in the project contribute ten per cent of the cost, which would provide enough money to pay for the cost of the eleventh uar. The proportionate amount contributed by each family unit would also determine, on a pro rata basis, the number of cattle out of the total of three thousand that each family would be able to run on the project.

On a recent visit of the Prime Minister of the Somali Republic to the area, the announcement was made that all work on the project should cease. Subsequent discussions between ICA and Somali Government officials resulted in an agreement that the project could continue. However, the people and local officials of the Bassa Giuba Region have been left with the definite impression that additional uars will be constructed in other areas (especially in a region northwest of Belis Cogani) probably in the next dry season, five or six months hence.

These developments raised the question as to the place this project has in current Somali thinking and so the USOM Director requested that I look into the matter. I spent approximately one week (March 16-22) in the area discussing the project with the project supervisor, local government officials, and the Somali people, and my findings are reported herein.

* Reprinted from *Community Development Review*, June, 1961, pp. 34-39, by permission of the publisher. Mr. Mahoney has served as District Anthropologist in the U.S. Trust Territories and was for two years Mission Anthropologist for the Agency for International Development in Somalia.

† *Uars* are natural or artificial mud holes which serve to catch and hold rain water.

Most of the Somali people in the area do not realize or understand that the work being undertaken is a project in range management. From their point of view the Somali Government is building uars for them just as it has built uars and dug wells for them in the past—to supply them with the water they so desperately need during the dry season. Since they do not realize that attempts at range management are being made (or for that matter even what range management is) they say that the uars are being built too close together and that there is not enough grass in the immediate area to take care of all the animals who will be watering there.

From their point of view also the large number of uars being constructed in a relatively restricted area will be of tremendous benefit only to the people moving about in the near vicinity of that area. This in turn evokes tribal sentiments, always latent beneath the surface, and exposes local officials to charges of favoritism. Thus the people are able to bring considerable pressure to bear, through representatives on the District Council, to have the benefits of a uar building program more widely distributed around the district.

In addition to being subjected to these pressures, local officials also had the notion that there was a limited amount of funds available for building uars in the district. Consequently they felt that it would be better to stop the building of uars in the project area so that the balance of the available funds could be used to build uars in other areas. The result was that, on the occasion of the Prime Minister's visit, the announcement was made that work on the project should cease.

As mentioned above, work on the project has been resumed but both people and officials have been left with the definite impression that additional uars will be constructed in other areas, probably during the next dry season. If these additional uars are not built, considerable frustration and disappointment will result.

The District Commissioner and other local officials have no more understanding, than do the people, of the ideas and concepts underlying proper range management. Local officials are, however, aware of the control measures we seek to enforce to bring about proper range management. They know that we would like to confine use of the area to a limited number of people possessing a limited number of animals and that we would like these people to remain within the project area and practice rotational grazing. However, they refer to these controls as "the American system," clearly implying that they may be alright for America but that they simply can't be applied in the Somali Republic.

Indeed, the District Commissioner and others, when the controls are explained to them, say simply but firmly that they won't work. Nevertheless they always agree to the idea of having some kind of control. But while we are thinking and talking about range management controls they are nodding and agreeing and thinking about the same kind of police control they exercise over every other permanent source of water. This consists of stationing policemen at the various water sources. The policemen's duties are to prohibit the use of certain supplies so they may be held in reserve, see to it that the first to come are the first to be served at the water sources in use, and generally to prevent and regulate any arguments or disputes that might arise. These are the kinds of controls local officials have in mind.

By long established tradition among the nomads, thirsty people have always been allowed to obtain water for themselves and their livestock at almost any permanent source of water. Any time any group has sought to keep a water supply for its own exclusive use, sooner or later the result has usually been open feuding and warfare. Thus, local officials have no intention of reserving use of the uars on the range management project to a particular group. In their eyes such an action would be tantamount to promoting warfare among the peoples of their jurisdiction. This they have no intention of doing.

For this reason Government officials have no intention of carrying through with our plan to have certain families or groups of people pay part of the cost of uar construction within the project area. By this method we had hoped that those directly involved would develop a proprietary interest in the project and help to maintain the area for their exclusive use. Somali Government officials have no such intention, however. If ten per cent, or any other part of the cost of the project is to be added to ICA funds, officials intend that the Somali Government, and not any special group, shall make this contribution.

In addition, local officials have no special intention of forcing or encouraging certain groups of people to remain within the project area, rotating their livestock around the different grazing areas of the project. Officials also have no special plans to encourage the culling and sale of surplus livestock.

Consequently, the end result of the pilot project may be to promote the very thing which it is trying to avoid, namely, over-grazing near permanent water supplies. For, with a relatively abundant supply of water in a limited area, and lacking official coopera-tion to control grazing, large numbers of people accompanied by their livestock will be attracted to the area during dry seasons. Thus the available grass and foliage may rapidly be exhausted. The people themselves recognize this possibility (though remaining ada-mant about range controls) when they voice one of their principal objections to the project as presently constituted saying that there is not enough grass in the project area to support all the livestock that will be watering there.

Is the situation therefore completely hopeless? Certainly in terms of the immediate success of the pilot project the situation does not seem very promising. To insist upon or demand conformance to proper range management controls at the present time would alien-ate a considerable body of Somali officials and public opinion. Pre-sumably this would not be desirable. But, simply because a quick and easy success is not assured for the entire program is no reason to abandon optimism.

The acceptance of range management controls would involve gross changes in the entire nomadic socio-economic system. It would involve changes in their concepts of land tenure and water rights, changes in their family-tribal organization, and changes in the way they manage and control their cattle. Perhaps such changes can never occur; perhaps they could occur in twenty years—but what-ever the eventual result, the effort towards change can be made.

The aspect of the project that is wholeheartedly accepted and eagerly sought after is the construction of the uars themselves. Everyone likes the uars and all would be happy to have as many of them as could be provided.

One naturally thinks of alternate methods of organizing the project as ways of dealing with existing problems. For example, the USOM could seek agreement with the Somali Government to set up a project area on its own, hiring laborers to do the necessary herding. Or the USOM might work through a group of businessmen who could incorporate a range management project as a business and who might agree to abide by our controls in exchange for our assistance. However, such alternatives would still not deal with the basic problem which consists of trying to change the thinking and socio-economic organization of the nomads to conform to accepted range management practices.

To effect such changes would require, we believe, a long term educational program. This, of course, is a large part of the reason why the pilot project was set up, to educate by means of an actual demonstration the benefits that could accrue through the use of proper range management practices.

In this effort, however, we are trapped in a vicious circle. One of the nomadic ideas that would have to be changed to develop proper range management is the notion that a family has the right to water and graze its livestock anywhere it wants, and that this is the best and most natural way of doing things. One of the things the pilot project would demonstrate is that this is not necessarily so. But, and this is important, this attitude would have to be changed even *before* the pilot project was set up to demonstrate that the change was feasible. For, in order for the project to work at all, the people of a given area would have to recognize that water and grazing rights be restricted to a certain small group of people and animals in the project area and barred to everyone else. Thus, the very thing the project would seek to demonstrate the value of is actually a precondition of the successful functioning of the project in the first place.

One way out of this dilemma, temporarily at least, would be suddenly to provide enough uars and wells at closely spaced intervals so that it would no longer be necessary for a large number of people and animals to congregate near the small number of existing, permanent water sources. (This is obviously impossible to accomplish for the whole country but it is instructive to follow the possible results of this hypothetic example.)

As it is now, the nomads move about during the rainy season(s) going to areas where there have been recent cloudbursts. In these areas pools of surface water and fresh, green grass and foliage can be found. During the drought(s) people move to the vicinity of permanent water sources. At varying intervals, depending on the type of animal, livestock are brought in to water, brought out again to graze. However, the animals cannot be grazed too far from the water. The result is that areas near water supplies are over-grazed, while areas far from permanent water are under-grazed. If more abundant supplies of permanent water could be made available at more closely spaced intervals, a better balance between the number of animals and available grazing could be achieved. In those few areas of the country where such water supplies exist we find that this is indeed the case.

However this more proper balance might only be temporary. With a better balance it would be possible for the number of livestock to increase rapidly. At the present time the nomad is loathe to sell his livestock, partly for reasons of prestige, and partly because he has the uneasy expectation that his herds may be decimated by long walks to water, prolonged drought, disease, or other factors. Although the situation might change, mental attitudes would likely remain the same. Thus, herds might increase to the point where instead of over-grazing around permanent sources of water, the entire area would be over-grazed.

Before this happened, education in proper breeding and selection and good range management practices might begin to take hold. If money became more important to the nomad and his fears of drought and disease abated he would more easily be encouraged to select and sell off his surplus animals. Thus, some measure of proper range management might be achieved.

What this means in terms of the pilot project is that it would probably be wise to build uars in the places requested, in other locations around the pilot project. Temporarily, at least (if there were no immigration from other areas) this would result in more proper use of the existing range. This would also take the pressure off the pilot project since, if people in areas nearby to the project had more abundant sources of water they would be less likely to invade the project area. Through the extension service, or by other means, educational efforts could be intensified. The best teachers in such an educational effort would be Somalis themselves, especially if they knew and had a sympathetic understanding for the nomadic way of life and at the same time had a good understanding of range management and were convinced of its value and utility. Thus it would be of great value if Somalis with a nomadic background and possessing some education or knowledge of English could be found and given the required training.

CONCLUSION

Although the concept of range management is little understood and not at all accepted by the officials or the people near the project area, all are requesting that additional uars be built in other areas of the district. If possible, it would probably be a good idea to construct these uars in the areas requested without incorporating them into a formal demonstration project. Meanwhile greater efforts might be made to educate the people in the whole field of animal husbandry including range management. One of the best ways of doing this would be to train Somalis who have a sympathetic understanding for the nomadic way of life. If such people could acquire the same attitude towards scientific range management, and at the same time be inspired to help their own people, real progress might be made.

12

Developing a
Village Co-operative in Israel

If the rural communities of the nonindustrialized world are ever to become the productive units that their equivalents in the Western world have become, the attitudes of the residents toward the outside world will have to be changed. Because they have lived in circumstances where their own efforts have produced so little and outside powers have been exploitive for so long, the people of many such communities have developed attitudes of apathy and acceptance of things as they are. They have resigned themselves to believe that change can take place only if powerful outsiders, from their own governments or foreign agencies, accomplish it. They do not know that their governments' resources are limited and that their ministries will not be able to do all the work that is needed, at least not quickly. Moreover, they do not know that the greatest resource any government has is its people. If the people are apathetic, the government is weak. Development can very logically be considered an effort to create positive attitudes among well-organized people, rather than the mere transference of technical skills.

In the following case history we find many good techniques used by the change agents to bring about this end. Probably the most significant actions they took were to be very scrupulous in establishing firm communication with the recipients and in requiring positive participation throughout. All forms of communication that we have learned about were applied. Basically, the villagers knew what was going on at all times, owing to the efforts of the innovators. One of the most significant kinds of communication that occurred was in demonstrating the advantages of new practices. This technique is an old standby in rural extension work in the United States, and it works equally well among peasants. It should be emphasized, however, that really effective demonstration takes place only where circumstances are the same as they will be where the new practice is to be adopted. In the case of agricultural innovations, this means the farmers' fields, not the agricultural station. The peasant is not sure that what happens at the agricultural station is possible on his land, but when he sees improvement in his neighbor's field, he is much more quickly convinced.

This case, also, strongly points out how quickly peasants will adopt ideas that are clearly advantageous. Practical economic benefits are very powerful incentives when they are recognized as such by the recipients. Improvements resulting from the use of machinery, fertilizer, and improved seeds, which are clearly demonstrated, will usually be adopted by farmers. They will even change traditional practices of their own accord, as they did with their planting schedule in this instance, when the benefits become obvious.

Participation by the recipients in a fully committed way is necessary if a new idea is to be integrated into the local society. Here we find that villagers were involved from the first in decision making, and were constantly given more responsibility, including the onerous task of collecting the debts of the co-operative. Though they started with the customary apathy of peasant peoples and were quite willing to go on forever with the outside agency acting in a paternalistic fashion, when the final decision had to be made as to the future of their co-operative, they knew what choice they had to make. That the change agency could step out of the picture completely was an impressive indication of the new confidence that had been built.

THE TUR'AN
AGRICULTURAL PROJECT *

A REPORT BY THE AMERICAN FRIENDS SERVICE COMMITTEE

INTRODUCTION

In late 1948, the American Friends Service Committee (AFSC) assumed responsibility for relief distribution to Arab refugees in Gaza and in Western Galilee on behalf of the United Nations. AFSC became interested in the problems of integration of Arabs

* Reprinted from *Community Development Bulletin,* Vol. VII, No. 4, September, 1956, pp. 79-85, by permission of the Community Development Clearing House, University of London, Institute of Education.

into the new State of Israel, and discussions were opened with
government officials in the fall of 1949. Permission for an agricultural project in an Arab village was granted in March, 1950, and
Tur'an village near Nazareth was suggested by the Ministry of
Agriculture.

The general purpose of the project has been to improve and
to modernise the agricultural methods and practices of the Arab
villagers, and thus to help integrate them into the economy of
Israel. The government operated a machinery unit for use on Arab
land in Western Galilee, and it was interested in AFSC bringing
in an agricultural machinery unit to this Eastern Galilee village.
There was expectation on the part of the government that a cooperative would be established among the villagers to purchase
the unit within two or three years. In the introduction of the project
to the notables of Tur'an village, the representative of the Ministry
of Agriculture emphasised that the Quaker project would be integrated with the plans of the government for the development of
agriculture in Arab villages. He also explained that all work to be
carried out by machinery would be against payment of a nominal
sum.

Tur'an village was suggested for at least two reasons. Its extensive fertile soil and level land was adapted to mechanical cultivation. The location of farm land near the main road from Nazareth
to Tiberias made it possible for the work to serve as an example
to other Arab villages.

The 1,600 Tur'an villagers own approximately 11,000 dunums
(about 2,750 acres) of arable land. There are fairly extensive olive
groves and sheep, goat, and cattle herds. The village is predomi-
nantly Moslem with a Christian minority. There is no electricity
and no piped water supply in the village. Cisterns and a spring
on a nearby hillside provide the water supply for Tur'an. At the
time the project opened there was no surfaced road into the village.

METHODS EMPLOYED IN THE AGRICULTURAL PROJECT

Farm Machinery. Farm machinery was introduced in Tur'an
by AFSC soon after the project opened. A horse-drawn mower and
rake used in the first harvest were followed by modern machinery
including tractors, ploughs, combine, manure spreader, lister planter,
drill, tool bar, etc. The AFSC purchased all the machines brought
to Tur'an with the exception of a tractor and plough purchased

by the village. The AFSC team and staff took major responsibility for the operation of the machinery until the fall of 1954. The introduction of machinery made necessary the clearing of stones from the fields by the villagers and the combining of small landholdings for cultivation.

Test Plots. Test plots were planted in 1950-51, 1951-52 and 1952-53 in co-operation with individual villagers to demonstrate the increased yield possible with improved seed, heavier and earlier seeding, and the use of manure and chemical fertiliser. The test plots during the last two of the three seasons were very satisfactory, and the villagers were impressed with the tall, thick grain and the high yields from the plots. New crops such as sugar beets, sorghum, flax, and vetch also were introduced to the village by means of the test plots.

*Co-operation with M.O.A.** There has been close co-operation with the Village Development Section of the Ministry of Agriculture from the initial stages of the project. Frequently the AFSC agriculturists served as liaison between M.O.A. and the Tur'an farmers. Through M.O.A., new and improved seeds, chemical fertiliser, and fruit and olive trees were ordered for villagers. Technical assistance and loans were provided by the Nazareth office of M.O.A. to the villagers.

Agricultural Education. Much of the agricultural education in the village has been carried on informally by the AFSC agriculturists through contacts in the fields, at the workshops and in the homes. During the first two years, agricultural classes were held for the youth on Saturdays, and as many as 40 attended regularly for a period of time. Then from January, 1953, to January, 1954, a training programme was conducted on a formal basis with nine youths from Tur'an enrolled. The programmes included a tractor driving course at Ruppin Agricultural School, field work in Tur'an, field trips to kibbutzim, experiment stations, etc., and lectures, discussions and demonstrations.

Co-operative Education. Various approaches were made to prepare the villagers for the eventual forming of a co-operative. From the beginning every effort was made to keep the village informed of the development of the project and to involve them in decisions such as the choice of machines to be brought to the village, policy

---

* M.O.A. will be used in the remainder of the report to designate the Ministry of Agriculture.

in the operation of the machinery, and rates for work. There is only a loose organisation in the village. The Moslem mukhtar is the nominal head, but he was chosen because he represents the largest clan in the village. He, the Christian mukhtar, and the other heads of family clans make up the Village Committee. Over the five years, many meetings were held with the Village Committee and with the whole village. Strong, effective leaders are lacking in this village in the opinion of the AFSC team and of representatives of M.O.A. and of the Ministry of Social Welfare who know the village well.

Home Visits. AFSC team members lived in Tur'an until April, 1955, and they did extensive home visiting throughout the five years. For example, in 1953-54, the two members of the Quaker team made 250 visits in the village to discuss the project and its future.

PERSONNEL OF THE AGRICULTURAL PROJECT

The overseas appointees of AFSC have included four agriculturists and one social worker-community organiser, each of whom served the regular two-year term of service. An American agriculturist opened the project, two agriculturists served the next two years, and an agriculturist and community organiser composed the Tur'an team from July, 1953 on. Two other professional persons served for brief periods of time. The local staff members have included a machine operator, a workshop attendant, who also served as blacksmith, and an administrative assistant who handled the office work and accounts and served as translator. These three positions were filled by villagers from Tur'an.

RESULTS OF THE AGRICULTURAL PROJECT

Agricultural Practice and Yields

1. *Acceptance of the Value of Machinery.* The Tur'an villagers accept the idea of machinery cultivation. They realise that the deep ploughing in summer eliminated the worms and the weeds which, in the past, often destroyed the crops, and that it also turned over new soil for crop growing. They have seen the results in thicker and higher growth in the fields cultivated and planted with machinery in contrast to the animal-cultivated fields.

The acceptance of machinery made necessary the clearing of stones from the fields. On the more stony land in Tur'an, as many as 20 tons of stones per dunum were removed. In one season, it is estimated that 1,500 tons of stones were cleared from the fields. Most of the flat land is now quite clear of stones.

Changes in time and methods of cultivation and seeding have accompanied the acceptance of machinery. For example, in 1950 the village for the first time planted wheat before the rains, or "afir." With their wooden ploughs used for centuries, they had to wait until the ground was softened by the rains. The villagers were cautious and afraid the first year, but the green wheat which came up with the late November rains reassured them. To seed the grain "afir" is now a generally accepted practice. The villagers were resistant to the use of the drill, which plants the seed more regularly and also applies the fertiliser with it, in contrast to the usual custom of general broadcast of seed and fertiliser. The acceptance of the grain drill came in the fall of 1953 with the villagers competing for its use on the fields before the rains. Cultivating summer crops, spraying of vegetables for insects and disease, and the use of a three-crop rotation plan of grain, vegetables, and grasses (rather than just grains and vegetables), have been accepted by some villagers.

2. *Use of Fertilisers.* In 1950, the villagers sold manure to the nearby Jewish settlements or burned it in their ovens, but they made little or no use of it on the fields. The success of the test plots gave them evidence of the value of fertiliser, and the manure spreader brought to the village early in 1952 also helped to encourage them. The report of the AFSC agriculturist in October, 1952, states: "We have been much encouraged by the interest taken in the use of manure. . . . Last year our first manure was hauled on September 17th. This year, one week before that date, we have hauled more manure than all together last year."

The Tur'an farmers had never used chemical fertiliser on their grain fields until the 1951-52 season when 4 tons were bought for this purpose and paid for by the villagers themselves. There has been a conspicuous increase in the use of chemical fertiliser from this beginning. An order was purchased in the fall of 1953 through M.O.A. by 50 villagers for 350 dunums. Then, in the fall of 1954, a sub-committee from the Village Committee purchased and brought to the village three loads of fertiliser. Seventy-two villagers ordered a total of 25,200 kilograms of phosphate and nitrogen, or approximately 25 tons.

3. *Improved Seeds and New Crops.* In co-operation with M.O.A., improved seeds have been introduced to the village. Now many of the villagers are planting improved wheat seeds, new varieties of wheat, and new varieties of barley. Various new crops have have been tried by the villagers, and vetch and sorghum have become popular with them. The test plots of sugar beets were only moderately successful, and there were problems in marketing them.

4. *Increased Yields.* Accurate data on the increased yields in Tur'an are not available. The typical villager estimates that the yields have doubled in the five years of the project. The M.O.A. representative and the villagers state that the grain crop for the spring of 1955 is a bumper one, the best yield which Tur'an ever has had.

5. *Additional Land Farmed.* Before the project opened in 1950, landowners who had no animals started early in the year to beg those with animals to rent their fields. Often they realised little or no yield, and they were forced to buy all their foodstuffs. Now they grow their own grain and vegetables, and are no longer dependent on the whims of those who have animals. The villagers who work outside Tur'an also are able to farm their land by means of the machinery. Now if a villager owns land, he can be a farmer. The machinery has released the farmer, in terms of time, to the extent that it is estimated Tur'an villagers now rent about the same number of dunums outside the village as they farm within Tur'an. In other words, the villagers are now farming with machinery the land in Tur'an, and in addition they farm with animals approximately an equal amount of rented land.

6. *Increased Income.* The increased yields and the increased acreage of land cultivated have raised the income level in Tur'an. The building going on all over the village in 1955 is one concrete evidence of greater wealth. Rooms are being added to many dwellings, and new units are being constructed.

Increased Responsibility Taken by the Village

1. *Change in Payment.* In the beginning it was agreed with the government that all machinery work would be against a nominal fee. Until the fall of 1954, the rates for work were much below those charged by government and private machinery units. The rates were increased greatly at this time in order to cover all expenses of the mechanical unit, including salaries of the local employees. The vil-

lagers have resisted any increase in rate for services, but the decisions on rates from September, 1954, on were made by the Village Committee. The Village Committee and the village were for the first time accepting the responsibility of covering the expenses of the unit.

Debts were allowed to accumulate in the early days of the project. Finally, in December, 1953, the village agreed that no work would be done for a villager who owed debts to the project. In September, 1954, a further step was taken when it was agreed that a down payment must be made at registration and that the Village Committee would accept responsibility for collection of debts.

2. *Advance Registration.* The early practice was to plough for everyone unless an individual protested. In March, 1954, this practice was changed, and each individual was responsible for registering at the project office in advance of any service desired. There was great resistance to this increased individual responsibility during the spring, but it became an accepted practice by the fall of 1954. There was also the understanding that the machinery worked by areas, and land must be registered before the machinery had passed the area.

3. *Purchase of Allis-Chalmers Tractor and Plough by the Village.* In 1952, when villagers began requesting that new machinery be added to the unit, the AFSC made clear that the village would have to purchase any additional machines. The heads of families, therefore, decided to purchase for use with the combine a new, heavier tractor and plough by doubling the rates then charged for services. The AFSC advanced the money for the purchase; the village completed payment for the tractor and plough by the fall of 1954. The ownership of this equipment is in the name of the village.

4. *Increased Participation by the Village in the Project.* The village participated at the time the project opened in the decision that a mower would be the first piece of equipment brought to Tur'an. From then on, there have been fairly consistent efforts to increase the village's co-operation with and responsibility for the project. There have been successes and set-backs, but, in general, there has been resistance and reluctance on the part of the village to accept responsibility.

In the summer of 1954, it was decided that the AFSC should not continue to operate the machinery unit without a definite agreement with the village of Tur'an. The village was informed that no further field work would be done without a signed agreement. As of September 21, 1954, an agreement for three months was signed by AFSC with the Village Committee. In this agreement, the Village Committee accepted definite responsibility for the operation of the unit, including the collection of past debts and of field income. The two AFSC team members worked closely with the Village Committee, and the Committee was encouraged to make the decisions and to take initiative. There were shortcomings and also many excellent results. The Committee raised the rates of work enough to make the potential income sufficient to cover the project expenses for the three months. Two of the three sub-committees functioned well. For example, the fertiliser sub-committee took orders, collected payment, purchased, and had delivered 25 tons of fertiliser for the villagers with a minimum amount of expediting by the Quaker team and staff. On the other hand, the Village Committee allowed the villagers to be lax in payment for field services, and debts to the amount of IL.1,680 (i.e. more than half of the potential income for the three months) were outstanding at the end of the agreement.

5. *Construction of Village Road.* One outstanding evidence of growth in village initiative and co-operation since 1950 is the completion of a paved road from the highway to the village early in 1955. There were sporadic efforts toward the road building beginning in 1950. At one time the sum of IL.1,500 was collected in the village for this project, but lack of co-operation and responsibility defeated this and other efforts. The AFSC project cannot be credited with the final success. However, there may be some relationship between the Village Committee's acceptance of responsibility for the machinery unit and their leadership of the village in the road building project during the fall and winter of 1954-55.

RELATED PROGRAMMES

Training of Youth. It is difficult to evaluate the informal educational efforts made in the early period of the project. The formal training course, which was conducted for one year, gave to the seven youths who completed it a survey of sound agricultural practices, training and skill in driving and maintaining farm machinery, and group experience in discussions and conducting of meetings. Two of the graduates are now employed in agricultural machinery units, one of them in Tur'an. A third also found employment in agriculture. It was hoped that these youths would be able to assist the village in understanding new methods and in operation of the machinery. As yet, the village has not been ready to accept their potential contribution.

Health Programme. The AFSC began a health programme in Tur'an in December, 1952, to introduce maternal and child care and to improve the general level of health in the village. A well-baby clinic was opened. Due to shortage of personnel and finances, the health programme was discontinued in June, 1953.

FINAL OUTCOME OF THE PROJECT

The agreement with the Village Committee ended December 21, 1954. No field work could be done by the machinery unit during the rainy season, and no interest was expressed by the Village Committee in another agreement or in fulfilling their responsibility for the collection of outstanding debts. After careful consideration the representatives of the American Friends Service Committee decided not to take the responsibility for operation of the machinery unit another season. It was very clear to all observers that the village recognised the benefits of the project and the value of the use of machinery. For AFSC to continue to carry the major responsibility for operating the unit after five years of educating the village to the use of the machinery presented the likelihood that the project would assume more the characteristics of a business than a Community Development programme. It seemed inappropriate for the AFSC to accept the role of business management. Moreover, it was recognised that it was desirable for the village to have a financial interest in the unit, in order for the village to have a true sense of responsibility for it and for the villagers to be more accepting of sound practice in the operation of the unit.

The American Friends Service Committee, therefore, offered the machinery unit for sale to the village on a lease-purchase plan in February, 1955. Insufficient interest was shown in this offer, perhaps because the village could not believe that the Quakers were serious in their statement that they would not operate the unit another season. The Village Development Section of the Ministry of Agriculture was approached in April to explore their interest in purchasing the unit. The M.O.A. decided in May to purchase the unit. The suggestion, made by the M.O.A. representative in Nazareth and encouraged by AFSC, that the unit be continued in Tur'an was accepted. AFSC offered as a gift the buildings and miscellaneous tools and shop equipment in Tur'an. The M.O.A. made the decision that the services of the unit would be extended to the neighbouring villages. As the arrangements for the sale of the unit to the Ministry of Agriculture were being completed in May, the Village Committee began to show belated interest, and steps were taken in the village to form a co-operative to purchase the unit. The M.O.A. generously agreed to sell the unit to a village co-operative, if it should be formed and be prepared to purchase the unit within a reasonable period of time. The bill of sale between AFSC and M.O.A. was drawn up to include these agreements.

The American Friends Service Committee is pleased with this outcome. One of the goals of this project has been to relate the Arab villagers to their new government and to assist in bringing together village interest and government resources. The withdrawal of the AFSC from Tur'an has been made at a time when this relationship of village and government has proved desirable and practicable. We are hopeful that the village, in co-operation with its government, will progress toward greater community responsibility.

13

Rural Development in East Pakistan

One of the basic characteristics of human life is that it is organized on a group basis. All men belong to social units which provide advantages that could not be obtained through individual action. However, the group also demands a price—principally, taking away some freedom of action in exchange for greater group strength. One of the most serious problems that faces the nonindustrialized nations is that the majority of their people, the peasantry, is not a vitally functioning part of the nation-group. Not only are they often uncommitted to national goals, they frequently do not even know what they are. The organizations such peasants do have are not usually functioning to fulfill the goals of the government. Therefore, a vital necessity is either to create organizations which can and will undertake roles of national responsibility or to endow those which already exist with these characteristics. Moreover, if the social group of greatest significance in this era, the nation-state, is to achieve viability, the lowest level of organizations, those in the villages, will have to be connected meaningfully to the highest government levels. Very impressive steps in this direction have been taken in East Pakistan, where a simple organizational structure has been built that incorporates the villager into a union with his government that can be meaningful for him as well as for his nation.

We see in the following account how much can be accomplished in a relatively short period of time, less than a year, when planning is done with a good understanding of village life and by putting a major share of the responsibility on local organizations and leaders. Perhaps one of the most significant lessons here is that it is unwise to underestimate the ability of the villager. He is a person who knows local conditions much better than any outsider, and he has the cunning of all persons who survive with little more than their wits as weapons. Although in the past most of the mental effort of the villager has been utilized to manipulate the powerful outsiders that he has had to deal with, these talents can be turned toward genuinely productive purposes when the villager realizes that the purposes are truly designed for his benefit. He has not avoided commitment to the national government in the past because he lacks patriotism, but rather because he had no opportunity to commit himself or because commitment appeared to promise more losses than gains. In this project we note that even the common practice of making fraudulent claims to satisfy government leaders was abandoned when it became clear that this was not expected and that the deceiving villagers would lose rather than gain by doing so.

Perhaps most development agencies operating in the non-industrialized world offer inducements to village people for participation in selected projects. Though these are partially given to subsidize the work of poverty-stricken communities, they can be more logically viewed from the viewpoint of the recipients as rewards. For co-operation, the workers will receive goods or money. If such rewards are large enough, there will practically never be any problem of co-operation by village-level people. When the rewards are partial, however, the villager will calculate at what point the losses of time and labor counterbalance the gains. When there is considerable commitment in other ways, through local leaders and organizations, the proportion of time and labor the people are willing to give will be greater than when all decisions are being made by the outside change agents. Punishment by withdrawal of such rewards is also frequently used by change agents and it, too, is effective, particularly when the villagers understand why the punishment is being applied.

Frequently there are traditional practices that are presumed to be difficult to change. One of the most important of these is dietary habits. In general, it can be said that village people are pragmatists and that their resistance to change is not as great as is sometimes supposed, at least when they see real advantages for changing. Thus, in this instance rice eaters did switch to eating wheat because they felt the losses for not doing so would be greater than the disturbance consequent on a change in diet.

Perhaps the final comment that should be made in regard to this case is the emphasis on maintenance through eduction and organizational incorporation. As the project was operated, there were persons equipped to fulfill the technical responsibilities, as well as leaders and organizations that could carry the social responsibilities.

MOBILIZING VILLAGE LEADERSHIP *

AKHTER HAMEED KHAN and A. K. M. MOHSEN

The Kotwali Thana, a 100-square-mile area, is for the Comilla Academy a testing ground for several experiments. First is the 5-year plan for the development of village cooperatives and introduction of supervised credit, use of machines, and joint marketing. Second, the Kotwali Thana Council is run as an experimental model to find an efficient pattern of rural administration. In addition there are school projects and work with youth groups and with women. Extensive records are kept and the results are analyzed to enhance our understanding of rural problems and to help us discover better methods.

PILOT PUBLIC WORKS PROGRAM

In September 1961 a Planning Commission official asked the director of the Academy whether it was possible to organize a public works program in the villages to increase employment and income, and whether the workers would accept wheat in part payment of their wages. Receiving affirmative responses, he suggested, that the American so-called Public Law 480 funds and surplus wheat might be used for rural development. The director welcomed this proposal because, during the previous two years, no other fact had become more obvious than that the two main obstacles to agricultural prosperity were the recurring risk of monsoon floods and the absence of winter irrigation. By putting the large and idle village labor force to work, these obstacles could be removed. A rural public works program would bring a double boon: supplementary income for distressed farmers and increased agricultural production.

Many kinds of development works are needed in the long neglected countryside, including roads, bridges, culverts, schools, houses, ponds. But measures of water control, including a network of drainage channels, with properly designed embankments, regulators, and sluice gates, claim an evident priority. Roads are next in

* Reprinted from the *International Development Review*, September, 1962, pp. 4-9, by permission of the publisher. Dr. Khan has served as Director of the Comilla Academy for Rural Development in East Pakistan since 1958, and Mr. Mohsen—who was previously working in the Village Agricultural and Industrial Development Program in Dacca—has been Training Officer in the Academy since 1959.

importance and, with skillful planning, can become an integral part of the water control system. Good drainage and irrigation is the first and most essential step in the direction of agricultural development, and though the fact is generally admitted, surprisingly little is done to assure that this step is taken. Enormous damage is caused every year by choked channels and unregulated excess of water or by drought. Yet thousands of sturdy farmers sit idle and unemployed during the dry months when they might be mobilized to solve the problem.

The Academy director agreed to organize a pilot rural public works project in the Kotwali Thana. There were several questions and doubts that could be resolved not by arguments but only by actual work:

• What kinds of public works can be started easily in rural areas?

• What should be the organizational and administrative agency to best execute such rural public works?

• What should be the role of Union Councils?

• Is the requisite technical competence available?

• Is it possible to mobilize village laborers extensively and in sufficiently large numbers to carry out such works?

• Will they accept wheat or other foodstuff as wages?

• How much will local farmers contribute voluntarily in labor, land, or money to the support of such works?

• What would be the economic benefits of such a works program and to whom?

Close contact with union councils and village cooperatives over the past two years has given the Academy staff certain insights that enabled them to make the following assumptions regarding these questions:

Public works to develop a comprehensive system of drainage, irrigation, and communications can usefully be carried on for several years in Kotwali Thana. Such works can be started quickly and easily.

The most effective and least expensive organizational and administrative agency would be the Thana Council and its constituent members, the Union Councils. The circle officer, as the representative of the civil admiñistration and as secretary of the Thana Council, should be the executive chief.

The role of the Union Councils is central and vital. They should prepare the schemes in consultation with the villagers themselves, organize the work (employ labor, disburse wages, keep accounts, ensure correct specifications, etcetera), and undertake subsequent maintenance.

The Union Councils and village leaders can supervise earth work competently. Farmers are very knowledgeable about local drainage. Small schemes prepared by them are generally sound. Engineering assistance, however, is needed in the case of large projects.

Large numbers of laborers can be employed from approximately November to May under the supervision of Union Councils on extensively scattered projects.

The laborers will accept wheat in part payment of their wages.

Local contributions in land, labor, and money would be forthcoming for projects designed and carried out by the local people for their own benefit.

Rural public works would relieve distress caused by unemployment; increase agricultural production; build the much needed development infrastructure of drainage, irrigation, and communication; create managerial and technical skills; strengthen local governmental bodies and enable them to raise more taxes.

PREPARATION OF A PLAN

The director of the Academy placed the rural public works proposal before the Kotwali Thana Council. Early in 1961 this council had located its headquarters at the Academy, and the Union Council members began to be trained in program planning and organizational leadership. This project provided an opportunity to test their ability. They might provide a model for the province if they could organize the work in Kotwali Thana. The following procedure was adopted:

• Union Council chairmen called meetings of the members and explained the proposal. The members, in their turn, held meetings in their wards and invited suggestions for local schemes of drainage and irrigation.

• The members' local project proposals were then discussed and consolidated by the Union Councils, and the Union Council projects were consolidated and approved by the Thana Council.

• The consolidated plan was then forwarded by the circle officer to the irrigation engineer of the provincial Water and Power Development Authority (WAPDA) for technical scrutiny. Some of the projects were modified according to his suggestions.

• After technical processing and revision, the plan was written on the appropriate Planning Commission form and after approval by the deputy commissioner and the district council was submitted to the provincial government's Agriculture Department, which had funds available for small irrigation schemes.

The proposal was first discussed in the Thana Council in October 1961. By November the consolidated thana plan was ready and all other formalities were completed. The official sanction was received before the end of December.

The Union Councils planned 21 drainage and irrigation projects, mainly re-excavations of existing channels that had been choked by encroachments and silt. It was estimated that more than 8,000,000 cubic feet of earth would be removed from 37 miles of these channels at a cost of Rs 150,000. Forty-five thousand rupees were estimated as local contribution. The rate of compensation for earth work was estimated at 18 rupees per 1000 cubic feet.

Two Union Councils planned 5 projects for prevention of flooding of a 12-square-mile low tract by reconstructing 12 miles of embankments and dykes, and by building one sluice gate and 10 water flow regulators. Here removal of 5,000,000 cubic feet of earth was estimated to cost Rs 81,000, while the masonry work was valued at Rs 97,000. Public contribution to the extent of Rs 23,000 was expected. The totals were impressive: 13,000,000 cubic feet of earth, 49 miles of channels and embankments. The works were widespread and farflung over the 100 square miles of the Kotwali Thana. Yet the government was requested to contribute only Rs 258,000, of which half was to be in cash, the other half in wheat.

THE REVISED PLAN AND ACTUAL WORK

The plan had to be revised, and it was fortunate that the revision could be done promptly. Planning at the village level is far from perfect, hence rigid adherence to initial plans may be fatal. A flexible approach, which allows corrections to be made in the light of experience, is much safer and wiser. Six projects had to be abandoned because of lack of interest or violent controversies among the local residents. The original plans for sluice gates and regulators were found to be too ambitious. Further study of the volume of water involved and other data were necessary, so much of the work was postponed till next year.

Since the work is still going on in some projects as this is written (15 June), final figures cannot yet be given. Out of the original 24 projects, 16 have been completed, 6 have been dropped, and work is in progress in 2. Out of 7 new projects, 3 have been completed and work is continuing in 4.

Nearly 8,000,000 cubic feet of earth have been removed at a total cost of about Rs 150,000, the average cost per 1000 cubic feet being Rs 14. More work remains to be done, but out of the total government grant of Rs 258,000, only Rs 146,000 have been spent so far, including the expenditures on regulators. Workers came from 195 villages, and their total labor days to date exceed 45,000. About 4,000 maunds of wheat flour were paid in wages [1 maund = 82.28 lbs. or 37.64 kgs.].

It is now possible to answer the questions raised at the beginning of this report and to examine the validity of the assumptions described. The facts and figures speak for themselves:

• A comprehensive program of public works was designed and carried out within the short period of 6 months.

• The Thana Council and the Union Councils proved themselves remarkably efficient in planning and executing the project.

• The Union Councils mobilized and supervised the laborers much better and more cheaply than private contractors would ordinarily do.

• The village leaders' own skills in earth work and their ability to follow the engineers' instructions were fully demonstrated.

• Employment was provided to a substantial number of laborers at widely scattered localities in the thana.

• The laborers accepted half their wages in wheat.

• Public contributions, except in the form of gifts of land and clerical and supervisory services, were hard to obtain. Our insistence on realizing them led some to attempt subterfuge and dishonest manipulation of accounts, as described later.

• The public works carried out by the Union Councils with the help of local leaders aroused much enthusiasm. Foundations were laid for a good drainage system. To a certain extent flood risk in the area was reduced. Managerial skill was created and the position of the Union Councils was greatly strengthened.

ORGANIZATION AND ADMINISTRATION

How was the plan implemented? How was it administered? What were the guiding principles? How were the local leaders trained? What sorts of difficulties were encountered and how were they overcome? All these topics are thoroughly treated in the full monograph report, of which this article is a summary. Here only some salient features are presented. The administrative setup was as follows:

The circle officer, who was also the secretary of the Thana Council, was both the drawing and disbursing officer and the chief supervisor.

Each Union Council established a committee for every individual local project. If a project extended over a rather wide area, it was subdivided into convenient sections, and each section was entrusted to its own committee. The Union Council member representing the ward in which the project was located was appointed chairman of the committee, and he chose influential local leaders to help him employ and supervise the laborers.

For technical advice the circle officer and the project committees depended on the subdivisional irrigation engineer of the WAPDA, and the American Peace Corps voluntary engineer posted at the Academy. Private surveyors were engaged for a few days as required.

The Kotwali Thana Council was fortunate to have some staff available to assist in the project—a supervisor and 12 workers. They had been engaged in training the Union Council members in program planning, budgeting, and coordination. First they assisted the members in planning the projects, then they checked earth measurements and payment of wages.

As the funds were sanctioned by the Agriculture Department, the thana agriculture officer and some of the union assistants were also involved in supervision and checking.

The training officer of the Academy, who is an experienced member of the East Pakistan Civil Service and a Village-Aid veteran, was the guiding spirit of the pilot project throughout—the planner, advisor, trainer, and recorder. He is the author of the full monograph report on the project and is also writing a rural public works manual. Later he will be responsible for training the other circle officers, if the government decides to have them trained at the Academy, for conducting similar works in other thanas. Help and advice were given by the director of the Academy as circumstances required.

The financial and supervisory procedures were streamlined for speedy execution.

In the first place, it was decided not to engage any contractors for doing simple earth work. Tenders were, however, invited for masonry work on gates and regulators. But the margin of profit permitted was so unattractive to the contractors that no tenders were submitted, and ultimately even the masonry work, like the earth work, was done under the direct supervision of the project committees and the Peace Corps engineer. Successful elimination of the exorbitant middleman—the ubiquitous contractor—has resulted in both very speedy execution of the projects and remarkably frugal costs.

(Every project committee was allowed to take an initial advance of money and wheat estimated to be sufficient to defray the wages required for one week's work.) A bond was signed jointly by the chairman of the project committee and the chairman of the Union Council holding themselves responsible for proper use of the funds. After being given the initial advance, the project committee was reimbursed only when the receipted muster rolls were produced and after the amount of work performed had been certified by the supervisors.

Funds were withdrawn from the treasury by the circle officer as required and disbursed to the project committees. There was no hitch or delay.

ENGINEERING ADVICE AND SUPERVISION

Doubts are most frequently expressed about the technical soundness of earth work not directed by engineers and contractors. Obviously such doubts are misplaced in the case of simple operations, such as removal of silt from old water channels or the construction of village roads. But sound engineering advice is essential before digging new channels or obstructing or diverting the flow of existing channels. Above all, a master plan for drainage, irrigation, and communications for the whole thana should be designed only after a thorough survey by qualified engineers. Unfortunately there is no precedent for such localized but comprehensive planning. In fact, the engineers are so preoccupied with either routine work or with big individual projects that none of them has cared to focus his attention on the fundamental problems of a single thana. But clearly enough the union plan and the thana plan are the bases of development. The Kotwali project is the beginning of a comprehensive plan for this thana. Both the Peace Corps engineer and the WAPDA engineer will observe the next monsoon flood and then design roads, channels, embankments, and regulators accordingly. Further surveys and further earth work may well be necessary during the next 3 or 4 years, as the problem is neither simple nor small, and it would be childish to expect a quick solution.

The first year's plan, as already stated, was scrutinized and revised by the two engineers. Actual work was also supervised, largely by the Peace Corps engineer. He also trained the Thana Council workers and the project committee members. He made the blueprints for the water flow regulators, and when the contractors refused to submit tenders, he engaged skilled masons, called them to the Academy, and built a model of the regulators for their instruction. He cautioned against placing the sluice gates and too many regulators this year without the benefit of full data, and consequently the plan was revised. His skillful and accurate measurement of earth work soon put an end to all attempts at cheating.

TRAINING AND DIFFICULTIES

The central idea of the pilot project was faith in the ability of Union Council members to undertake responsibilities that had never before been given to them: to carry out cheaply and quickly a public works program that cannot be carried out by engineers and contractors except at great cost and with inordinate delays.

Much depended on the training imparted to the members. First a change of attitude was required. The traditional image of the councillor was that of an advocate, a spokesman or a petitioner. The new role was that of an organizer, a planner and supervisor. Instead of writing petitions or making speeches, the member was expected to mobilize local labor and actively direct the solution of a problem. Secondly, the skills for performing the new tasks had to be taught and taught quickly. Several training camps were therefore held. All members of one council were called to the Academy at a time and the principles of program planning and of coordination and group work were explained. When the project committees were formed, their chairmen and secretaries were trained in measurement of earth work, in keeping accounts and muster rolls, and in the use of wheat.

That so much work was done with such speed and so few breakdowns proves without doubt that a vast reservoir of true leadership exists in the villages waiting only to be tapped. And the quick response also proves the importance of persistent training. A manual is therefore now being written at the Academy that will explain the methods of organizing public works and the principles of training local leaders as executive agents.

Though much work was done in the relatively short period of 4 months, some difficulties were encountered, which are here described very briefly; details will be found in the full report. Similar difficulties, it is feared, will be met in other places if such projects are undertaken.

As this was the first lesson in assumption of responsibility by local leaders, a great deal of imperfection need not cause much surprise. It was found that some of the schemes were drawn up carelessly and without consulting the villagers. Some members depended mainly on guesswork. Others could not resolve local conflicts; they were not persuasive or influential enough. A few had vested interests in certain encroachments and secretly sabotaged a project or two. Others were slow to learn the importance of punctuality and accuracy in the keeping of accounts. But on the whole, initial lack of skill or interest was soon remedied, and the majority of project chairmen and secretaries became good workers. Many of them displayed extraordinary ability. There is no substitute for learning by doing. These projects have created a numerous body of managers in the nooks and corners of Comilla Thana who are now ready to undertake bigger tasks.

The worst obstacle at the initial stage was the tradition of corruptness. Government officers are assumed by the public to be dishonest; hence public work conducted by them is considered a fair opportunity for graft. Well informed village leaders are willing to participate in dishonest dealings and are not much troubled by pangs of conscience in defrauding the government or the public. Test relief operations, V-AID community works, and small irrigation schemes have not been completely free from such taint. And often the Union Councils' earth work has been inflated to the disadvantage of the taxpayer.

The Kotwali Thana public works were at first considered by the villagers to be similar in kind to what has gone before and goes on everywhere. Strict checking of measurements, verifications of payments to laborers, and inspection visits by the overseers all came as a surprise to the village people. Even more surprising to them were the suspension of work at the least sign of fraud and the firm announcement that work would be done honestly or not at all. Meetings of Academy personnel with laborers in the villages and on the work sites had a most wholesome influence, as did also a lot of plain speaking to the assembled chairmen of Union Councils and the project committees. Though various fraudulent practices as well as the counter steps are described in detail in the full report, it may not be too optimistic to state that the crisis caused by a corrupt tradition was overcome by strenuous efforts to impose rigorous standards of honesty, and that after the first difficult month the work proceeded with acceptable integrity. Whether similar strenuous efforts would invariably be made in other areas it is impossible now to say. But strenuous efforts would undoubtedly be needed to establish a reasonable standard of integrity in the execution of such projects.

PUBLIC CONTRIBUTION

One main source of fraud was the so-called public contribution. The evaluation reports of the Indian Community Development Program have pointed out that in many cases the "local share" is purely fictitious. The estimates of costs are inflated, thus allowing the work to be completed by means of government funds alone, while the manipulated accounts give fraudulent credit to the locality's spirit of sacrifice and participation. There are good reasons to believe that similar fictitious contributions are not uncommon in Pakistan. In the very first fortnight of this project it was discovered that the old trick was well known to the Union Councils of Kotwali Thana. Misleading attempts were made to show public contributions in either of two ways. (a) Cost estimates in the plan contained a labor rate of Rs 18 per 1000 cubic feet of earth moved. Project committees were actually paying only 9 or 10 rupees to the laborers but obtaining a receipt for 18 rupees, this fulfilling the condition of a 50 per cent public contribution. (b) Sometimes the earth work measurements were inflated—for example, 20,000 cubic feet in place of the 10,000 of actual digging—to make up the public contribution.

The chairmen seemed surprised when both these practices were denounced as cheating and fraud. "How else," they asked innocently, "has the public contribution ever been raised?" They had done it so many times before. But they were firmly advised not to do it now. And the fiction of a public contribution was discontinued. Actually, however, nothing was lost because, even though the laborers were paid at the rate of 10 or 12 rupees, the actual cost was much less than the estimated cost.

There was, nevertheless, a genuine contribution in three ways. The laborers accepted very low rates of pay—almost half of what is quoted by the contractors for departmental works. All organizational, supervisory, and clerical work was done by the project committees without remuneration, thus bringing the establishment charge down to almost nothing. All land required for digging, or for new channels or roads or embankments, was donated without any compensation.

Further genuine contributions may be expected after the benefits of the projects have been demonstrated. It is hoped that the Union Councils would in future be able to raise taxes to maintain the drainage, irrigation, and communications works in good condition, and that the farmers would not grudge the expense when they realize that it is incurred for the sake of their own security and prosperity.

PAYMENT IN WHEAT

Comilla farmers are rice-eaters, hence their resistance against part payment in wheat as an innovation was expected. A lower price for wheat, which was to be the chief incentive, was unfortunately not fixed till the middle of April. Thus for 3 months the project committees had to persuade the laborers to eat wheat flour that cost them 20 rupees while they could easily have bought their favorite rice at 22 rupees—not a very attractive margin. Naturally there was much grumbling, yet the project committees had sufficient influence to obtain labor at their terms—half wheat, half money. When the price of wheat was reduced to 12 rupees it became readily acceptable.

There were some minor problems—about the transport and distribution of wheat, shortages due to bulk purchase, and retail supply —but these were easily solved by the ability and good sense of the project committees. In the course of 4 months, 3,000 maunds of wheat worth Rs 60,000 was paid to hundreds of laborers as wages.

LONG-TERM PLAN AND RECOMMENDATIONS

The development of a well designed system of drainage, irrigation, and communication in a 100-square-mile area calls for long-term planning. This can be demonstrated in Kotwali Thana, and the Union Councils have been advised to prepare a 3-year plan in the light of their recent experience. At the end of each year the plan should be revised and extended for another year, till in 7 or 8 years the entire system would be fully developed. By that time there should be sufficient skill and increased wealth to maintain this portion of the infrastructure of an agricultural economy.

There are 301 miles of village roads in the thana. These roads are generally in bad shape. There are 28 scattered markets. Now the Union Councils are planning to build good roads linking the villages with the markets, the provincial highways, the town, and the three railway stations falling within the thana. These roads will not only improve communication and marketing facilities but will also serve as dykes for the low-lying lands. Bridges and culverts will be constructed, with flood gates to control the water. The 3-year plans will include re-excavation of the remaining channels, building of old and new link roads, sluice gates and regulators, bridges and culverts, excavation of large ponds for irrigation, and afforestation and erosion control.

These works will provide employment to thousands of distressed farmers and also improve agricultural production to a considerable degree.

The pilot project has resolved many questions for us and clarified the pattern of planning. Though much remains to be learned by the painful process of trial and error, for the present the following recommendations are made with considerable confidence:

A rural public works program of far-reaching significance, both economic and political, is feasible, but it should be suitably phased. Its successful effectuation demands a high standard of integrity and competence on the part of executive officers and intensive training of the village leaders. Sound engineering advice and supervision are also essential. It would be advisable, at the outset, to start the program only in the 50 thanas adjacent to district and subdivisional headquarters. Experienced officers could subsequently be moved to outlying areas and all 400 thanas of East Pakistan may be covered in a period of 8 years.

The executive agencies should be the Thana Council and the Union Council, and chief authority should be vested in the thana circle officer. A supervisor, an accountant, and an overseer should be provided to the selected Thana Councils as extra staff.

Funds should also be given for training and contingencies. Fifteen thousand rupees at most should be enough to pay the salaries of the extra staff, and to cover training and contingent expenditures. Without the extra staff it would be impossible to train or supervise the council members, and without intensive training and supervision, especially in the first year, the program would end in a fiasco. Therefore Rs 15,000 should be budgeted as the establishment cost of the public works.

If the government seriously desires the success of rural public works (which can make it immediately and immensely popular) it will have to choose the first group of officers very carefully. They must possess integrity, energy, and a capacity not only to organize but also to teach and train Union Council members and other village leaders. The selected officers should be sent for a month to the Academy to study the work in Comilla Thana and acquaint themselves with its theory and practice. They should come in small groups so that individual attention may be given to each of them. If begun promptly, such training can be completed before next winter. Similar training can also be imparted to the supervisors, accountants, and overseers.

A manual and other materials, which would help the officer in his training of the Union Council members, would be supplied to him at the Academy.

After these officers are trained and placed in charge of their areas they should assist the Union Councils and the Thana Council in preparing good plans. There must be constant consultations and meetings with the villagers, and the councils should be authorized to revise or amend the plans. Impersonal planning by letters and official directives would lead nowhere or give birth to bogus projects.

The plan for each thana should also be phased, the volume of operations gradually increasing with the growth of local managing ability. An investment of one lakh in the first year and two lakhs each in the second, third, and fourth years seems to be a reasonable estimate [1 lakh = 100,000 rupees].

Sound engineering advice must be obtained. By placing the first projects near the district and subdivisional headquarters the services of WAPDA engineers can be made available most conveniently.

In order to ensure the success of the program the officers should not only be selected with care; they should also have an incentive to make it succeed.

14

Community Development
in India

There is probably no large culture area in the world in which Western-derived innovations are as difficult to introduce as in India. Besides the usual resistances to change that occur in rural areas world-wide, India presents several additional difficulties. Though traditional social structure is important in all cultures, nowhere is it as complex as in India. The system of caste affects individuals in a multitude of ways, and the egalitarian ideas that have emerged in the Western world rarely fit easily with Indian customs. Also, the necessity for ritual purity is deeply rooted in the Indian personality, so much so that many everyday actions are controlled by the requirements for keeping pure. The sacred and profane cannot be logically separated in the Indian village. On top of these complexities, the dense population and low level of subsistence promote very strong competition among villagers and reduce the opportunities for co-operative effort very markedly. It might be said that anyone who can successfully introduce Western innovations based on communal effort into Indian villages can do so anywhere in the world.

Thus, the following case history is particularly valuable, presenting a high quality of analysis and providing detailed descriptions of the outcome of various kinds of innovation attempts in the same Indian village area. It is thus possible to compare the reaction to different Western ideas, when the innovation techniques and the recipients were the same.

The first lesson we learn is that innovations which depend on an understanding of Western health concepts are very difficult to transfer, a fact which we have noted before. It might be well, though, to mention here that the specific kind of health change attempted unsuccessfully in this village area—latrines—is one that Westerners have tried to introduce all over the world, usually unsuccessfully. Of all possible changes in public health practices, the advantages of privies are probably the most difficult to demonstrate, while at the same time the adopters need to invest considerable time and effort in the construction and

191

maintenance of these devices. These are difficulties encountered in villages all over the world, and when the problems of ritual cleanliness are added, as in India, the chances for early adoption are slight indeed. It is significant that sanitary wells frequently will be adopted when latrines are rejected. The reason is not far to seek. The sanitary advantages of wells rarely convince village people to adopt them, but the convenience of a new water source provides a kind of convenience not found with privies. It is significant that when this kind of convenience motivation is operating, local people will even go against their traditional beliefs to a certain extent. In this case, they were willing to partially ignore caste restrictions in order to get the new wells, even though when they had their choice, they again raised the old social walls.

Ritual purity and caste lines also influenced the adoption of new kinds of food production practices. Probably nowhere in the peasant world are food restrictions as marked as in India, although they operate to a certain extent elsewhere. Therefore, to attempt to introduce new food production practices without learning the attitudes of the local people regarding different types of food is a foolhardy practice. To attempt to get Muslim villagers to raise pigs or orthodox Hindu villagers to raise chickens would be somewhat similar to trying to get American farmers to raise dogs for food purposes. It must be re-emphasized that all peoples have a traditional culture, including industrialized Westerners, and new ideas that ignore the existing prejudices have relatively little chance of being accepted unless the rewards are enormous. In this area, vegetable production faced no such bias, though it might in a society of animal herders. An additional positive influence in this case was positive timing. The new vegetable production was introduced just at a time when conditions for producing vegetables had improved.

Co-operatives have worked well in the Western world, but they face certain special difficulties elsewhere. In particular, people of the nonindustrialized rural areas often have developed very competitive tendencies toward their neighbors and have little inclination to get involved in mutual endeavors. There are groups that are co-operative, but these may be composed of individuals who are not members solely because of their occupation. For instance, Indian farmers belong to a multitude of castes which do not usually work together on an equal basis. In this case history the individual castes worked together, though the multicaste co-operative found little basis for group harmony.

As in a previous chapter, a final note of importance derived from this case history is that participation in decision-making activity is vital if people are to continue with any new organization. It is almost always easier for the change agent to take on the most difficult responsibilities, but when he does, he jeopardizes the possibilities of independent continuance by the adopters. The most fortunate accident that took place with the co-operative that survived was that the recipients made the most critical decision independently.

SOCIOCULTURAL PARAMETERS IN DIRECTED CHANGE *

THOMAS M. FRASER, JR.

The charge has been made that the methodological tools and theoretical models available to anthropologists are insufficiently precise to enable accurate prediction in the field of directed social and cultural change. It has further been charged that in their *ex post facto* analyses of the dynamics involved in such situations, anthropologists as well as other social scientists tend to give far more attention to attempted innovations that "didn't work" than to those areas where change has been successful. While the second charge is belied by many studies such as those included in the volumes edited by Spicer and Paul and the special issue of *Applied Anthropology*, anthropologists have, for the most part, been hesitant to extend their generalizations, based on the analysis of change, to the task of specifying, more or less concretely, the conditions favoring or

* Reprinted from *Human Organization,* Spring, 1963, pp. 95-104, by permission of the publisher. Dr. Fraser, who has had considerable field experience among village people in Thailand and India, is Assistant Professor of Anthropology at the University of Massachusetts.

inhibiting social and cultural change. Thus, in spite of a growing theoretical corpus there appears to be reluctance to put it to the practical test of prediction or planning.

While the conclusions presented in the present paper have also been reached in retrospective analysis, the attempt is made to present them in such a way that they may be tested as predictive tools. Both the data and their analysis are based on a larger study by the author of a program of directed change conducted by the American Friends Service Committee in the Sambalpur district of Orissa, India. The material for analysis will be presented below as a series of paired cases, where one change-directed program in each pair was a success and the other a failure. Data not pertinent to the present analysis will not be included in the cases. An attempt will then be made to "factor out" those aspects of the innovative situation which on the one hand fostered or permitted the desired change, and on the other inhibited it. Further general consideration will be given to the possibilities of developing a predictive methodology on the basis of this analysis.

THE SETTING

The programs of directed change to be discussed below were all undertaken at Barpali Village Service, a small community development project operated by the American Friends Service Committee in the plains area of District Sambalpur, Orissa. Barpali *thana,* or police district, consists of seventy-seven villages with a population of somewhat more than sixty thousand. The main village of the *thana,* Barpali (population about six thousand), lies just north of the center of the *thana* at the junction of two highways. One of these is the paved road connecting Sambalpur, some forty miles to the north, and Bolangir, headquarters of the adjacent district. Frequent bus service along this road provides easy communication between Barpali and the administrative and commercial facilities of Sambalpur. While of less significance in regard to modern transportation, the east-west road passing through Barpali is also of importance to the community. Not only does this road link together a number of weekly markets within the *thana* and beyond, but it also forms part of the ancient highway and pilgrimage route joining the religious centers of Banaras on the River Ganges with Puri on the coast of Orissa. During the dry season thousands of pilgrims pass over this route through Barpali. Thus there is not only easy communication with the relatively urban center of Sambalpur and beyond that with Calcutta, but also contact with two of the traditional centers of Hinduism and with the religious devotees journeying to and from them.

Originally, and in large part still today, the area has been devoted to a single, monsoon-irrigated crop of rice. In addition to the single rice crop, small quantities of winter vegetables have been traditionally grown by the Mali caste of cultivators, while other cultivators have grown a few peanuts and pulses on the dry uplands as well as a very limited quantity of irrigated sugar cane for sale. In 1957, canal irrigation from the Hirakud Dam on the Mahanandi River first reached Barpali *thana,* allowing a second and even a third crop of rice for those cultivators desiring it, and facilitating the production of supplemental or cash crops. In addition to agriculture and the usual complement of occupations in an Indian rural area, a significant minority of the population has long been engaged in the production of cotton and *tussah* cloth. The cotton weavers, in particular, are renowned throughout a large area for their colorful saris employing a variety of intricate woven and *ikat* designs.

Barpali *thana* had been chosen for the establishment of Barpali Village Service in 1952 because of its agricultural and economic backwardness, and because of the potential for growth which would be provided by the introduction of irrigation facilities and eventually electric power from the Hirakud Dam. Although the staffing pattern of the project has varied over its ten years because of the difficulties of obtaining suitable personnel, it has aimed at maintaining one Indian and one Western technician in the fields of agriculture, public health and sanitation, village industries and cooperatives, and education, as well as an Indian rural life analyst and a Western director. In addition to the technical staff, the project has trained and assigned to villages a number of multipurpose village level workers recruited from within the state of Orissa. This pattern is essentially the same as that which had been in use at Allahabad Agricultural Institute and at the Etawah project and which was subsequently adopted by the Community Projects scheme of the government of India. The aim of the Barpali project has been to improve the economic standards and living conditions of the area by enlisting the efforts of the members of the community and, wherever possible, by letting the direction of the program be guided by community needs, either explicitly recognized or developed by antecedent work of the project.

Although most of the programs undertaken by Barpali Village Service have resulted in neither complete success or acceptance nor in complete failure or rejection, the programs discussed in the following analysis all tend to approach one of the extremes of success or failure. These extreme cases have been chosen to facilitate the isolation of sociocultural factors influencing their acceptance or rejection. Once such factors are identified, situations in which a larger number are involved or in which a balance between opposing factors is approached should yield more readily to both retrospective and predictive analysis.

PAIR 1—PROTECTED WATER SUPPLIES AND SANITARY LATRINES

Early in its efforts to improve health conditions in Barpali *thana,* Barpali Village Service undertook to tackle the two greatest problems in the control of disease germ transmission: unprotected drinking water supplies and unsanitary disposal of human excreta. The general practice in the villages was to collect drinking water from large open catchment tanks or ponds which served for bathing, laundering, and stock watering as well. Villagers defecated in the open fields just outside the villages, or, frequently, along the banks of the tanks before bathing.

The program to provide protected water in the villages had two phases. During the early years of the project no reliable, economical pump appeared to be available, so project technicians attempted to organize entire village populations to decide upon and contribute labor and materials for the construction of open wells for common village use. Money was made available by the state government for material not obtainable locally (mainly cement) and for specialized labor. During the first year of the program four wells were started, one of which was completed during the dry digging season. In the next and final season of the open well program fifteen wells were started, seven of which were completed that year and five more during subsequent seasons. By the third year of working on the problem of protected water, Barpali Village Service technicians cooperating with pump manufacturers in Calcutta developed a mechanically simple hand pump which could be installed over a well having half the diameter of the previous open wells at a substantial saving in *total* cost.* By the close of the 1961 well-digging season, 154 pump wells had been installed in the villages of Barpali *thana,* and nearly one hundred had been installed outside of the *thana* by project personnel. The figure of 154 represents an average of exactly two wells for each of the seventy-seven villages of the *thana,* and, while not *every* village had in fact installed such a well, the goal of a protected water supply was largely realized.

A program to introduce sanitary water-seal latrines to the villagers was launched at the same time as the first phase of the well program. A molded concrete latrine was developed which could be manufactured at the project and sold to the villagers at an extremely low cost. While the purchase and use of a latrine was essentially an individual decision in contrast to the group or total village decision involved in the construction of a well, Barpali Village Service attempted to create group opinion and pressure in favor of latrines by holding village meetings, demonstrations, and eventually a two-week intensive village-wide campaign in one village in which the active participation of most of the village leaders was obtained. However, by the end of 1960, only about three hundred latrines had been sold within the *thana,* and of these only 120 were in even irregular use. On the other hand, there was a relatively great demand for "Barpali latrines" from towns, particularly Sambalpur, and from government installations.

Neither of these programs was based on an explicit felt need of the villagers, but they were undertaken by the project in view of the enormity of the problem of water-borne diseases in the area. In the interpretation of Barpali Village Service, both programs were directed at the same set of village problems; the need for the acceptance of one was approximately equal to the need for the acceptance of the other. Why did one program achieve a large measure of success, while the other was almost a total failure in the villages of Barpali *thana?*

The factors operating to cause the differential reaction to these

* These wells comprise a covered reservoir made of three precast concrete rings, and a concrete slab, set at the bottom of the pit (approximately thirty feet). From the reservoir a chimney of six inch diameter precast concrete pipe, through which the water pipe is inserted, leads to the surface and is sealed at the pump platform. Earth is then filled in over the reservoir and around the chimney. This arrangement not only reduces digging labor, but obviates the necessity of a costly masonry lining for the entire pit.

two programs are perhaps the most direct and striking of any encountered in the work of Barpali Village Service. As will be seen
from the following discussion and from Table 1, the great majority
of cultural linkages in the areas affected by wells and latrines would
point to the failure of *both* programs. However, one aspect of the
situation was of sufficient importance to outweigh the inhibiting
factors in the case of the well program. During the hot dry months,
water was in very scarce supply in many of the villages of Barpali
thana. The women, who carried all water for household needs from
the village tank, often half a mile to a mile from their homes, frequently found the tanks dried up altogether, requiring an even
longer trek to an adequate source of water such as a dry river bed
where water could be collected in holes dug in the sand. The significance of this factor in causing acceptance of the well program
can be judged by comparing these villages with the few where pre-
existing water supplies had been entirely adequate. In these latter
villages little or no progress could be made in introducing improved
(from the sanitary point of view) wells. In addition to the acute
need for an adequate supply of water was the convenience of having it located right in the village, and, of course, the fact that much
of the cost of these wells was borne by the government.

In the case of the latrine program there was no such significant
objective or situational reason or set of reasons fostering acceptance.
On the contrary, all factors of this type, except the low cost of the
latrines, militated against acceptance. While wells were a convenience to life in these villages, latrines were a decided inconvenience.
In order to flush these latrines properly at least one quart of water
was required each time one was used, and in a large family, the
mere provision of flushing and cleaning water would add a considerable water-carrying burden to the woman or women of the household who had little interest in the latrines or their use anyway. A
further significant fact was that in the villages of Barpali *thana*
almost all of the men are cultivators whose work is in their fields.
These men could hardly be expected to leave their agricultural work
and return home, often a considerable distance, simply to make
use of a latrine. It was pointed out earlier that there has been a
relatively good demand for latrines in large towns such as Sambalpur; similarly the acceptance of latrines in Barpali *thana* has been
greatest in those villages which have the largest population (and
thus greater average distances from the homes to the open fields

used for nocturnal defecation) and where there was a greater proportion of individuals carrying on sedentary occupations such as
priests, teachers, weavers, and smiths. While problems of initial cost
were not great either in the case of wells, which were largely sub-
sidized, or in the case of latrines which could be bought for as little
as five rupees (about $1.05), subsequent maintenance and care
were resented by the villagers. Proper installation of a latrine required the digging of a pit and the erection of some sort of fencing
for privacy. In roughly half the cases of newly installed latrines, the
cause for discontinuation of use has been that the fencing fell into
disrepair and was not mended or replaced. Pump and well maintenance has been under the supervision of the techicians of Barpali
Village Service, and they have attempted to build up a cadre of
mechanically trained men in the villages and also to organize village
and *Gram Panchayat* well-maintenance funds. However, without
this supervision by the project, lack of proper maintenance and
repairs might well prove an important negative factor in the continued acceptance of village wells. A final situational factor has to
do with the timing of the installation of wells and latrines. While
the dry season which is the most suitable time both from the point
of view of other activities and in order to avoid cave-ins, is the
time of most acute water shortage (i.e. mutual reinforcement), this
season presents fewest problems which might be eased by the use of
latrines. It is during the rainy season that people complain of the
unpleasantness of going to the open fields at night over the muddy
streets, and when the streets themselves tend to become muddy
sewers. And it is then that the catchment tanks are filling up and all
the new and accumulated debris is being washed down the banks.

While situational or environmental factors are generally not
sufficient to ensure the acceptance of an innovation when it conflicts with aspects of the value system or with institutional patterns,
this has been the case in the Barpali well program. The strongest
factor which had to be overcome initially by the well program was
involved in the policy of the project that wells (open type) should
be a joint community effort and for the benefit of the whole community. This, of course, meant not only that members of the upper
castes were expected to contribute manual labor along with *harijans*
(untouchables), but that the completed wells should be used by both
the ritually pure and the ritually impure or untouchable. It is an
indication of the acuteness of the water problem that at least half

of the fifteen open wells completed were used by both of these divisions of the community. However, after the pump wells were made available at one-third to one-half the price of an open well, and when Barpali Village Service dropped its demand that wells be used in common by the whole village, the practice of caste separation in the use of water sources was quickly reestablished, and now the general pattern is for a village to have one pump well in the *harijan* section and one or more in the upper-caste sections.

Concepts of ritual purity were considerably more important in inhibiting the latrine program than they would have been in the case of the well program even had there not been a scarcity of water. Contact with human excreta is considered extremely defiling; when necessary its removal is a task relegated to the lowest of the *harijan* castes. Villagers interpret the flushing, cleaning, and even the use of latrines as defiling contact. It was considered extremely offensive to have a latrine located close to a dwelling house where a family not only lived, but prepared food and worshiped its deities. As a consequence of differing value systems of the villagers and the project technicians, it was impossible to translate the most significant reason for *initiating* these programs as a reason for *accepting* them. Although it was attempted, it proved impossible to give the villagers an understanding of the germ theory of disease transmission. It was much more credible to them that diseases were caused, as they had always been, by minor deities and spirits who had in some way been displeased.

It was usually the younger village men who were contacted by the project concerning latrines, and these men were most susceptible to purchasing them because of various types of pressure from project personnel and because of a degree of prestige in taking on an urban trait, but it was among the wives of these men that resistance was perhaps the strongest. Being either the only adult woman in a small family or a junior wife in a large joint family, burdensome tasks such as hauling water for latrines fell to them. One of the few periods of relaxation and gossip with other young women available to them was the time of the morning and evening bath. These women felt that having a latrine near their homes would do away with much of the reason for these expeditions to the tank, and consequently they were strongly opposed to having and/or using latrines.

While the foregoing discussion has not touched upon all the factors involved in the acceptance of the well program nor the re-

TABLE 1

FACTORS OPERATING FOR/AGAINST WELLS AND LATRINES

Wells		Latrines	
For	Against	For	Against
SCARCITY OF WATER Subsidy Digging Season	Maintenance	Low Cost	*Inconvenience* Digging Season
Separate Caste Pump Wells	*Caste Purity* Disease Theory		*CONTACT WITH EXCRETA* 1. Near house 2. Near gods Disease Theory
	Caste Segregation	Prestige	*Division of Labor* Men Approached

Note: Factors in capitals and italicized are considered *DECISIVE;* those merely italicized are *important;* those in plain type are of secondary importance.

jection of the latrine program, it has at least mentioned those which appear to be most important. Table 1 summarizes these factors, roughly indicating the weight or effectiveness of each. These are grouped according to the sociocultural nodes discussed below.

PAIR 2—MORE AND BETTER VEGETABLES AND POULTRY

Although both the vegetable and poultry programs of Barpali Village Service were given priority because of nutritional deficiencies in the area, both were also responsive to an explicit need in the villages: the need for more production in an expanding cash economy. Before the establishment of Barpali Village Service only very small quantities of such vegetables as chilis, edible greens, onions, garlic and small tomatoes were grown by members of the Mali caste, whose traditional occupation was gardening. Vegetable products, other than pulses grown by a few of the other cultivating castes, had hardly any place in the diet of the villagers except as seasoning. High-grade protein intake was likewise extremely low. Many *harijan* families kept a few diminutive, local chickens whose small and infrequent eggs were sold to wealthier village families. On special occasions the birds themselves might be sold at one of the weekly markets.

While sporadic efforts to increase the quantity and quality of vegetables grown in the area were made by the project during its first two years, it was not until drought in 1954 threatened to destroy the rice crop completely that a serious program to encourage vegetables in the area was undertaken. By that time cultivators had become aware of the success of vegetable growing in the project's demonstration garden and in the kitchen gardens of many of the village workers, and were themselves ready to attempt it in the face of potential crop failure and the concomitant hoarding of available supplies of rice. During the drought and in the ordinarily cool dry season following, many cultivators planted such vegetables as eggplant, cabbage, cauliflower, beans and beets. With the help and advice of project technicians a good yield was produced which the cultivators were able to market in order to purchase stocks of rice. During the following two years there was a slow increase in the number of cultivators planting vegetables and in the varieties planted as people realized the economic advantages of growing vegetables. With the coming of the first canal water in 1957, there was a tremendous increase in vegetable production, but because of insufficient preparation of the plots and lack of protective fencing, the yield that year was disappointing. However, since that time there has been a steady increase in variety, quantity, and quality of the vegetables grown in Barpali *thana*. The problem today is one of marketing the vegetables produced, because increasing quantities have greatly depressed local prices.

Among the earliest programs of Barpali Village Service was the attempt to upbreed local poultry. While the raising of chickens was carried on by many low-caste families as an adjunct to their customary occupation, the technicians hoped that some of these families might raise improved stock as a full-time occupation. Considerable emphasis was given to this program. The first phase aimed at complete eradication of local cocks from several pilot villages,* and later from a larger number, by the exchange of one purebred Leghorn cock for two local cocks. The second phase provided purebred eggs for hatching in the villages at minimal cost. In addition to

---

* In the village of Chiknipali where local cocks have been completely eliminated, a non-poultry raiser obtained a local cock for sacrifice. He brought the cock into the village the afternoon of the day on which the ceremony was scheduled. However, due to inauspicious circumstances the ceremony was postponed for four weeks. The cock was allowed to roam in the village, and by the time of the ceremony much of the upbreeding work had been undone.

these parts of the program, village workers and technicians spent considerable time giving advice in the villages and helping with the care of the improved birds. During this intensive phase of the poultry program there was apparently a fair degree of acceptance: during the first year of the program over fifty men had joined in the improvement scheme. However, once it appeared that the program had become established and the project technicians and village workers relaxed their intensive efforts in the villages, the villagers relaxed their own efforts with the result that the small local strain of poultry gradually reasserted itself. In spite of the fact that even first and second generation crosses were producing eggs almost double the size of those of the uncrossed local birds, and that the improved birds were significantly larger than their local ancestors, there seemed to be no concern on the part of the villagers to halt the rather rapid reversion to local type. By 1960, with the exception of two well-tended poultry farms maintained by *upper-castemen,* there was no trace of the improved poultry to be seen in the villages of Barpali *thana.*

Both the vegetable and poultry programs of Barpali Village Service were conceived by the project with the double goals of increasing the nutritional standard of the villagers' diet and of affording villagers an additional source of cash income through the marketing of their increased production. Demand for both vegetables and poultry products was good, both locally and in the town of Sambalpur: the marketing of eggs for village producers was even undertaken at no cost by the local branch of the state Animal Husbandry Department. Both programs seemed to receive good initial acceptance. What are the factors which caused one program to take firm hold in the area (to the point of creating a surplus problem) while the other program withered away?

The success of the vegetable program can be attributed to a relatively large number of moderately positive factors (see Table 2). Likewise, the poultry program encountered a series of moderately negative factors, but also one significant conflict involving both the institutional and value systems of the local culture. In addition to the positive effect of the drought and of the coming of irrigation in 1957, the potential for increased cash income through vegetable growing was clearly perceived by most of the cultivators. In the case of poultry raising the potential for increased profit was also present but it was far less certain. As the poultry program aimed at *improving* village poultry populations it was directed at individuals already raising fowl. Thus direct comparison between the old poultry raising practices and the new was natural. It immediately be-

TABLE 2

FACTORS OPERATING FOR/AGAINST VEGETABLES AND POULTRY

Vegetables		Poultry	
For	Against	For	Against
Income Drought Irrigation Slack Season		Income 1. large eggs	Maintenance
Neutral 　Ritually 　1. To grow 　2. To eat Varieties not 　Traditional			*Unclean* 　*Ritually* 　1. To grow 　2. To eat *SANSKRITIZATION*
High Castes	Tradition of Malis		*POTENTIAL* *OCCUPATION* Low Castes

came obvious that the improved birds required far more care and expense in every respect than had the small, local birds. For instance, the Leghorns required fencing, feeding of special diet, and inoculation, while the local birds wandered freely, scavenging for their own food and managing to protect themselves from predatory animals and birds and from diseases.

Vegetable growing and eating were in no way ritually tainted, in fact the ritually purest diets were vegetarian. (The exceptions to this generalization, onions and garlic which are not eaten in some of the purest diets, were traditional vegetables of the Mali caste and did not form a part of the improved vegetable complex.) On the other hand, the raising of poultry is considered an unclean occupation and is confined to *harijans*. Chicken and eggs are eaten by many members of the clean castes, but there are also many non-vegetarians who will not eat poultry products. These facts were recognized by the technicians of Barpali Village Service when they instituted the poultry program. However, the project felt that because untouchables were already raising local poultry, they would be receptive to improving their flocks. This assumption was not borne out. In this situation some of the processes described by Srinivas as "sanskritization" appear to have been operating. The majority of poultry-raising families belonged to an untouchable weaving caste. These people were aware of the fact that within the memory of most adults another similarly untouchable caste of weavers had elevated their status, through the assumption of rit ually pure behavior, to that of a clean caste. While poultry raising was unclean in itself, it was carried on by these people as a sideline, simply as a convenient way to bring in a little bit of additional cash income, but something which could be given up at any time. The intent of the Barpali Village Service poultry program was to elevate poultry raising to a full-time, or at least systematized *occupation*. As members of a caste aware of the possibility of their own upward mobility these people were unwilling to assume formally an unclean occupation which would preclude such mobility. It is the assumption of the present analysis that, while the villagers were not consciously aware of this reasoning, these factors were (and are) of sufficient importance to assure the failure of poultry raising in any kind of *systematic* fashion among *harijans*. It is significant in this report that within the *thana*, two individuals who have taken over the raising of improved poultry are not *harijans* but both members of a higher cultivating caste. Their ritual status is assured and they have simply taken on a new, potentially profitable business which may even have for them a certain prestige value as a form of Westernization.

In the acceptance of the vegetable program by traditionally non-gardening castes there was the slightly negative, or perhaps only neutral, factor that there was in the area already a caste of vegetable growers. However, because there was no important overlap in the area of varieties grown, there was apparently no opposition from the Malis who might have had a vested interest in vegetable growing. On the other hand, the very possibility of poultry raising becoming a caste occupation for the *harijans* already engaged in it as a sideline was enough to defeat the program. A further factor related to caste which has been found to operate in a large number of community development programs all over India is that it is always the economically and socially more secure castes or groups that most readily accept innovative programs. A final incentive to taking over vegetable growing was the fact that the yearly round of the cultivators created slack periods between the initial planting and cultivation of rice in the monsoon period and the harvest some months later in the middle of the dry season, and again after the rice harvest. The fact that the activities involved in vegetable growing fell neatly into these two slack periods further contributed to the success of the program.

As in the preceding section, the factors discussed above are summarized in Table 2, and the attempt is made to indicate the significance of each.

PAIR 3—COOPERATIVES FOR LEATHERWORKERS AND WEAVERS

In working with both the weavers and leatherworkers, Barpali Village Service sought to accomplish two goals: more economical and efficient production and marketing operations and improvement of the quality standards of the products. These goals would help to increase the individual income of the artisan and lead to improvement in his living condition. The situation of the Barpali weavers had been one of almost perpetual indebtedness to cloth merchants and middlemen in the area: the weavers received advances in cash and in kind, and were forced to contract their total output to the middlemen or merchants. Because of the desirability of the cloth woven in this area the merchants were able to realize large profits while the weaving families subsisted in substandard housing on an average wage (advance) of one rupee (about 21¢) per day. While the situation of the local Chamars (Hindi: *camār*), or leatherworkers, was in no sense as extreme as that of the weavers, they were finding that one of their most profitable occupations was becoming less and less profitable. This was the collection of dead animals in the villages of the *thana*. Whereas removal of carcasses had been a *duty* of the Chamars alone, other low castes in the villages were now competing for the dead animals, parts of which had a ready market in Sambalpur. Thus, Chamars were either deprived of these saleable commodities or were forced to pay for them. In addition, the sale of hides to Sambalpur and the subsequent repurchase of leather by the local Chamar shoemakers funneled a large portion of potential local profit into the hands of the Muslim hide dealers in Sambalpur.

Encouraged by the Cooperative Department of the state government, Barpali Village Service began a program aimed at organizing the shoemaking Chamars of Barpali and providing instruction in tanning and the preparation of their own shoe leather. Although this scheme threatened to cut into the business of some of the Barpali Chamars who acted as middlemen between the village hide-collecting Chamars and the hide dealers in Sambalpur, the organization took shape and grew gradually. This growth was, however, more apparent than real, as it represented mostly simple shareholders in the co-operative organization rather than actual shoemakers. By 1956, the third year of the organization, a transition occurred rather abruptly. One of the products traditionally salvaged by the Chamars is the bones of dead animals. During the past decade there has been a steadily increasing market for processed bones as a source of fertilizer. In view of this it was decided *by the Chamars* to devote the major efforts of the organization to the collection and processing of bone for fertilizer. The organization, now consisting of at least the family head of each Chamar family in Barpali village, was registered as a cooperative by the state; the cooperative has provided a pump well for the use of all Chamar families; and bone processing equipment has been purchased to replace crushers and digesters originally loaned by the government. While in the beginning some financial assistance on the part of Barpali Village Service was required, the cooperative has repaid all debts and is now operating entirely independently of the project.

The initial project work with the weavers of Barpali, while aimed at improving the quality of their goods and raising their economic standards, was not directed toward the goal of any sort of a permanent organization. The idea of a cooperative did not arise for some years after Barpali Village Service had been successfully handling several aspects of the weavers' production and marketing operations. Essentially, the role of Barpali Village Service during these first years was to purchase the entire output of a small group of weavers, selected on the basis of their weaving ability, at the rate of three rupees for each day of labor involved. This rate was determined by the weaver himself and represented three times the average rate of payment for other local weavers not working for Barpali Village Service. The project then undertook to market these materials either through outlets in Indian cities or through private orders from the United States. Cooperation between project technicians and Indian chemical companies resulted in fast dyes of standard colors which were used by the weavers jointly before taking their yarn home for weaving. In 1957, the initial group of weavers in addition to a few more members were registered as a cooperative under the laws of the state of Orissa. Barpali Village Service had been largely responsible for this step, hoping that it might lead the group of weavers to take over all the functions of purchasing yarns and dyes, supervision of quality, and marketing, which were then being performed by the project. In addition, it was hoped that the cooperative might be able to repay the project for at least some of its financial assistance in the beginning. Not only did this repayment fail to materialize, but the cooperative was forced to contract even larger debts to the project. At the end of 1960, the outstanding debt amounted to over thirty thousand rupees (about $6,300). However, more than this amount was tied up in the cooperative's inventory. The handling of both domestic and foreign sales by the cooperative was generally unsatisfactory and has required more or less constant supervision by project technicians. And finally, no consistent policy, nor even the beginnings of one, could be agreed upon by the members of the cooperative. With the withdrawal of Barpali Village Service set for the autumn of 1962, it seems reasonably certain that the weavers' cooperative will be totally unable to maintain itself as a viable organization.

Both the weavers' cooperative and the Chamars' cooperative were outgrowths on the part of Barpali Village Service to improve the economic condition of these groups of artisans and secondarily to improve product quality. A subsequent goal was the establishment of a permanent organization owned and controlled by the producers to maintain procurement and marketing functions on a joint basis for the sake of efficiency and profit to the members. In both cases the economic standards were raised through the effort of the project; even weavers not belonging to the cooperative became able in time to demand a higher rate from their middlemen. Particularly in the case of the weavers, quality control has risen markedly; and this too is reflected in the work of weavers not belonging to the cooperative. However, in terms of organizational viability, one group has succeeded to the point of becoming totally independent of the project in both finance and supervision, while the other group is hopelessly in debt and will probably collapse entirely once supervision and technical aid of the project is withdrawn. On the basis of what factors can such a difference be explained?

In terms of the situational factors alone there appears to be more reason to expect the weavers' cooperative to succeed than the

Chamars' cooperative. For instance, the weavers by working with Barpali Village Service and later by being members of the cooperative were assured a reasonably steady flow of orders throughout the year, their marketing was undertaken by the organization, they were encouraged to improve and widen their repertoire of types and designs of material, and a cash wage was provided by the cooperative which was two or three times that prevailing in the *thana*. On the other hand, the original work and organization among the Chamars was confined to improvement in shoemaking techniques. Not only were there few Chamars actually engaged in shoemaking, but the reservation of hides for local processing was at least a potential threat to those Chamars whose business it was to collect local hides and sell them in Sambalpur. However, there were balancing factors in both cases. The fact that the activities with the weavers had been organized within the framework of the project itself, and that Barpali Village Service had not realistically accounted for the services of its technicians in developing markets and handling orders and books, has made it difficult for the locally based organization to assume responsibility and understanding of the established pattern of operations. Likewise, through urban and overseas contacts of the project technicians an extensive system of external relationships was set up with which it would be difficult at best for a rural organization to cope. The positive balancing factors in the case of the Chamars' cooperative were largely associated with the change of function from shoemaking to preparation of bone meal. In the first place, this was a program developed by the internal leadership of the organization, and it coincided with increasing demand for fertilizer in the area as a result of the efforts of Barpali Village Service and the local community development block. In effect the function of the Chamars' cooperative was satisfaction of local demand with processed local resources, while the weavers' local production had become involved in a completely external pattern of demand.

In the case of both cooperatives the fact that their activities corresponded with the traditional caste occupations of the membership provided a strong positive factor, and in the case of the Chamars this was reinforced by a very marked sense of caste solidarity, more highly developed among the Barpali *thana* Chamars than in other castes of the area, to the point of members subordinating their own interests to those of the cooperative and caste. The decisive differential factor in these two programs was the way in which the activities were related to the caste structure. In the case of the Chamars, the program was directed at a single caste group, largely localized in Barpali village, and having already a pronounced sense of caste solidarity. On the other hand the members of the weaving coopera- tive, and indeed the original group of weavers worked with by Barpali Village Service, were largely from outlying villages of the *thana,* and represented two different castes whose interests were not identical. The initial intent of Barpali Village Service had been to work with weavers on the basis of their skill and ability regardless of their caste affiliation, and indeed, it had at least been an implicit goal to work toward the weakening of caste differences and barriers. For two reasons the two lowest weaving castes did not become in- volved in the organization. First, their output was confined to plain white or colored garments with only the simplest border designs, and second, the higher-caste weavers would have refused to work in the same organization with the untouchable Ganda weavers or the recently sanskritized but still very low Kuli weavers. Although the two castes making up the cooperative have been able to work together in relative harmony *under* the direction of Barpali Village Service, they have recently exhibited complete inability to function together as a decision-making body. Invaria- bly, when there are two sides to an issue for decision, all mem- bers belonging to the Bhulia caste will take one position and all Kusta weavers will take the opposite side. Beyond this there is friction in the actual operation of the cooperative because the Kusta weavers, producing cloth of hand-spun *tussah* silk would ordinarily be eligible for various government rebates on the pro- duction of *khadi* (hand spun, hand woven cloth). However, because the Bhulia weavers use mill-made cotton yarn in their goods, the cooperative cannot be considered a *khadi* organization, and thus all rebates are denied.

As has been pointed out elsewhere the likelihood of a coopera- tive in India surviving, or even developing, in a form similar to Western cooperative organizations is negligible. The concept of member-owner is alien to the Indian villager. It appears that while even economically insecure villagers are often willing to go into business for themselves, they are unwilling to enter into risk- taking situations where responsibility is *shared.* That is, if they cannot be in reasonable control themselves as entrepreneurs, they will relinquish all opportunity for responsibility in favor of the security of an employee status. This has certainly been the case among the Chamars and weavers of Barpali as well as in other cooperative ventures encouraged by Barpali Village Service. Among the Chamars this situation has in no way hindered the development of a viable organization (although not a true cooperative) as the caste structure itself provided a framework on which to add the functions of the cooperative. Decision-making and managerial authority was naturally assumed by the already strong and effective caste leadership, and support (financial and organizational) was given by the whole caste. Active members considered themselves employees of the cooperative/caste and followed the directives of their traditional leaders.

Among the weavers, however, no such structure existed. Not only were two distinct and independenct castes involved in the cooperative, but neither one of them alone had the cohesion and centralized authority of the Chamars. There are at present several other weaving cooperatives in Barpali *thana*. However, these are quite simply private businesses of individual entrepeneurs, legally registered as cooperatives in order to benefit from the preferential regulations governing this type of organization. Weaving has traditionally been a family occupation carried on in relative isolation from other weaving families in many villages dispersed throughout the area. Consequently the structure of the weaving castes has been extremely loose and with no clear patterns of authority. This, coupled with the dominant management position of Barpali Village Service in the initial stages of organizing the weavers, has resulted in *all* the members of the cooperative looking on themselves as employees ready to follow orders but none ready to assume any sort of responsibility. In spite of efforts of the project to educate the members in cooperative management, no effective leadership either joint or individual has emerged, nor has any outside individual with managerial skills been willing to assume responsibility for the organization.

Table 3 presents a summary of the above discussion. As in the preceding tables, the attempt is made to weight the factors operating to assure the viability of the Chamars' organization and likewise to assure the failure of the weavers' cooperative.

CONCLUSION: TOWARD DEVELOPING A PREDICTIVE METHODOLOGY

From the foregoing analyses the fact emerges that factors decisive to the acceptance or rejection of programs of directed change may lie at any point along the sociocultural spectrum. However, the factors do tend to cluster about institutional and/or normative nodes which are important to the recipient culture. It hardly need be said that these nodes usually do not coincide with institutional and normative nodes of an alien donor culture (in this case Euro-American). The importance of these nodal points is that they serve as cultural foci or reference points for orienting normal behavior as well as defining deviations from traditional practice (which is the condition of an innovative program when

TABLE 3

FACTORS OPERATING FOR/AGAINST CHAMARS' AND WEAVERS' COOPERATIVES

Chamars		Weavers	
For	Against	For	Against
Resource/ Need—Local Increased Demand *Self-Developed Program*	Hide Dealers Few Shoemakers	*Income Marketing Steady Orders*	*BVS Management* 1. finances 2. external markets 3. programmed by BVS
Traditional Occupation *STRUCTURE OF CASTE* 1. Solidarity 2. Leadership 3. Totality *Employee Security*	Member- Owner	Traditional Occupation	Member- Owner *MIXED CASTES No Caste Leadership* Family Pattern of Weaving

it is first presented). Because of their function as foci of orientation, the pure nodes are connected by extensive linkages with many other aspects of the sociocultural system. It has been seen that the caste structure, through its linkages with the economic, occupational, and power patterns in the villages, had a *direct* effect on every program discussed except latrines, and that in the case of three of them (poultry weavers' and Chamars' cooperatives) this effect was decisive. Furthermore, through ideological linkages with ritual purity, this node has far wider effect, and at this point becomes a decisive influence on reaction to the latrine program.

While the caste structure node is of tremendous importance in determining the response to potentialities for cultural change, the material presented may have exaggerated its significance. It is not the only such node operating to facilitate or hinder the acceptance of new practices or items. Although linked with caste, ritual purity can be justified as an independent node. Likewise, the seasonal and agricultural cycle appears to represent a nodal point, particularly when its linkages with the pattern of income and expenditure are considered. Factors stemming from the organization of the family and domestic division of labor have only been mentioned here twice, but these factors have been of considerable importance in other programs undertaken by Barpali Village Service. Another node which has been significant in many of the project's programs is village factionalism. Village factions entered into the differential acceptance of the well program, but the problem is too complex to be dealt with in an article of this length. The problem has been outlined by the author elsewhere, and is given full treatment in a forthcoming work.

What implications can be drawn from the foregoing that will be of assistance in planning programs of directed change and in predicting their outcome? Of course, no short-cut or formula will ever be devised which can substitute for complete and detailed knowledge of the recipient culture. However, it is often impossible to gain such knowledge before the initiation of a program of change, either through field work or even from existing literature. Consequently, the administrator or his anthropological advisor must be alert for clues to important areas of the recipient culture which may be expected to have significant influences on the reactions of members of the society to the attempted innovations. This must be more than an intuitive feel for the culture, or an awareness that it is somehow different from Western culture. A cultural model composed of nodes and linkages could serve to provide such clues objectively to the program planners. It could have the initial advantage of being immediately useful in an outline form, and capable of further elaboration as the innovating group became more familiar with the recipient culture.

The construction of such a model can be accomplished in numerous ways, depending on the recipient culture itself and on the perceptiveness, training, and amount of time at the disposal of the initial and subsequent investigators. The following outline suggests some of the steps which might be useful in the preliminary identification of nodes in rural Orissa. Needless to say this would represent only a beginning; there are other equally valid first steps, and, of course, a succession of subsequent steps of increasing specificity leading eventually to a virtually complete knowledge of the culture. The following steps, then, are presented as an example of how a planner might first approach a village in such an area as Barpali *thana:*

1. What is the largest building in the area? What is it used for? Who uses it? Answers to these queries could indicate important areas of ideological culture (temples), economic (factories, store-houses), social organization (segregated usage, landlordism), etc.

2. Are there significant differences in size and type of residential dwellings? Do there appear to be distinct living areas in the village for different groups? Investigation of the bases of such differences and their significance in the village would reveal factors related to social and economic stratification, and might ramify into areas of occupational distribution and land tenure, etc.

3. What is the relative proportion of men, women, and children engaged in different observable activities? Does this proportion vary from one group to another? Does it vary according to season? Such findings would point out information about family structure such as domestic division of labor, about social stratification and occupational distribution, and about the yearly cycle of economic activity.

4. What do the villagers feel to be the "real" objectives of the outsiders in establishing a project in their locality? What kinds of changes do they think the project plans to introduce? Answers to these questions in Barpali tended to cluster around a) the caste system, b) land tenure, and c) religious beliefs, all significantly related to local cultural nodes.

5. Does one group respond in a markedly different manner to the project than do other groups? Can such groups or their differential behavior be related to previous findings about stratification, land holding, etc.? Or can they be identified as factions operating

on another basis? If factionalism is identified, consideration should be given to the desirability and implications of trying to exploit it to further program objectives.

6. What reactions can be observed among villagers, or different groups of villagers, toward a) the project staff, b) other villagers or groups, c) natural objects, d) strange objects? Answers to any of this group of questions, such as friendliness, interest, indifference, avoidance, hostility, fear, whether generalized or differentiated, can be of value in bringing to light aspects of the value system (eg., the concept of ritual purity,) supernatural beliefs, expectations from external relationships, etc.

Having begun the construction of the model by isolation of nodes, the next stage in program planning would be a careful consideration of the ways in which proposed programs might relate to the identified nodes. On the basis of the above outline, a considerable amount of predictive evidence would be available about the six programs discussed earlier. It should be immediately evident that because of the strong patterns of group (caste) segregation probably identifiable in all six of the steps outlined, the formation of an organization involving the cooperation of members of different groups (i.e., the weavers' cooperative) would have little chance of success. Likewise, evidence of strong organization and solidarity within a group would indicate the probability of success in fostering an organization (i.e., the Chamars' cooperative) whose functions were related to a traditional occupation of the group. The yearly cycle of seasons and of agricultural and other activities would permit acceptance of wells and of vegetable growing. The technical feasibility of wells (ie., a high water table) and their relatively low cost should tend to give weight to a prediction of success if no negative factors appeared in other nodes. In the case of vegetable growing, the existence of a traditional gardening caste should suggest caution at least in trying to introduce the program to other cultivators. The fact that the range of vegetables promoted in the Barpali Village Service program did not overlap the traditionally caste-tied vegetables could certainly be considered a positive factor. Given this situation, the specific drought conditions and the recognized potential for continued cash income would constitute evidence for a fairly bright prognosis. Once the concept of ritual purity had been identified by project planners, either through the sixth step, the caste structure, or through other evidence, the latrine program could have been considered doomed to almost certain failure. With further information on domestic division of labor and occupational patterns, this prediction would have been confirmed. Of the programs discussed, the only one which might have been misjudged on the basis of such preliminary investigations as outlined, is the poultry program. While certain caution signs might have been present, such as the ritual impurity of poultry raising and its relegation to definitely secondary importance among the occupations of the raisers, probably the overriding evidence would have been that the group of people aimed at were *already raising poultry*. It is probable that sufficient refinement of the working model would not have been attained early enough to take into account mechanisms for caste mobility, and the difference between incidental and routinized association with unclean objects or jobs.

The conclusions presented here are by no means new or original. Furthermore, they are relatively limited in their ability to probe the deeper, often most important, areas of a cultural system. They do represent, however, examples of the kinds of first steps that can be taken in undertaking a program of directed change. There is a real need, particularly in community development programs, for even such a limited type of investigation systematically carried out toward a clearly conceived analytical end. All too often development programs having neither the resources nor the time for full-scale socio-cultural research, abandon all attempts at this sort of analysis and guide their programs "by the seat of their pants." Perhaps the point of view represented in this paper will stimulate further consideration and research toward the development of a precise methodology for dealing with the process of directed culture change.

15

Health Education in Village India

Although we stated in the introduction to the previous case history that India has one of the most complex cultures in the nonindustrialized world and that Western-derived innovations face very severe resistances there, change can be induced when the innovators understand and adapt to Indian beliefs and values. The difference between village India and village life elsewhere is that there is a greater variety of more complicated beliefs in India; consequently, there is more need to understand the culture.

The community development program of India has had serious difficulties in implementing socioeconomic change in villages, even though it has been staffed by Indians. However, the urban educated in many non-Western countries often do not have very deep understanding of their own rural people, although they may share the same general values and beliefs. But proof that change can take place in village India when the the proper methods are used has been amply illustrated by an unusual collection of cases, of which the selections in this and the following chapter are samples. The authors claim that they deliberately attempted to describe "success stories," which means that the accounts are not necessarily typical of what has happened throughout the country. Nevertheless, we think these studies indicate that change can take place, even in India, when efficient techniques are used. If space had permitted, we would have used more of these graphic accounts; however, if readers want to read further, they can write to the authors. We have selected one dramatic success story and one failure (Chapter 16), the only unsuccessful project in the volume. We include it, as the authors did, to show a more "typical" outcome in village assistance.

The "success story" is the introduction of a frightening new idea to village people: vaccination. It clearly indicates the normal villager's dependence on traditional methods. Some

Westerners might call it superstition to depend on placating village goddesses to avert sickness and death, but they can do so only because their culture has been fortunate in developing scientific medicine. In societies where this has not happened, people rely on beliefs and methods that seem logical within the limits of their knowledge, which include placating gods and goddesses. To act as if such traditional beliefs do not exist adds to the uneasiness of village people, at least when no clearly demonstrated alternative has been offered. For the change agent merely to tell them that he has the answer is not sufficient to promote a positive reaction, particularly when their welfare is at stake. The alternative is to present the new idea as an adaption to the old one. Then the risk is minimized in their minds.

The other significant lesson in this account is the power and influence of the traditional leader, in this case the Hindu priest. All leaders have vested interested in their positions, and priests are no exception to this rule. They may often obtain economic benefits from their followers and to outsiders they may appear to be charlatans. But they do provide important services to the believers and they can do enormous harm to any development effort if they are bypassed. They are a fact of life in the villages of the world, and the change agent who ignores or opposes them is building a wall of resistance that can easily destroy his efforts. By incorporating them into projects, powerful allies can be gained or, at the very least, powerful enemies will not be created. As this case clearly indicates, when a religious leader obtains an advantage from co-operating, he can become a positive force for change. We see again the constant necessity of adapting to traditional ways, whether they be local beliefs or local leaders.

A NEW GODDESS FOR AN OLD *

EUGENE P. LINK and **SUSHILA MEHTA**

THE CASE STORY

When smallpox broke out in a village of Kalahandi district of Orissa State, the people knew that the Goddess "Thalerani" was in a rage. Some of the villagers formed a delegation to call upon the headman who was expected to do something to pacify the Goddess. He, in turn, thought it fit to consult "Gurumai," the village priest.

When the priest saw the crowd which was gathering before his house, he sat quiet, his legs crossed and closed his eyes. Then suddenly his body jerked, his eyes danced and he was overcome with a spasm. The spirit of the Goddess was upon him. He then scolded the crowd for not contributing enough money to the Goddess, "Thalerani." "She will now take her toll."

The poor villagers were terrified to see the mysterious antics of the priest. They fell at his feet and implored:

"Goddess, Mother, be pacified."

"Forgive us."

The priest declared that the Mother would be pacified only after a great sacrifice followed by a feast, and the headman promised to take an oath on behalf of all the people to offer the goat sacrifice and follow it with a feast, if only the children were saved. At once a procession was organized, with musical instruments and all trappings, to offer worship to the Goddess, and to seal the vow of the headman to sacrifice a goat if the Goddess would spare the children.

When the Block authorities heard about the outbreak of smallpox in the village, they sent immediately a vaccinator with medical

* Reprinted from *Victories in the Villages—India,* State University College, Plattsburgh, New York, 1964, pp. 33-39, by permission of the authors. Dr. Link, who is Research Professor of History at State University College, Plattsburgh, N.Y., was twice a Fulbright professor in India and on a third trip worked with the National Fundamental Education Center on village development problems. Miss Mehta is a sociologist on the staff of the National Fundamental Education Center and worked with Dr. Link to provide training materials for village level workers. This case history is also printed in *Working with Village People,* Sushila Mehta, National Council of Educational Research and Training, New Delhi, 1965.

supplies. On arrival, he went from house to house, telling the mothers to bring the babies and children in order that they might be vaccinated at once. The women, who knew about DDT spraying but not about vaccination, were nonplussed to have a stranger come right to their door and ask for their babies. Some of them thought that the movements of this stranger were suspicious and that he bore watching.

The first woman he approached could not understand what he was talking about. When he tried to explain she stared at him in amazement, and when he asked her to bring her child to him to be vaccinated, she was positively alarmed. She turned around and walked away murmuring that her husband was not at home, and that she could not allow this strange man to touch her baby in his absence. Others overhearing this conversation, made it a signal for them, on one pretext or another, to shun the vaccinator. All kinds of excuses arose: one said that her mother-in-law was out; * another said this was the wrong day for it; still others had to follow the cows. Some just closed their doors and went to the fields.

After two hours of fruitless effort, the vaccinator gave up because fear of him had spread throughout the village. The people even passed around a name for him: "The one who makes the babies cry." All the women were alerted and now, no one wanted to oppose the public opinion that this man was dangerous. They would not offer him even a glass of water. In desperation the real benefactor was forced to leave the village.

At the Block headquarters the vaccinator met the social education officer, who had never visited this village, and was speechless on hearing about the experience. Something must be done. Suddenly, the cruel trickery of the village priest, shameless as it was in using suffering and disease to collect money, gave him an idea.

"Why don't we use that "Gurumai?"", he muttered grimly.

"What? that old grabber? I don't think he will do anything unless he gets paid for it. He is only after feasts and fees. Nothing else will interest him. Still something must be done, the next day if possible." The Social Education Officer and his vaccinator headed toward the priest's residence.

It was dark when they reached the house. They both greeted

* The mother-in-law dominates her daughter-in-law almost completely in most of the folk cultures of India. The girl is often at her mercy, and can make few decisions on her own.

cordially and conversed with him for some time about the raging disease and their own concern. When the matter of necessary action came up the social worker took over and said:

"Gurumaiji,* the people have great faith in you, so they seek your advice. In a disease so serious as smallpox wouldn't you like to offer them medicine as well as religious guidance?"

The priest seemed interested. "Yes," he said, "I help them in my own way. What else can I do? After all, I have no medicines."

"That is right, we have the medicines, but we need you, their spiritual guide, to explain the use of medicine and to show that the goddess favors its use. These people have faith in you, so they will believe your word of blessing on the medicine, if you will give it."

"Medicine? What medicine? These village people have faith and that faith cures them. Why bother further?"

The social worker's heart sank, as he said: "But don't you see this is a serious matter?"

"Whatever it is, I must see that the Goddess becomes pacified. It will take a good feast, then trouble will end."

"Yes, yes, that is a fine idea for you could have a ceremony, hold a feast, and bless the treatment," quickly added the desperate worker.

"Why should I get involved in all that trouble? There is a village headman, you know, who took care of the spraying," said the priest.

After a time the Social Education Officer and the vaccinator left the priest without an iota of success. They talked for awhile then slept at the village chaupal.†

Next morning while they are getting ready to leave, they saw the old priest coming toward them as fast as his legs would bring him. He almost fell at their feet and implored:

"Please help, please help, my favorite nephew is ill. My

---

* The suffix "ji" is almost like saying "the honorable" or "the revered," hence Gandhiji, or Nehruji (more often Panditji), and here the astute worker is giving the priest special honor.

† The chaupal is a meeting place for a caste usually, although it is often used by a gossip group, too. The village chaupal is supposedly for panchayat, and all-village meetings. Traditionally it has also been used as a place for a traveller to rest over night, where food will be offered free in the morning. The small building for shelter is usually under or very near a large tree. Women and Harijans are never permitted in the caste chaupals, and seldom indeed in the village wide ones.

brother has just come to me very much worried, that the Goddess Mother will take him too. He is the only son, so you must stay and save him. Give him that medicine you were telling me about last night."

The two men were thunderstruck for a moment as they looked at one another and then at the begging holy man. The Social Education Officer felt like throwing the gauntlet and said:

"But what about that faith? Don't you have faith?"

"Sir, that is for those simple village folks who understand nothing else. My nephew must be sure and be saved by getting some medicine. Please help us?"

"And what will you do for us? What about the other children who also need vaccination?"

"Anything, sir, whatever you want me to do. I am your humble servant."

"You must help us explain to the people the need for vaccination. You must assemble all the people at one place, talk to them, and help us proceed with vaccinations."

"Yes sir, please come to my house and I will do the needful." The priest was compliant.

That same morning, he again worked himself into a kind of frenzy. A large crowd gathered before his house, to get the latest word from the goddess. She declared through her agent that she desired to save only those children who were vaccinated with a magic herb! Therefore, all the children must be vaccinated without delay. A hubbub spread through the crowd and up the lanes of the village.

Numbers of people followed the priest and the vaccinator as they walked to the priest's home. They all watched as the nephew took the little scratch on his arm with only a whimper.* This soon got the message across and changed the whole atmosphere. One by one the men got up and went to bring their babies. Vaccination was in full swing, with the priest standing by to assist as much as possible.

As a matter of fact the priest became friendly with both the medical aid and the social worker. He accepted instruction from them and then collected the parents to give them advice on the care of the children and of the sore created by the vaccine. Later

* If the child really had smallpox, the vaccination was too late. He probably didn't.

on he showed a willingness to incorporate some general ideas about better health practices in his nightly sessions of religious discourses and Bhanjan singing. Unwittingly, a new goddess was speaking through him.

Through the priest the workers found a ready and effective contact with the people. He became willing to call public meetings to discuss village issues. Here, with the confidence people had in him, he became a leader for village progress. The ideas of social education captured his thoughts and energies so that he wanted to do more. The Social Education Organizer felt the value of his friendship more than ever. Regularly, he invited the priest to the Block Headquarters to see the work being done in other villages. This was an inspiration which increased his own influence and effectiveness. Social education was launched in still another village in India.

COMMENTARY

It is disturbing to read the sentence that "the social education worker had never been in this village." Therefore, if the smallpox emergency was to be met, he must try to motivate action through a local leader. Fortunately, he found a holy man who was willing to cooperate. But what if he hadn't? What could have been done if a fortuitous circumstance of a nephew's illness had not so timely appeared? Could the villagers in any other way be turned from a miseducated priest and his sacrifice.

Some standard characteristics of a public or a crowd are evident here, too. When one woman reacted against the vaccinator, who incidentally was brash in his too bold approach, others followed. In Indian villages news spreads fast. "He who makes babies cry" became a slogan that permeated the village quickly. A mass opposition carried with it even those not so religiously oriented. The "band wagon" (everybody's doing it) emotion slammed and bolted the door for the work of those who came to help. Only an equally powerful social force such as religion and the priest, could break through.

In helping people to accept health and medical changes one can be mindful of the fact that there is almost a natural resistance to inflicting pain for good. Even people who are accustomed to the most advanced medical operations are fearful and would avoid the experience if possible. Villagers can be expected to be over-concerned with shots and vaccinations and great care should be made to prepare them for these experiences to eliminate as much trauma as possible.

In this situation, seeing was believing, so that the worker invited the people to come and see the priest's nephew actually take the vaccine. This was wise, for this kind of object lesson broke resistance much more rapidly and turned the tide in favour of science and health.

This case further illustrates that if emergencies arise, and they do, perhaps drastic action needs to be taken. However, people should not be left in this state. Careful, respectful explanation should follow. The villagers can understand and will accept scientific truths and explanations if carefully handled.

16

Factionalism in
Village India

The "failure" we mentioned in the previous chapter is concerned with a very important problem in village development:
factionalism. The principles of community development have
been devised in the belief that organized group effort is a very
efficient means of galvanizing rural communities. Although
much fine work has been accomplished in the United States
by this means, as well as in some nonindustrialized countries,
there have been serious problems also. One of the most basic
questions that is rarely asked is, "Is the rural village of Asia,
Africa, or Latin America really a co-operative unit?"

Some social scientists have questioned this premise and
have advanced the thesis that the peasant is basically very non-
co-operative, at least on a village-wide basis. This belief is
based on the fact that the peasant's resources are very limited
and that he views the gain of his neighbor as his own loss.*
His slice of the economic pie is so small that he cannot afford
to share it. There is undoubtedly much logic in this point of
view. It has been noted frequently that the man who takes a
chance on a new idea in a rural village is almost always the
one who is better off than his neighbors. His piece of pie is a
little larger. On the other hand, it should be stressed that social
units exist only because the individuals composing them have
some common interests. A peasant village is no exception to
this fact. If rural villagers did not gain something by living together in one settlement, they would disperse over the countryside. Thus, there is some basis for co-operation, but it should
be stressed that very powerful divisive forces may also exist.
In any event, it will be rare that peasant villagers in general
will be co-operative because they believe in the abstract notion
that co-operation is noble whereas competition is base. Their

* See George M. Foster, "Peasant Society and the Image of
Limited Good," in *American Anthropologist,* Vol. 67, No. 2, April,
1965, pp. 293-315.

co-operation will almost always be tied to economic or social benefits of a practical nature.

Factionalism, or the association of informal groupings of individuals for some special benefit, occurs in villages in all parts of the world, but perhaps nowhere is it carried to such lengths as in India. Factionalism, of course, does constitute co-operation among the members of one particular group, but this kind of co-operation often brings about divisiveness in the larger social unit, the village. The Indian villager is addicted to group effort, but usually this occurs on a level below that of the village. Thus, village unity and co-operation is often difficult to obtain.

We find in this case history a good account of how such groups formed in one village, what their common interests were, and how high the tensions became when these interests were threatened. We see how changes in the economic pattern, in this case land values, can foster the development of such groups.

Group action and organizations are vital parts of any cultural system and consequently must be taken into account. No idealistic philosophy by outside change agents will change this situation quickly. The alternative is the same as with religious leadership—to be truly effective the change agent will have to adapt to such traditional groups. And when village unity is precluded, the only kind of innovation that will succeed is one which is tailored to groups that do co-operate. Obviously, this course requires understanding of what cultural groups are significant, but this is a constant requirement—to know the characteristics of the recipient population.

WHAT TO DO *

EUGENE P. LINK and SUSHILA MEHTA

The Problem

About a year ago a Social Education Program had been started in the village Ayanagar—a village in Mehrauli Block near Delhi. The worker had established a reading room, a youth club and a radio-listening group. But it was found that the youth club was merely on paper and very few people showed any interest in common activities. The worker realized that there were several factions in the village. When he approached members of one faction he became identified with it so that others regarded his activities with suspicion. What little participation had developed was deteriorating. What could be done?

Economic Factors

Ayanagar is a small village of Delhi State with a population of 1,675. The village is situated about two miles from Mehrauli, the block headquarter town. It is ten to twelve miles from the metropolitan area of Delhi city. Daily a large number of private buses run between Delhi and Ayanagar. Due to the nearness to a large metropolitan area the village has been experiencing strong urbanising influences.

A large number of people in neighboring rural areas depend on Delhi city for their livelihood. Many families in the village keep milk cows, buffaloes, and goats. They sell milk in Delhi and gain a steady income. Each day a large number of milkmen cycle to the city carrying the milk in two big drums balanced on both sides. Some have taken up jobs in the city.

Many of the people are also agriculturists. They keep small farms. The expansion of the metropolis causes land prices to shoot up. People want to sell all their land so that they can make big money. Because of this some families have encroached upon village

* Reprinted from *Victories in the Villages—India,* State University College, Plattsburgh, New York, 1964, pp. 62-67, by permission of the authors. This case history is also printed in *Working with Village People,* Sushila Mehta, National Council of Educational Research and Training, New Delhi, 1965.

owned common land called the "Gaon Shamlat Zamin" (village common land) and thus introduced bitter feuds.

Sociological Factors

The social structure of the village is much influenced by one dominant caste called the *"Gujjars."* The Gujjar caste has the largest number of families, nearly two hundred thirty five. Another big caste group is composed of the Harijans and chamars who have nearly forty families. There is a large kin group of Brahmins who call themselves one family, but they are divided into several smaller families. Their total number is sixty.

Among the Gujjars there are four different factions called "Panas" or "Juthas," living in four different streets and each having its own "Chaupal," the common meeting place of a caste group.

A large group of Gujjar families called the "Ghodewalla pana" so named because formerly they all kept horses (Ghoda) live in what is considered the front portion of the village in a long winding street. This group is economically more prosperous than the others and is a dominant faction, having its own chaupal and four members sitting in the village panchayat.

A second group inhabiting another stretch is called, for reasons unknown, the "Babawalla" pana. It too has its own chaupal. It is the second most powerful group and maintains a keen rivalry with the first one.

The third faction is called the "Bhoobhadia" pana. Again the origin of this name is not known. Its people live in a street next to the "Babawalla pana," but it maintains its own chaupal.

A fourth group is called the "Gandia pana." It is located at the end of the long winding street of the "Ghodewalla pana." It too has its own "Chaupal" and a leader who is a member of the panchayat.*

Nearby, and yet to itself is the "Harijan Wada" (Area) where all the Harijan (lowest castes) families live.† Again they have

---

* The origins of these names of the panas are obscure. "Baba-walla' could relate to a renowned forerunner (gotra), a sort of holy grandfather. "Boobhadia" could be named after a group migrating from Sind territory in the Gujarat. "Gandia" derives from the classical Mahabharata and one of its mythical heroes, "Arjun."

† Harijan is the name given to the lowliest people, the outcastes, in the social structure of Indian society by Mahatma Gandhi. It means "children or people of God."

their own meeting place. Their houses and their chaupals are kept clean and tidy.

In the opposite corner of the village there is a walled area with a big gate inside which live the Brahmin families. They are not a large number, but they do add a sixth faction to this small village.

Political Factors

The village elected a panchayat in 1958. There are eight members and three members of the village are in the circle panchayat.* Of the eleven members, four belong to Ghodewalla pana, five are divided among the other groups, and two are from the Harijan families. It is noted however, that the panchayat was not active, it had not met as a body for a year and very little work for the improvement of the village had been undertaken.

This body, representing the entire village, was expected to take legal possession of and manage the village common land, the "Gram Shamalat Zamin." Of this land nearly fifty-five acres was earmarked for school buildings; a higher secondary school for boys, and a girls' School.

Course of Events

Before the village panchayat was established in 1958, certain families of Ghodewala pana had already started occupying illegally some village land set aside for the schools. The new panchayat's duty was to recover the village land but it was heavily influenced by the fact that four of its members came from the dominant pana that had taken over the land.

Following the example of the more influential Ghodewalla pana, others like those from Babawalla pana also tried to occupy village lands illegally. Tension among the factions was keen.

Some members of the panchayat proceeded to file a suit against the families who had taken over the village land. To complicate

---

* This is a statutory elected panchayat, and is to be distinguished from the traditional social panchayats, which exist within each caste to manage its affairs. The laws of India establish the statutory "Gram" or village panchayat and usually require the election of at least one woman and one Harijan. Although "panch" means five, the number of elected representatives are often several more. The circle panchayat is characteristic of Delhi and the Punjab and is usually a body representing a number of villages.

matters, certain families had started building houses on this land. Bickering increased even more. Members of Gandiawala pana wanted all the land given for the school buildings to be vacated, while others favored a compromise. The court, however, was slow to make a decision and the animosity gathered momentum.

In the meantime a social education worker was appointed in this village. When he started his work he was not aware of the painful tensions and sharp rivalries that were hidden under a superficial appearance of good relationships. However, the worker soon found that his efforts were not successful. The rivalrous factions were not ready to trust him, and misinterpreted any contact he made with those in another pana. He was deeply hurt and discouraged.

Intensification of the Conflict

In August of 1961, two boys, one belonging to the Ghodewalla pana and other belonging to Bapawalla pana grazing cattle in the common pasture land of the village, had a quarrel. This spread and developed into considerable violence. One boy "beat up" another severely. When the lad came home crying and showed his wounds to his father, the father's anger flared. He picked up a long stick and went to the house of the other boy and there he found the father sitting on a "charpoi" (cot), smoking a "hookah" (a water pipe). He shouted at him and told him of the beating of his son. When he saw the fellow was not much impressed by his account he could not control his anger. He hurled his "lathi" (a long heavy stick) and then started pummelling him with his fists. Most men from the Ghodewalla pana gathered on one side, and when word spread about the quarrel, the men from Babawalla pana came running to help their man. Abuses were showered upon one another and lathis were wielded freely. Elders of the village came to separate the quarreling men, but they were brushed aside. Then some members of the panchayat tried to intervene but without success. Somebody finally ran to the police station and the police succeeded in separating the groups, rounding up the most quarrelsome. In this fight four persons were seriously injured and had to be taken to the hospital, one so serious that he died soon after. The remaining were treated in the hospital for several days. Upon their release, the police arrested them and other ring leaders, bringin charges against them under the criminal code. All of them were released on bail, and the case was still pending in the courts.

Later Course of Events

This violence, death and court action seemed to sober the people to some extent. They now go about their work quietly. They will go to the court when they are called for the case. But they do not talk about the tragic incident. The rift between Ghodewala pana and Babawala pana is wide and deep. It seems impossible to get them together for any village activities or development.

Some time after this incident the worker organized a Five Year Plan publicity week for which he arranged a public meeting. People from both the groups came and listened to the lecture and talks.

When the building for the higher second school, erected by the education department on public lands, was ready, its inauguration was attended by some prominent leaders from the outside. A public function was organized. For this, some panchayat members wanted to collect Rs. 100/—as a village contribution. It became a factional issue as usual. The proposal was carried by a bare majority. During the ceremonies many people were apprehensive about the behavior of the faction-ridden audience. The situation was tense and had to be handled carefully. However, without any untoward incident, it passed off.

The Present Position

The factions to this day are apathetic to any program involving their rival groups.

All the panchayat members seldom if ever meet together. During recent months no meeting has had the full membership present. The village level worker has tried to enlist the cooperation of the youth by forming a youth club and initiating a common program. But the thirty names of the youth club remain on paper and little enthusiasm is shown for any welfare activities. They have taken up some minor work such as cleaning and whitewashing the chaupals of their own pana, but they are not willing to come together for projects beneficial to all.

The worker has opened a literacy class in the Harijan Wada and has found some interest among them to attend. But only Harijans attend it. The others keep aloof and away.

The Bharat Sevak Samaj (Indian Service Society) has a health centre for women in this village. It has not created much enthusiasm among the women. The feeling seems to be that they might have to meet and associate with rivals.

The village worker is confronted with a knotty and complex problem in human relations. Much careful study and patient effort will be needed gradually to heal these old wounds.

COMMENTARY

It may be said that this outlined study ended in failure. Probably the village worker "acted before he thought" or studied about the situation. He must have been misled by the veneer of good will be needed gradually to heal these old wounds.

A social education worker must see the village in its area or regional setting. The social control of sky rocketing land prices is important to keep in mind while dealing with the immediate problems of the village. Instead of this being a divisive factor, could it be a unifying influence in resisting urban encroachment except under the guidance of an area planning commission? Perhaps the village could cooperate and demand even higher profits and use the extra money for community betterment.

Let us ever be mindful of the seeds that have been planted. Literacy work among the Harijans was started. These literate Harijans can be involved in other community efforts or involved in a competition with another village engaged in literacy efforts. There is a health centre and in a crisis it can be used. Could the worker perhaps find a community health problem?

The village should be surveyed with the people themselves participating and thus focus effort on some serious common difficulty. Could cooperative transportation to Delhi be organized? Or could piece work from city factories be introduced? The reader probably has other suggestions.

17

Buddhism and Development
in Laos

The following account is particularly timely in view of recent occurrences in the neighboring country of Vietnam. We refer in particular to the problems that have arisen between the Buddhist fraternity in that country and the secular South Vietnamese administrators, along with their American advisers. Although there are significant differences between the variety of Buddhism that exists in Laos and that of Vietnam, we believe that the difficulties that have occurred in the latter country with the traditional religious fraternity stem from similar relationships with the government. The problems have mainly developed because highly organized traditional priesthoods have been ignored in the Western-oriented development efforts. The priests have seen their prestige and influence diminishing, and like those with vested interests anywhere, they have banded together to resist the force of change that is excluding them. This process is taking place in many areas of the non-industrialized world, whether the religious leaders are Christian, Hindu, Muslim or Buddhist.

The following article attempts to put the religious fraternity into proper perspective, and in particular to counter some of the stereotyped views of Asian religious beliefs and practices. The most common Western conception of Asian religions is that they are tradition-bound and other-worldly, and thus inimical to change. But it must be remembered that all religions, including Christianity, are other-worldly in their emphasis that the most important task of the believer is to satisfy his deity and provide for life after death. However, it is more important to remember that in all cultures there is usually a wide variance between theological principles and day-to-day behavior. This is nowhere more apparent than among peasant villagers. Furthermore, it can easily be argued that the apathy toward change that is often found among rural folk is more a product of truly limited possibilities than of religious beliefs. The beliefs serve only as rationalizations for unsuccessful change agents.

But what of the religious fraternities themselves? Are they not archaic survivals of a premodern age when asceticism was the goal of men? We believe that this is also a stereotype—that religious leaders in Asia, as well as the ordinary citizens, have been caught up in the waves of change that are sweeping the twentieth-century world, and that they are attempting to adapt to these new conditions. But their traditional organizations are still largely intact, which makes them an enormous potential force for positive or negative effect. They can act as a group that still has considerable prestige in the villages.

In the following account we see the religious leaders become involved in several village development programs in Laos, not because they were sought out by the change agents but because the villagers turned to them when they needed direction and advice. We see them as the potential organizers who could obtain participation when no one else on a village level had that ability. Moreover, they provided the most readily available source of maintenance of new ideas, in this case wells, when the change agents neglected this final necessity. And it must be repeated that the ultimate requirement for the continuation of any new idea is that patterns of organizational and technical maintenance be established.

THERAVADA BUDDHISM:
A VEHICLE FOR TECHNICAL CHANGE *

ARTHUR NIEHOFF

Buddhism, particularly the southern variant (Theravada), has been consistently singled out by Western specialist-technicians as a resistance factor of primary importance, impeding the introduction of new ideas or techniques into the countries of Southeast Asia. The negative aspects of belief have been stressed almost exclusively.

* Reprinted from *Human Organization*, Summer, 1964, Vol. 23, No. 2, pp. 108-112, by permission of the publisher.

And although these do exist, they are probably no more important than the positive ones. In fact, there is adequate evidence that the attitudes stemming from Buddhist religious beliefs can be usefully employed to introduce change.

Probably most foreign aid technicians in the countries of Laos, Thailand, Cambodia and Burma have taken the attitude that the traditional religion, Theravada Buddhism, produces only negative influence on technical aid projects. This attitude is based on the belief that the religion is tradition-bound and thus resists change. I have heard comments expressed by technicians on many occasions that Buddhism in these countries keeps people satisfied with what they presently have and uninterested in improving their material circumstances. Such technicians often construe their role as that of trying to convince the local people to accept innovations, since it is believed that there is no felt need already existing.

It is widely believed that acceptance of the conditions of life as they exist is a product of Buddhist disinterest in earthly existence. This belief is based on the two doctrinal ideas that this world is unreal and that the worst evil man has to struggle against is his limitless desire, which in this world is incapable of being satisfied. In order to attain salvation, the individual must therefore disengage himself from the affairs of this world and concentrate on spiritual matters.

Now, although Buddhism may carry the idea of the importance of spirituality to a greater length than some other world religions, it must be agreed that all stress the primary importance of spiritual salvation. Christianity is no exception to this rule, the difference being one of degree only. And certainly the other two major religions of Asia, Islam and Hinduism, emphasize other worldly goals. However, I believe there is enough historical evidence to indicate that none of the religions has prevented their believers from striving for purely worldly goals on a scale as great or greater than that which occurred in Europe before the age of discovery and colonial expansion. Islam, with its doctrine of "kismet" (fate), was still capable of spreading its faith and profoundly influencing the lives of people from the Atlantic to the Pacific Oceans, in a secular as well as religious manner. Hindu and Buddhist peoples were capable of establishing impressive colonies throughout Southeast Asia, the most spectacular of which were Pagan in Burma, Borobadur in Indonesia, and Angkor Wat in Cambodia. Indeed, without the secular aggressiveness of the royalty, Buddhism might never have spread to the extent it did. It appears that the concepts of the ascetic or priest have had only a minimal influence on the everyday conduct of secular affairs, whether this influence was Christian, Muslim, Buddhist, or Hindu.

BARRIERS TO CHANGE

The question still remains though, *Why doesn't the modern Buddhist villager accept the changes offered by technicians faster than he does?*

I believe that in his day-to-day life the peasant is interested in improving himself, quite as much as a peasant of another religious faith, although perhaps less than a Western industrialized farmer. The main reason that he is not as enterprising as his Western counterpart can be explained more logically as being a result of limited possibilities. The Lao, Thai, Burmese and Cambodian peasant has been exploited and used by authoritarian rulers for so long, in conditions where true economic expansion was next to impossible, that he has developed an attitude of resignation and acceptance. Where this relationship is changing rapidly, notably in Thailand, the peasant is accepting innovations of a worldly sort very rapidly also.

The second basic objection of Western innovators toward Buddhism in these countries has been that so much wealth is spent for religious affairs and such a high percentage of able young men spend their best years as monks. It is true that a considerable amount of village wealth goes into the support of monks and their establishments and that many young men do spend time in service as monks. Furthermore, little can be done about this in countries where the official religion is Buddhism.

The second objection is less serious, I believe. The attitude toward service as a monk is changing rapidly. Even though every young man is supposed to spend some time in the *sangha* before assuming the duties of a householder, it has been estimated that no more than fifty per cent actually do nowadays in Thailand. The percentage in Laos would probably be smaller. However, the brotherhood still remains one of the most active in the world and probably will remain so for some time. But it is my thesis that rather than condemning this organization, the foreign innovator would do best to utilize it.

Secular leadership in Buddhist villages of Southeast Asia is weak. Ordinarily, there is a headman, either elected by the villagers themselves and then approved by the central government or else appointed directly by the government. Such a person is expected to help in the settlement of minor disputes in the village. The normal procedure in Laos is for the village chief to call a meeting when there is a dispute. The disputants call in the respected older men of the village for support. Evidence is presented, after which the village chief makes a pronouncement. However, the headman has no power of enforcement. If the disputants do not accept his verdict they take the dispute to higher authority, to the chief of district, *Tasseng,* or the chief of county, *Chau Muong.* The *Tasseng* has more authority than the headman and the *Chau Muong* is a government civil servant who in the village situation is quite powerful. The situation in Thailand is roughly the same. The headman, called *kamnan* serves only to settle minor disputes. Any criminal actions or land disputes are taken to the district officer, a government civil servant. Previously, it was the villagers themselves who were responsible for maintaining law and order in the village. What this means is that with the rise of national, centralized states the former village patterns of law enforcement and village authority have been replaced by modern police systems and authority based on Western models. The village headman is relatively impotent and there is no other secular authority on the village level who replaces him. Village level leadership is a basic problem in the operation of development projects on a community level, those which can utilize the labor of the peasants to fulfill their own needs without large scale investments. Schools, access roads, small dams, fish ponds, wells, small irrigation facilities, village markets, and drainage systems are some such projects which have been undertaken in this part of the world. In general they fall in the category of "community development."

One of the primary requisites for such projects is that they be done with the willing cooperation and understanding of the villagers themselves. In fact, community development has been considered as serving two purposes—to produce self-help projects on a village level and to assist in the process of building a national consciousness in the villagers. The process is believed to promote some measure of decision-making among the villagers who will then become a functioning part of the local government. One important difficulty that has been found in trying to implement such programs is that the village headman is often incapable of bringing his villagers into such programs and there is usually no one else of the lay community capable of doing it. The constant need in the community development program of Laos was to find capable leadership for such projects. And up until 1961 none was truly found. It is the thesis of this article that an important potential leadership group, that of the Buddhist monks, was ignored. And although the field data are from Laos, it is my belief that roughly the same conditions prevail in the other southern Buddhist countries.

THE ROLE OF THE BUDDHIST BROTHERHOOD

The Lao village is normally built around a *wat,* a pagoda compound, which serves as the one center of interest to all villagers. It would be similar to the situation which prevails among Latin American peasants in regard to the Catholic Church or to Muslims in regard to the mosque. The Buddhist monks are the most highly respected men in the village because of their dedication to religious work and also because of their assistance to villagers in religious affairs. They read horoscopes and conduct rituals for blessing the houses, for bringing rain, for counteracting evil spirits, for death rites, and for most of the other supernatural needs of villagers. The villagers support the monks, feeding them daily when they pass with their begging bowls, although also carrying food to the *wat* on special occasion. The villagers build and maintain the *wat* buildings, both with money and labor. They gather or make the materials needed for construction or provide the money needed to buy them. The highest act of merit a Buddhist can perform is to assist the local temple. Besides providing the construction material, the villagers usually provide the labor, which is done under the supervision of the monks. Buddhist temple buildings are almost always the best constructed and maintained in their villages. And there is no type of communal building in which the villagers are more interested.

A village self-help program was begun in Laos in 1959 in which there was very little supervision of projects undertaken. The program was operated on the basis of the villagers doing the labor and providing the material they could get, with the United States aid mission providing the material the villagers did not have, mainly cement, roofing materials, and metal hardware. The villagers selected their own projects although these had to be approved by members of the Lao ministry and their American counterparts. The program worked adequately until it was interrupted by political events in 1960. Several hundred village projects were carried out, including the construction of schools, dispensaries, irrigation canals, roads, markets, bridges, and dams. However, within six months of the beginning of the program it became apparent that roughly half the constructions were Buddhist *wat* buildings. Out of 114 inspected projects in the three southernmost provinces 61 were *wat* buildings. These included a type of meeting house, *salahongtham,* which is one of the buildings found in a *wat* compound but which is used by villagers generally, and the Buddhist religious school, *hocheck.*

By law the United States government is not allowed to engage in the construction of religious structures in its aid program on the assumption that this is not economic development. This policy is a reflection of the separation of church and state in American home government. For this and other political reasons it was decided that future self-help projects could not include religious structures. The *hocheck* and the *salahongtham* could be built with aid funds but not the *pagoda* itself. The important fact that emerges from this data is that, if left alone, most effort of a communal nature would be for the construction and maintenance of religious buildings. The most efficient organized cooperative group in the village is the Buddhist brotherhood. Not only can they organize their own people toward a given communal task (of a religious nature) but they can draw upon the resources of the community freely and successfully.

This organizational ability of the monks finds many avenues of expression. Young monks work regular hours, keeping the *wat* clean and actually repairing and constructing the buildings as a part of their discipline. They have efficient money-making schemes. When money is needed for religious purposes, the *wat* has recourse to religious fairs, *bouns,* which among other activities involve considerable gambling. The Lao are very fond of gambling, and attend the games most assiduously. Their liking for this sport is so great that the government took steps to halt it in 1961. One of the contributing factors in the government objection to gambling was that the local Chinese got in control of the games and of course made a large profit. Even gambling at the *wat bouns* was usually in the hands of the Chinese, who paid a percentage to the monks for the right to run the tables. Quite apart from the gambling though, the *wats* collected money or material for new buildings or special purposes by simple solicitation. Nowhere in the Lao village is there any system comparable to that of the *sangha* for collecting money.

Even if it were agreed that the Buddhist brotherhood is a highly developed organization, the objection of foreign technicians might still remain that it is too tradition-minded to be interested in new ideas. This attitude is far from certain. There are, it is true, many practices which indicate an interest in asceticism and other-worldly goals. Monks do not take food after noon each day, they do not take alcoholic drinks, they isolate themselves from women, they spend most of their creative energy in the learning of Buddhist ritual and Pali, and they wear special clothing to mark their monastic status. And yet there is much evidence that monks in Laos are quite interested in the changes taking place in the world around them. Although there are specific prohibitions like that against the taking of alcohol there are many modern practices which the monks have adopted. Smoking cigarettes is almost universal in the brotherhood, carbonated drinks are consumed freely, and the use of modern mechanical implements and gadgets is controlled only by the monks' ability to buy them. Modern methods of construction are brought into the *wat* as soon as they are practically available. The monks in Laos have adopted galvanized iron roofing widely to cover their temples, on the ground that it is cheaper than tile, and easier to install. Esthetically this has been disastrous to the appearance of the traditional *pagoda* but the monks, like other Lao, have ignored esthetics in favor of ease of installation and cheapness. In neighboring Thailand the use of galvanized roofing for *pagodas* became so widespread that the government made its use illegal.

Also in discussing traditionalism versus modernity it is significant that the desire for learning English is widespread among the monks. The two groups most interested in learning English in Laos were the Chinese merchants and the Lao monks. The Chinese were interested in learning the language primarily for business purposes. The monks wanted to learn it because it was a means of travel, both to the other Theravada Buddhist countries and to the English-speaking Western countries. Educated monks in Thailand, Burma and Ceylon speak English, so a knowledge of English by a Lao monk could mean the difference in getting a Buddhist scholarship. Moreover, many wanted to come to the United States, either as monks or after leaving the order.

A final point of interest concerning the monks is their involvement in politics as an indication of modernity and worldliness. The years 1959-1961 were a period of great political unrest in Laos, most of which time there was leftist guerrilla action. One constantly unknown factor was how much the monks were involved in actual political campaigning. There were incidents in South Laos where monks were caught in direct participation with the leftist party, the Pathet Lao. On one occasion a *wat* in Pakse distributed leaflets for this party in secret and in defiance of the civil authorities. At least one monk was defrocked as a result of this incident. It was also generally believed that the terrorists travelled throughout the country in the garb of monks, staying overnight at the *wats*. How many of these individuals were actual monks and how many were people merely using the costume for disguise was not known.

At the time of a coup d'état in Vientiane in August, 1960 the monks took direct political action. An army captain, Kong Le, staged a bloodless coup and established a neutralist government which, however, had at the time certain anti-American overtones. He attempted to get mass approval through public harangues and did get a certain part of the population stirred up enough so that they marched on the American compound shouting anti-American slogans. The processions which I witnessed were made up of a majority of monks, who marched in the forefront, throwing rocks and tearing down signs from the compound fence. After seeing such a sight it was impossible to accept the stereotype of Buddhist monks as being merely meditative, ascetic, religious scholars. It will be remembered that the man who assassinated the former prime minister of Ceylon, Bandaranaike, was a Theravada Buddhist monk.

WELLS THAT MOSTLY FAILED

A program of the American aid mission in introducing wells into villages and poor neighborhoods in and around the southern provincial town of Pakse provided some of the best evidence of the utility of involving monks in technical assistance programs. There were three separate programs to introduce wells, all of which ended in failure, although if they had been managed properly at least two of them probably could have been partially successful. The main difficulty was that the problem of responsibility for maintenance and repair was almost completely ignored. And it seems from analyzing what happened that the best group to have given this responsibility to would have been the Buddhist brotherhood. The first project was a group of seven wells dug in the town of Pakse in

1956 by the public works department, although with the advice and
financial assistance of the American aid mission. These were deep
wells and fairly expensive to construct. Most were made by dyna-
miting through layers of solid rock. They were placed in various
neighborhoods in the town where they could serve large groups of
people. There was a high demand for good water, since most people
had to carry it from the Mekong River or buy it from water car-
riers. However, no one was designated to be responsible for these
wells, and they were consequently regarded as government property.
By 1958, all were broken. The American aid advisor of the area
repaired them all in that year, but again not bothering about the
problem of designating responsibility. Before he left the country a
year later, some were broken again and in 1960 all were out of
order.

In 1959 two more well-drilling projects were undertaken in the
same area. One was experimental in nature and did not develop into
a useful technique. It consisted of a method of drilling shallow
wells by using hand equipment only, a drilling system which theoretically could be managed by village people themselves. Two wells
did produce water for a short time, although both dried up when
the water level dropped during the dry season. There was a lot of
publicity about this technique, however, and the idea spread that a
new easy method was available for bringing in water. For many
months afterward there was a procession of Buddhist monks to the
local American aid advisor requesting assistance to put wells on
their *wat* grounds. Unfortunately, all these people had to be turned
away because the system was unreliable. The point is that the
Buddhist monks were willing and able to organize parties to drill
wells and were the only rural people who took the initiative to do
this.

The third project was one in which a contract American well
driller came in to drill deep wells with a professional rig. His technique was to consult with the Lao officials to find out what villages
needed wells most, then go out with his rig and paid crew and put
them in. Technically there was no problem. He put in about fifteen
wells, but five of them were at government installations or at the
homes of Lao officials. In each of the other ten the villagers were
quite happy to get the wells and used them fully as long as they
were operating. Within a year, though, at least half of these village
wells were not operating. Usually, the breakage was minor and

could have been repaired in the local town but the government assumed no responsibility for this. The village people wanted the wells but no individuals assumed direct responsibility for them. Sometimes they made very crude attempts to keep the pumps going. The cast iron handles frequently broke and on one occasion when this happened some village people got together and put a wire on the end of the suction rod, attaching the other end to a pole about four feet long. Two women would put their shoulders under the two ends and do a kind of knee-bend exercise to raise and lower the rod, thus bringing up water.

Not only was there no organization to keep the wells maintained, but there was also no effort to keep the well areas in good condition. The villagers pumped water constantly while the pumps worked, some of them all day and night. They allowed the children to play with the handles and permitted excess water to fall on the ground where it created mudholes for the water buffalo and ducks to puddle in.

There were two exceptions. These were wells which had been put on *wat* grounds. These were not only maintained but improved upon. The grounds around them were kept neat and dry. The *wat* grounds were fenced off so animals could not wander about. Around one of them a concrete base about 20 feet in diameter had been built so excess water would not accumulate. On this same well one of the metal parts of the pump had broken, as it had on so many others. The monks, however, had duplicated this part in very hard wood, which surprisingly enough functioned quite satisfactorily. With these and all other wells located on *wat* grounds, the villagers were quite free to take water but they had to keep the grounds neat and clean, as *wat* grounds are always kept. Incidentally, the Buddhist *wat* is always the cleanest area found in any village, the young monks themselves sweeping it daily and keeping it in order. If village sanitation programs were embarked upon, there could be no better place to start than here.

HELP FROM THE BROTHERHOOD

Now, although many principles of introducing innovations into non-Western villages were violated in these programs, two of the most important were neglecting to get the participation of the recipients and neglecting to designate responsibility. No one was ever made responsible for these wells, except in a very perfunctory manner. Where this was done at all, the village headman was considered the leader. But the headman in a Lao village has a very limited control and cooperation from the villagers. Two other potential leader types could have been designated—the village schoolteacher or the Buddhist brotherhood. It is difficult to decide which would have been most appropriate because both have the respect of villagers, although for different reasons. The members of the Buddhist *wat* have certain advantages over the teacher. They are a group of men, most of them strong and well nourished, with a pattern of organization which is understood by villagers and which could be applied to innovations which the monks are interested in as much as are the villagers.

An additional motivation for the Buddhist layman to participate in projects backed or controlled by the monks is the positive value placed on ritual merit-making. There is no more laudable or beneficial action by the individual than effort in assisting the brotherhood in its ritual activities. By so doing the lay Buddhist obtains the approbation of his fellow villagers in this life and merit which will the leader. But the headman in a Lao village has a very limited common types of merit-making activities have been to support the monks physically by providing the necessities of their everyday life and to contribute to the construction and maintenance of the buildings and grounds used for ritual purposes. To build a new *pagoda* is perhaps the highest achievement to which a Buddhist layman can aspire. This, of course, is the reason why the self-help village improvement project described before was converted into a means for building or repairing *pagodas*.

The point is that a high value is placed on sacrifice entailing behavior which could be utilized in conjunction with the efficient organization existing in the priesthood. If the monks supported a project they could expect cooperation from the lay population and could moreover direct these efforts efficiently.

CONCLUSIONS

Other uses of the Buddhist brotherhood easily suggest themselves. They could be a focal point of village sanitation programs since they already keep their own establishments quite clean. Village drainage and refuse disposal system could be centered at the *wat*. The monks might be used in school construction programs. Formerly the *wat* school was the only one in the village. When Western-type governments were established, these *wat* schools were by-passed and the present government schools operate quite independently from the *wats*. However, there is no reason why combination schools for both religious training and secular schooling of the village children could not be constructed and maintained. In such a way the villagers could take advantage of the money-raising ability of the monks, as well as organize work parties more easily and efficiently for construction. There is indication that the monks themselves are interested in certain types of secular training, especially in English language training. It might be possible to construct schools that the villagers would use during the day and the monks at night, a time they favor for study anyway. Since American aid expressly forbids building religious structures one could not approve the construction or staffing of *pagodas* but schools, meeting houses, village wells, sanitation programs and other projects which require communal action could be managed with the direct participation of the monks.

The idea of strict separation of church and state is not so valid in countries where the secular ruler is the official protector of the faith. In the long run the secular government organization will probably become stronger and the need for such groups as the Buddhist monks will be less. But this will not happen for some time and until efficient secular leadership is provided at the village level it is probably sensible to utilize the already established organizations of the monks. The attitude of present technicians that monks are a quaint vestige of the past and should only be ignored is a product of the Westerners' cultural biases. New village projects should be undertaken either with the active participation of the monks or at least their approval.

18

Community Development
in Hong Kong

Our next two case histories take us into a distinctive culture area, China, where one of the most significant social characteristics is a penchant for formal organization. If Americans are the "organization men" of the West, the Chinese are the "organization men" of the East. It has long been recognized that practically no type of behavior exists which the Chinese have not incorporated into some organized group. Their traditional family and clan systems have been noted for their high degree of formally organized behavior. The governmental structure of China, both the old imperial system and the current Communist regime on the mainland, have been characterized by their elaborate organization. The Chinese have even been able to organize crime in their "triad" societies to an extent no other people have been able to achieve. Thus, it would seem that ideas of community development would fall on fertile soil among the Chinese.

It might appear to some readers that we are contradicting the view stated earlier about the lack of over-all co-operative tendencies among village people. We think that view still stands as a general charactericstic of most peoples, but it is probably least applicable to the Chinese. Moreover, a significant difference occurs in our two case histories on the Chinese, in that the social environment in both instances was urban and even industrial. We are no longer considering peasants but a people who are progressing visibly and already recognize themselves as a part of the world community. Although change can come more easily to these people, it must be recognized that new ideas will be resisted by the most advanced community in the world if no real benefits are recognized. Even in such ideal circumstances proper innovation techniques will have to be used.

In this instance we get a clear picture of the ideal role for the change agent to play—to establish effective communication in the initial stages and, as the project progresses, to move as rapidly as possible into the background. The most successful socioeconomic innovator is a galvanizer and no more. His project increases in strength in proportion to the amount of responsibility he is able to transfer to the recipients. In this effort, we note that the change agent was so scrupulous about his background role that he even refused to take steps to rid the newly formed groups of potential personal manipulators. The necessity for controlling them was put on the shoulders of the groups' leaders. This takes self-discipline on the part of the innovator, but the risk is worth taking if the effort is to become a part of the local social fabric.

By delegating responsibility rapidly to the leaders of a new organization, the problems of participation will largely take care of themselves. People will work for their own organization and leaders much quicker than for any outsider. Moreover, the local leaders have means of social control unavailable to an outsider.

Also, useful new ideas emerge easily in such circumstances. The initial idea of building a new welfare group on the foundation of the old *kaifong* association, a very fruitful kind of adaptation to the traditional culture, undoubtedly gave it much strength that it might not have had as a completely new kind of group. The final criterion for a successful project, maintenance, is automatically taken care of when people organize themselves so fully. And although the accomplishments in welfare activities were striking, from the point of view of successful innovation the most significant occurrence was the spread of the idea to other communities.

THE KAIFONG WELFARE ASSOCIATIONS *

J. C. McDOUALL and K. KEEN

The word kaifong is a Cantonese collective noun for the residents of a particular street or locality. Kaifong under one name or another are said to have been known in China for a very long time, and have existed in parts of Hong Kong throughout the Colony's history. At its best a kaifong was always something more than a chance collection of neighbours: it would have its own spontaneous leaders who for all practical purposes *were* the kaifong. These unofficial kaifong of old had very practical social responsibilities which included repairing bridges, mending roads, promoting educational facilities, providing free medical aid for the poor, and providing free coffin services for the destitute dead. Another undertaking was the organisation of holiday festivals on the anniversary of a locally venerated deity, and of processions to avert or diminish the effects of a disaster attributable to a god's negligence or anger. During the twenty years before the Pacific War the old kaifong in Hong Kong gradually died away. The Japanese occupation killed for good all but the remnants of one of them.

EARLY EFFORTS

At the beginning of 1949 the Social Welfare Office (S.W.O.) decided to try to encourage nearby residents to interest themselves personally in the work being done and in the people who attended at the Welfare Centres. If this were to succeed, the next step would be to build up a still wider local interest in all social problems affecting the neighbourhood. Clearly some kind of neighbourhood association might then be encouraged to play an active and constructive part in local social affairs. Though it was difficult to forecast the patterns which would most suit the different parts of modern urban

---

* Excerpts reprinted from *Community Development Bulletin,* Vol. VII, No. 1, December, 1955, pp. 2-9, by permission of the Community Development Clearing House, University of London, Institute of Education. Mr. McDouall has served in the Hong Kong Colonial Service for approximately 24 years and presently holds the position of Secretary for Chinese affairs. Mr. Keen worked with Mr. McDouall for 18 years in Hong Kong as a specialist in Chinese affairs, and retired as Director of Social Welfare for Hong Kong in 1958.

Hong Kong, there could be no question of blindly copying foreign community associations. Against this there was the common assumption that most of the residents of Hong Kong, of whom over 90 per cent were drawn from different districts in China, had come to the Colony merely to make a living or money for themselves, to seek asylum, or to take advantage of Hong Kong's social services. Their hearts would be with their families' homes. Alternatively, if local interest could be awakened, there were very real dangers of exploitation by triad societies or under-cover political agents.

In January 1949 the first attempt was made to enlist the interests of families and small shopkeepers living near the S.W.O. Welfare Centre in the Shamshuipo district of Kowloon. The attempt failed. A second approach was made, this time to include certain locally prominent Chinese from all parts of Shamshuipo which had an estimated population of 100,000. Some interest was kindled, and the first informal meeting was held in the Welfare Centre. It was then that the local Shamshuipo "representatives" suggested reviving the old term kaifong as a part of a new association's name. Throughout the spring and summer lengthy evening meetings were held, at which new plans, draft constitutions, often delicate questions of personalities, and other practical details were discussed over and over again. The Social Welfare Officer never took the chair after the first meeting. From the start the role of the S.W.O. was to encourage a healthy independence in this embryo Kaifong Welfare Association.

The work threw a heavy additional burden on the small staffs at the Welfare Centre. Even the coolies frequently and cheerfully stayed up working for long hours, sometimes as late as midnight, with no overtime pay or bonuses. The members of the Chinese public who were the founders of the Shamshuipo and later of other Kaifong Welfare Associations, put up an astonishing record of self-denial and hard work.

OBJECTIVES

In October 1949 the Shamshuipo Kaifong Welfare Association celebrated its inauguration. Its founders believed that the old kaifong and their traditions of public service were by no means forgotten. They were convinced that social welfare did not mean mere relief work or socially unprofitable "charity," but should include a whole network of constructive services designed to help people improve in practical ways their own welfare, and to maintain that improvement. They believed that these two sets of ideas, the one springing from the best traditions of the old kaifong and the other drawn from broad and constructive Western interpretations of social welfare, could be blended together. The whole emphasis was to be on practical interest and work by as many residents as possible for the welfare of their own community.

At the Inauguration Ceremony a general meeting of 500-600 people (the number rose to nearer 2,000 at a later Kaifong's inauguration) adopted the draft constitution with a few amendments and elected the appropriate committees and officers for a twelve-month term. Inevitably something fairly impressive was to be expected as a face-giving and enjoyable accompaniment to this inaugural meeting; the smallest Chinese club or society is always ready to celebrate even its annual general meetings by spending what to Westerners may seem far too much money and effort on obtaining suitable premises, on gay decorations and exhilarating fire-crackers, possibly on entertainments, and on light refreshments if no full dinner can be financed. The Shamshuipo Kaifong set the example for their kind of association by demonstrating their anxiety not to spend money on these essential but often expensive outward shows, when that money was so badly needed for constructive community welfare work. They solved the problem by holding the meeting in a suitably and gaily decorated school assembly hall (kindly lent free of charge by the chairman of the school's board of directors, who happened to be an energetic member of the new kaifong), by suggesting to a local bakery (also represented on the kaifong) that it should donate light refreshments only, and by having simple entertainments provided by local musicians and the flattered members of the local S.W.O. Welfare Centre's Children's Club.

CONSTITUTION

Another way in which the Shamshuipo Kaifong set a precedent was in the form of its constitution, which at the wish of the founder members was long and detailed. The S.W.O.'s part in the hours of debate and discussion spent on it was confined to suggesting alterations to parts of drafts which might be unfortunately misinterpreted by government officials or members of the public; as far as possible the Preparatory Committee was encouraged to make all the constructive suggestions.

In brief the main provisions of the final Chinese written constitution were:

(*a*) Full name of the association to be the Shamshuipo Kaifong Welfare Advancement Association.

(*b*) Object of the association to be to develop friendly neighbourliness and the spirit of mutual help, and to advance all welfare activities in the neighbourhood.

(*c*) Address to be, temporarily, c/o S.W.O. Shamshuipo Welfare Centre.

(*d*) Principal activities to include mass moral education, evening classes or schools for non-school children, vocational training especially for the unemployed, employment bureaux, public health campaigns, establishment of a public library, and charitable and public assistance work generally. (Note: later practical experience was to widen the scope of some of these aims and to shift the emphasis in others.)

(*e*) Membership of the association to be open to all "who live or work in factories, shops or houses in Shamshuipo, irrespective of nationality, sex, or age if over 20, if they are of good conduct with no bad habits, are of sound mind, are willing to to work faithfully and loyally for the welfare of the neighbourhood, agree to the Association's regulations, obey resolutions passed by the majority, and are introduced by two members," as well as being approved by the association's executive committee.

(*f*) Membership may be for life (one donation of $50), by firms (one donation of $10 and a yearly subscription of $10), or for individuals (one donation of $5 and a yearly subscription of $5). There is also provision for the receipt of additional voluntary donations, e.g. by wealthy members, should they be offered. (Note: there have been very considerable voluntary donations of this sort given in cash, kind and services in all the Kaifong Welfare Associations.)

(*g*) Supreme power to be vested in the members' General Meeting which ordinarily meets only once a year. Its principal duties at these yearly meetings are to pass or reject any proposed amendments to the constitution, to elect by secret ballot the executive and supervisory committees and principal officers for the forthcoming year, and to determine all general questions of policy and finance.

(*h*) The Executive Committee to be a comparatively large body elected for one year and which in its turn shall elect from itself the powerful Standing Executive Committee of twenty-one. (The Chairman of the Executive Committee is elected as such by the General Meeting and is *ex-officio* the Chairman of the Standing Executive Committee: he is the Association's principal official representative, spokesman and chief executive.)

(*i*) A Supervisory Committee of not more than 15 members to be elected for one year and to be responsible for checking all financial transactions and for enquiring into the faithfulness and zeal with which the Executive Committee carries out the Association's affairs. (Note: in practice, election to the Supervisory Committee usually means honourable recognition for elderly or exceptionally busy members who cannot be expected to serve more than once, if ever, on the Executive Committee, but whose advice and goodwill are valued.)

(*j*) Special provisions for the election, appointment or employment as the case may be for various Honorary Advisers or Officers, Vice-Chairman, a Treasurer, Secretaries, Clerks, and members or co-opted members of sub-committee.

(*k*) Receipt, care and expenditure of the Association's funds to be properly conducted in accordance with the regulations laid down in this constitution.

THE IDEA SPREADS

Four to five months before the Shamshuipo Kaifong Welfare Association was formally inaugurated, the Chinese Press had interested itself in this experiment, and had enthusiastically written it up as soon as it became apparent that other districts were beginning to follow Shamshuipo's example. Only the Communist Ta Kung Pao and Wen Wei Pao tended to ignore the whole matter, but even such reports as they carried for the next two years were meant to be objective and were never hostile. A few off-the-record conversations were held between senior members of S.W.O. and representatives of the Chinese press when the latter seemed to be getting on a dangerously wrong track; these never appeared in print, and as far as Chinese newspaper readers were concerned, all their information came either from the Kaifong Welfare Association's officers or from records of public speeches made at formal kaifong meetings. The English press on the whole remained silent, until 1950, and then started fairly full coverage.

By December 31, 1949, four Kaifong Welfare Associations had been formally inaugurated and six more urban ones were in an advanced stage of preparation. Tai Hang district's post-war Resident's Association had associated itself with kaifong welfare principles, and so had the hundred-year old Stanley Land and Sea Citizens' Association. The Social Welfare Office continued to try to keep as far as possible in the background, pursuing the same aims as it did during the Shamshuipo experiment. During the last quarter of 1949 Mr. C. N. Ei had to attend an average of 30 meetings a month, nearly all out of office hours, as well as taking part in many informal discussions; the Social Welfare Officer and certain other members of the Community Development Section also attended or assisted at large numbers of meetings. By March 1952 there were 18 fully established Kaifong Welfare Associations or similar bodies.

LATER INNOVATIONS

As already mentioned, the early history of the Shamshuipo Kaifong Welfare Association was not essentially different from that of any other new Kaifong Welfare Association. The principal later divergences and innovations, some of which were in turn adopted by Shamshuipo, were:

(a) It was never again necessary for the S.W.O. to take the lead in stirring up local interest, though in two districts it was involved in local antagonisms.

(b) In some districts there were long-established Chinese social or benevolent organisations whose leading members were not only anxious to devote themselves to kaifong work as well, but who also put some of the amenities and services of the existing organisations temporarily at the disposal of the new movement. This was especially useful in districts where there was no nearby S.W.O. Welfare Centre.

(c) The aims and objects and the approved principal activities set out in some constitutions were both wider and more detailed than Shamshuipo's.

(d) Appropriate measures were quietly taken to ensure the elimination of undesirable but powerful individuals who would bring discredit on an association, even if they did not set about manipulating it for their own ends. (Care was taken that the S.W.O. did not direct or demand the elimination of such people, for this would have implied an assumed power of direction of all an association's activities. This would, of course, have been a complete reversal of the fundamental S.W.O. policy of encouraging self-help and independence amongst these new Kaifong Welfare Associations.)

(e) In due course the women's side of kaifong activities were persistently encouraged by the S.W.O.

(f) Strenuous efforts were made for land to be made available on which each approved Kaifong Welfare Association could develop its own particular community centre suited in form and function to the needs of its district.

(g) At intervals of about two months the S.W.O. produced a Chinese "Kaifong Bulletin" containing some 50 or more pages of news, comments and information of special interest to Kaifong Welfare Associations and similar bodies. The small cost of producing this on a privately owned duplicating machine was at first borne by members of the S.W.O. staff; subsequently a generous cash donation disposed for the time being of all financial difficulties. The intention was that in due course the Kaifong Associations themselves should produce their own regular bulletins.

(h) A closer personal, as opposed to official, liaison was built up between the S.W.O. and certain key sections of the police force.

A list of all the achievements of these associations would take several pages. However, they can be summarized as follows: until March, 1952, a considerable amount of social welfare work was accomplished, including the operation of schools, provision of medical services, assistance to squatters, organization of ambulance brigades, sports teams, and sewing classes; from 1952 to 1955 they concentrated on three activities—increasing the numbers and membership of associations, extending medical and educational programs, and expanding the role of women. By 1955, there were 22 such associations and 277,760 members.

CONCLUSION

Kaifong Associations have indeed succeeded in winning the confidence and esteem of a large proportion of the local populace, 99 per cent of whom are Chinese. The Associations have chosen October 23rd to be observed each year as Kaifong Day. The first celebration of this event took place during 1954 and tens of thousands of local residents took part. Knowing the zeal of the kaifongs in carrying out their dedicated task of promoting the welfare of their communities, one can hardly expect public support to be less.

19

Family Planning in Taiwan

Remaining in the Chinese culture area, we turn to a type of innovation which is relatively new in international development, though it is one that will undoubtedly become more important very rapidly. Although those concerned with the developmental problems of the nonindustrialized world have paid lip service to the population explosion in the last decade, it is only very recently that they have taken practical steps to influence the situation. As a consequence of avoiding the problem previous to this time, there is little information on which to base such programs. Although we felt that this kind of effort was highly significant, it is pertinent that this case history is the only instance of family planning we could find that meets our conditions. There are some others, but they are few in comparison to accounts of efforts in agriculture, community development or health innovations. It is particularly significant that there are many studies on how to prevent deaths but so few on how to prevent births, the precise problem that has caused the tremendous world population increase of the last two decades.

But the following account is more than merely a case history of a unique kind of innovation; it illustrates many principles that are valid for all efforts to induce change in non-Western societies. We find here a very conscientious effort to know the community toward which the new ideas were aimed. Information was produced that belied many of the clichés of arm-chair planners. In particular, we learn that there was no requirement to stimulate any "need" for the new idea; it already existed. The people simply did not know how to solve the problem. There is no doubt that the Taiwanese are much more advanced than most of the populations toward which new ideas are aimed, but we believe that such felt needs exist even in less developed populations much more often than is believed.

Also, it is important to note that even though they were

dealing with a fairly sophisticated population, the innovators utilized to the fullest the techniques of communication. All the techniques that we have been able to identify were used. It will be remembered that we specified two different kinds of communication in our outline of the change process, that of communication from the innovators to the recipients and that of communication among the recipients which occurs spontaneously. This is one of the very few case histories in which the innovators clearly recognized the importance of this latter type and consciously tried to build it into their project. We believe this could and should be done more often. We have learned recently that the government of India has recognized this kind of influence in regard to their own family planning program and has talked of instituting a department of "gossipology" as the only effective way to get through to village women. Perhaps they have been influenced by what occurred in Taiwan.

Our final comment is that this case represents a new and very promising development in social science—experimentation in field situations with existing human organizations. If such techniques can be carried on in many spheres of human activity, there may be a possibility of learning as much about human social behavior as has been learned about human technology.

A STUDY IN FERTILITY CONTROL *

BERNARD BERELSON and RONALD FREEDMAN

It is widely recognized that in many parts of the world there is a "population problem": the high rate of increase in population makes social and economic development difficult if not impossible. Can anything be done about the problem? Practical means of fertility

* Reprinted with permission. Copyright © 1964 by *Scientific American*, Inc. All rights reserved. Available separately @ 20¢ as Offprint No. 621 from W. H. Freeman and Company, 660 Market Street, San Francisco, California. Dr. Berelson, a distinguished social scientist, is now Communications Research Director of the Population Council. Dr. Freedman is Professor of Sociology and Director of the Population Studies Center at the University of Michigan.

control are available to individual couples, but can the control of fertility actually be implemented on a large scale in the developing areas? This article will describe an experiment designed to find out what can be done in one of the world's most densely populated places: the island of Taiwan off the coast of mainland China.

Large-scale efforts to control fertility are, to be sure, not unknown. A number of governments have assumed the responsibility of providing their people with information and services on family planning, and some countries have organized major national programs. Lowering a birthrate is a novel objective for a government, however, and no country has yet managed to achieve widespread family limitation through a planned social effort. Current programs are therefore handicapped by a lack of information on attitudes toward fertility control and by a lack of experience with programs to implement family planning.

Since any change in birthrate depends on individual decisions by large numbers of husbands and wives, it is essential to know first of all how the people concerned feel about family size and limitation. Do they need to be motivated toward family planning? If they are so motivated, how can they best be helped to accomplish their aim? To investigate these questions the Taiwan study was inaugurated a year and a half ago under the sponsorship of the provincial health department of Taiwan with the support of the Population Council, a U.S. foundation that advances scientific training and study in population matters. The most significant preliminary finding is that the people do not need to be motivated. They want to plan their families, but they need to know how. Teaching them how —implementing a family-planning program—has proved to be feasible.

Taiwan has a population of about 12 million in an area of 14,000 square miles, and its population is increasing rapidly. In recent years mortality has fallen almost to Western levels: life expectancy is more than 60 years and the death rate is less than eight per 1,000 of population per year. The birthrate is about 37 per 1,000, so the rate of increase is almost 3 per cent per year, or enough to double the population in 25 years. Nevertheless, compared with other parts of Asia, Taiwan provides a favorable situation for the diffusion of family planning. The island is relatively urbanized and industrialized, the farmers are oriented toward a market economy, literacy and popular education are fairly wide-spread, there is a good transportation and communication system and a solid network of medical facilities. The standard of living is high for a population of this size in Asia outside of Japan. The society is highly organized. Women are not sharply subordinated and there are few religious or ideological objections to contraception.

The birthrate in Taiwan has been falling slowly since 1958. When fertility rates are analyzed by age group, it becomes apparent that they have decreased first and most for the older women of the childbearing population. This is exactly what one would expect if many women wanted to have a moderate number of children, had them with low mortality by the age of 30 and then tried to limit the size of their families in some way. The same pattern was observed earlier in a number of Western countries at the beginning of the declines in fertility that have tended to follow declines in mortality.

Although the situation in Taiwan was quite favorable for family planning and the birthrate trend had been downward, this was not to say that it would be a simple matter to accelerate the decline in fertility. As a first step in that effort the Population Studies centers in Taiwan and at the University of Michigan undertook a survey that would serve as a base line and also as a guide for a program of action. Between October, 1962, and January, 1963, public health nurses interviewed nearly 2,500 married women of the city of Taichung in the prime reproductive age group (ages 20 to 39) as to their attitudes toward family planning, their information about it and what they did about it. The survey made it clear that these women as a group wanted to have a moderate number of children, were having more children than they wanted, approved of the idea of family limitation and were trying—ineffectively—to limit the size of their families.

The number of children most of the women wanted was four, and women who had already borne more than that number acknowledged that they would have preferred fewer children. More than 90 per cent of Taichung's wives (and their husbands too, according to the wives) were favorably inclined toward limiting family size. They had few objections in principle, they saw the value of such limitation for the economic welfare of their families and they did not believe that the number of children should be left to "fate" or "providence." In this regard (and the same has been found to be true in other countries) their attitudes are more advanced than some officials believe them to be.

The women were in general poorly-informed about family-planning methods and indeed about the physiology of reproduction. About a fourth of them had employed some means of contraception, but in most cases only after four or five pregnancies and in many cases without success. The women expressed strong interest in learning and adopting better methods. And in their own minds family planning did not conflict with their traditional feelings about the Chinese family or its central role in their lives.

Experience with contraception or other methods of limiting family size was naturally most common in the "modernized" sectors of the population: the best-educated women, the most literate and those with an urban background. The women's actual and desired fertility were also related to these characteristics, but we found that on every educational level the average woman between 35 and 39, when childbearing is not yet over, had borne more children than she wanted. This was true even of groups in which substantial numbers of women had tried to limit the size of their families: contraception had arrived on the scene too late and was too ineffective to enable such women to attain their goals.

The survey data made it clear that the women had become aware of the decline of infant mortality in their community. This is an important perception, and one that does not follow automatically on the event. (Other surveys have shown that women sometimes perceive a decrease in infant mortality as an increase in births.) Because they recognized that more children were surviving, the women appreciated that, unlike their parents, they did not need to have five to seven children in order to see three or four survive to adulthood.

The salient message of the survey was that in Taichung people have more children than they want. There are indications that the same thing is true in many similar societies. It seems clear that if throughout the world unwanted children were not conceived, a large part of the "population problem" would disappear.

The next task was to facilitate the matching of behavior to attitude—to implement family planning. Several things were required beyond the mere wish to limit the number of children: information and knowledge, supplies and services, public acceptance and social support. To study how best to enable the people of Taiwan to do what they themselves said they wanted to do, the provincial health authorities undertook to develop a program of action to make the practice of family planning more readily available in the city of Taichung. This effort, we think, is one of the most extensive and elaborate social science experiments ever carried out in a natural setting.

Taichung has a population of about 300,000, including about 36,000 married women from 20 to 39 years old, of whom 60 per cent have had three or more children. Most of the people live in a central region of shops, offices and residences, but there are also rural areas within the city's administrative limits. A number of government health stations and hospital clinics provide focal points for the action program.

The city as a whole was exposed to only two aspects of the program: a general distribution of posters pointing out the advantages of family planning and a series of meetings with community leaders to inform them about the program, get their advice and enlist their support. That was the extent of the community-wide effort; the remainder of the program was designed as a differentiated experiment involving various kinds and degrees of effort. The objective was to learn how much family planning could be achieved at how much cost in money, personnel and time. To this end the local health authorities and a cooperating team from the U.S. devised four different "treatments," and applied one of them to each of the 2,389 *lin's,* or neighborhoods of 20 to 30 families, into which Taichung is divided. In order of increasing effort, the treatments were designated "Nothing," "Mail," "Everything (wives only)" and "Everything (wives and husbands)."

In the "Nothing" *lin's* there was no activity beyond the distribution of posters and the meetings with leaders. In the "Mail" *lin's* there was a direct-mail campaign addressed to two groups: newlywed couples and parents with two or more children. It was in the "Everything" neighborhoods that the major effort was made to increase family planning. The primary procedure was a personal visit to the home of every married woman from 20 to 39 years old by a specially trained staff of nurse-midwives. The fieldworkers made appointments for people at the health stations, provided contraceptive supplies, answered questions and did whatever else was necessary to satisfy a couple's desire for family-planning guidance. In half of the "Everything" *lin's* the visits were made to wives only; in the other half the visits were extended to both husbands and wives, who were seen either separately or together.

Rather than apply each of these treatments to a different part of the city, the investigators decided to arrange matters so as to test a central economic issue: How much "circulation effect" can one expect in a program of this kind? To what extent can one depend on the population itself to spread the desired innovation, and how large an initial effort is required to prime the process? There has been substantial testimony that word-of-mouth diffusion played a large role in spreading ideas about family planning in the West and Japan; any such effect would clearly be of major importance to national efforts in the underdeveloped countries, which must influence large numbers of people and do so with limited resources.

In order to investigate this question of "spread" it seemed advisable to apply the four treatments in different concentrations in different parts of the city. Taichung was divided into three sectors roughly equivalent in urban-rural distribution, socioecenomic status and fertility, and designated as areas of heavy, medium and light "density." In the heavy-density sector the two "Everything" treatments were administered to half of the *lin's,* in the medium sector to a third of them and in the light sector to a fifth. In each sector the remaining *lin's* were assigned equally to the "Nothing" and the "Mail" treatment groups. The *lin's* were assigned at random, although always in the proper proportion, and those designated for a particular treatment received exactly the same program regardless of their location in the city. They differed only in their environment; in the heavy-density sector, for example, "Nothing" *lin's* were much more closely surrounded by "Everything" *lin's* than were the "Nothing" neighborhoods in the two lighter-density sectors.

The program got under way in mid-February of 1963: the posters went up, meetings were held, 18 fieldworkers fanned out through the "Everything" *lin's* and the health stations prepared to receive inquiries. A set of educational materials was prepared for group and individual discussion, primarily visual aids dealing with the elementary facts about the physiology of reproduction, the reasons for practicing family planning and the major methods of contraception. The fieldworkers offered a wide choice of methods, encouraging couples to select whichever seemed most suitable: jelly, foam tablet, diaphragm, condom, rhythm, withdrawal, the oral pill and the new intra-uterine device. (The last is a recent development that holds great promise for mass programs to reduce fertility because it does not require continued supply, sustained motivation or repeated actions on the part of the user. A plastic ring or coil is inserted in the uterus by a physician and remains there; it is extremely effective as a contraceptive, although its mode of action is still unclear.) Contraceptive supplies were provided at or below cost, or free if necessary; the pills sold for the equivalent of 75 cents for a cycle of 20. The same charge was made for the insertion of an intra-uterine device.

By the end of June fieldworkers had visited each of the nearly 12,000 designated homes at least once and more than 500 neighborhood meetings had been held. Between then and the middle of October follow-up visits were made to women or couples who had indicated interest and to women who had been pregnant or had been nursing infants earlier in the year. A final phase began in late October and is still continuing; direct action has been terminated, but services and supplies are still available at the health stations, and the momentum of the program is continuing to have effect as of this writing.

There are three ways in which the effectiveness of the whole program will be measured. One is through case records kept for all couples who were visited in their homes or came to clinics as a result of the action program. The second is a before-and-after survey of a random sample of 2,432 women of childbearing age. The final story will be told in fertility statistics to be compiled eventually from the official register.

So far one result has emerged from the before-and-after survey, and it is a key measure of the outcome: at the end of 1962, 14.2 per cent of the women in the sample were pregnant, and at the end of 1963, 11.4 per cent were pregnant, a decline of about a fifth.

Aside from this one statistic, only the case records are available. Even for the people directly involved it is too early to measure the effect of the program on fertility; an immediate effect would take at least nine months to begin to show up! A presumptive effect, however, can be gauged from the record of "acceptances," defined as the insertion of an intra-uterine device or the receipt of instructions and the purchase of supplies for other methods, together with expressed intent to practice contraception. In the 13 months ending in mid-March of this year the action program was responsible for a total of 5,297 acceptances of family planning, 4,007 of which were from women living within Taichung proper. (The remainder came from outside the city even though no direct action was carried on there.)

How good is that record? There are different ways to appraise the figure of 4,000-odd acceptances within the city. First, the accepters constitute 11 per cent of the married women from 20 to 39. Not all the women in that age group, however, were "eligible" to accept family planning as a result of this program. About 16 per cent were already practicing contraception to their own satisfaction. Another 16 per cent had been sterilized or were believed to be sterile. Nine per cent were pregnant, 3 per cent lactating and 1 per cent experiencing menstrual irregularities of one kind or another. If these women are eliminated, only about 55 per cent of the 36,000 in the age group were "eligible." Of these 20,000 or so women, the porgram secured about 20 per cent as family planners. Included in that definition of eligibility, however, are women who actively want another child—young wives who have not completed their families or those who want a son. If they are considered not really eligible for contraception at this time, the "currently eligible" category is reduced to some 10,000 women, and those who have taken up contraception in the first 13 months come to about 40 per cent of this truly eligible population.

This arithmetic helps to define a "success" in the spread of family planning in the underdeveloped countries. At any given time somewhere between half and three-fourths of the target population is simply out of bounds for the purpose. If a program can get as many as a half—or even a third or a fourth—of the remaining group to begin practicing contraception within a few years, it has probably achieved a good deal. In this kind of work, then, having an impact on 10 per cent of the target population in a year or so is not a disappointing failure but a substantial success; one should report "Fully 10 per cent," not "Only 10 per cent"! Another way to appraise the Taichung results to date is to recognize that whereas in February, 1963, about 16 per cent of the married women from 20 to 39 were practicing contraception, by March of this year about 27 per cent were doing so, an increase of nearly 70 per cent.

The impact of such a program is not felt immediately or at one time or evenly. At the outset, the acceptance rate was remarkably constant, but after some seven weeks, when 40 per cent of the home visits had been made and word-of-mouth reports of the program were well established, the curve began to climb steadily. It hit a plateau in about four weeks and stayed there for about a month before declining. This was the height of the program, when two-thirds of the home visits had been completed and interest was strong. By the beginning of June, when nearly all the visits had been made, the cream had been skimmed: the women who were strongly motivated toward family planning had heard of the program and had decided what they would do about it. By the end of the summer follow-up visits were reaching less motivated women and the curve returned to its starting point. In the fall, when home visits ended but supplies and services were still available, the acceptances settled to a lower but steady rate.

A program of this kind, then, apparently starts off reasonably well, builds up quite rapidly and achieves roughly half of its first year's return within the first four months. The important thing is to develop a "critical mass" that can generate enough personal motivation and social support to carry on without further home visits. A poor country simply cannot afford visits to the entire population, so any realistic plan must rely heavily on personal and informal contacts from trusted sources; it may be that the job will have to be done by relatives, neighbors and friends or not at all. The task of a planned program will thus be to develop enough knowledgeable and convinced users of contraceptives to start a movement that reaches out to the ill-informed and unconvinced.

The indirect effects were extremely important in Taichung. The most dramatic indication is the fact that by the end of 1963 some 20 per cent of the acceptances had come from women who did not even live in the city. (That figure has since risen to almost 25 per cent.) Within the city about 60 per cent of the acceptances were from "Everything" *lin's;* the other 40 per cent were divided about equally between the "Nothing" and the "Mail" *lin's.* Even in the

"Everything" neighborhoods about a sixth of those who accepted contraceptives actually came forward before their scheduled home visits had been made. Direct home visits, in other words, accounted for only some 40 per cent of the acceptances by the end of December.

As for the effectiveness of various concentrations of effort, the proportion of those who accepted contraceptives was indeed higher in the heavy-density sector, but this effect was almost completely within the "Everything" *lin's* themselves. The indirect effect—the "rub-off" from the home-visit areas to the "Nothing" and "Mail" *lin's*—was remarkably constant in the three sectors. Our tentative conclusion is that the maximum return for minimum expenditure can be obtained with something less than the heavy-sector degree of concentration. Finally, the added effect of visiting husbands as well as wives was not worth the expense, perhaps because in this program the preferred contraceptive method was one involving the wife alone.

The nature of the contraceptive method, as a matter of fact, has more of an effect on the success of a program than may have been generally recognized. A "one-time" method requires far less field effort over a long term than a method dependent on resupply and sustained motivation. In Taichung the choice turned out to be overwhelmingly for the intra-uterine devices, which were preferred by 78 per cent of those who accepted contraceptives; 20 per cent selected one of the more traditional methods (mainly foam tablets or condoms) and 2 per cent chose the oral pill (which was, to be sure, the most expensive method). The women themselves, in other words, elected the "one-time" method. This was particularly significant in view of the method's high effectiveness and what might be called its "accountability" through scheduled medical follow-ups. The six-month checkup shows that only some 20 per cent of the devices have been removed or involuntarily expelled, whereas about 30 per cent of the women who chose the traditional methods are no longer practicing contraception regularly.

The Taichung study revealed another significant advantage of the intra-uterine device: a striking tendency for information about it to be disseminated indirectly by word of mouth, obviating much of the task of communication and persuasion. Nearly 75 per cent of the new devices were accepted without the necessity of a home visit, compared with only 15 per cent in the case of the traditional methods. The intra-uterine devices "sold" themselves; what the home visits did, in effect, was to secure acceptance of the traditional methods. Since last October, when the action program proper was terminated, more than half of those who have accepted contraceptives have come from a widening circle around the city, and almost all of these women have chosen the new devices. This is presumably what happens when word of the method reaches women who are ready for family planning but want an easier and "better" way than they have heard of before.

Family planning does not, of course, diffuse evenly among the different kinds of people in a community. Acceptance varies with education and age and—in Taichung at least—above all with number of children and number of sons. When couples in Taiwan have four children, they have all they want and they are ready to do something about it—if there is something available that is reasonably effective, inexpensive and easy to use. The evidence here is that whereas the slow long-term "natural" spread of contraception through a population reaches the better-educated people first, a deliberate and accelerated effort like the Taichung program can quickly have a major impact on the families that already have large numbers of children.

Taiwan is one of many low-income countries where rapid increases in population thwart economic development and threaten to slow further improvements in the standard of living. In the long run, to be sure, it seems likely that economic and social pressures combined with personal aspirations will lead individuals to limit their families. The underdeveloped countries, however, cannot wait for a long-term solution to their present crisis. The program in Taichung suggests that fertility control can be spread by a planned effort—not so easily or so fast as death control, but nevertheless substantially, in a short period of time and economically. (The cost of each acceptance was between $4 and $8, far below the eventual economic value of each prevented birth, which has been estimated as being between one and two times the annual per capita income.)

A good deal of the story in Taiwan remains to be told, of course, including the results of the sample survey and the critical check of official birth statistics over the next months and years.

Health agencies in Taiwan are now extending the program to a larger segment of the population, testing the Taichung results and trying out new approaches in the slum areas of cities and in poor fishing and mining villages. At this point one can at least say that fertility in Taiwan is changing and can be changed—changing over the long run as the result of unplanned social processes but, most significantly, changeable in the short run as the result of a planned effort to help people have the number of children they really want.

20

Village Improvement in
the Philippines

Although both of the case histories embodied in this chapter are of value in themselves, we believe the greatest benefit will be derived by the student of cultural change if they are read comparatively. We have no other accounts that go together so well in the sense that one shows dramatically how change can be accomplished while the other just as clearly indicates how change will not take place. Of particular value is the fact that both are in the same culture, both attempt to accomplish very similar goals, both utilize generally the same kind of change agent, both are sponsored by the same change agency, and yet their outcomes are completely different. In the first account (by Sibley) the project was almost a complete failure, whereas in the other (by Orata) almost all phases of the effort were achieved. Thus, we have a very good opportunity to examine in detail the particular differences that caused opposite results.

Probably the first aspect of both projects that should be considered is the type of change agents involved. In both they were schoolteachers, since the particular village development effort was sponsored by the national educational system. Sibley makes a strong case for the fact that local schoolteachers, though highly respected, are rarely regarded as technically competent in village agriculture. We believe that in general this is true and moreover, since village teachers are educated and relatively well-paid, they tend to exist in a different social world from the peasants among whom they work. The fact that they can take another role is dramatically illustrated by their actions in the village described by Orata. But it should be emphasized that a new type of leader has come into the village in the person of Orata himself. He is a person well-grounded in social science concepts, a man capable of disengaging himself from the customs and values of his own village upbringing to the extent of being able to take up a shovel and help dig the canal and the road. Of course, there are not enough Ph.D.'s in social science to go around to all the villages of the world. However, what is important to realize is that the concepts developed within the social sciences are capable of galvanizing village communities to productive action. This means that the schoolteacher can be a positive force for action, but only if he attempts to learn some of the principles that produce change and does not overextend himself technically.

There is a marked contrast in the two situations in the role of the young. Sibley points out the usual deference given to elders in Filipino village society and the difficulties of the young in influencing their elders. There is no doubt that in practically all peasant societies age is deferred to and that the ability of young people to influence their elders is limited. However, change is possible, if the young are willing to stay in the background and incorporate the traditional elderly leadership in any efforts rather than bypassing them as they did in the village described by Sibley. It has been noted by observer after observer that the young are much more prone to accept new ideas, which is of course a very real advantage for the change agent. But it has also been noted that the young frequently will attempt to shoulder their ideas through, treating the conservative elderly as archaic survivals. This is usually a mistake. For although the elderly may be more conservative and the society may be in the throes of change, the usual circumstances are that the elderly still wield real power. Therefore, the only practical choice, short of coercion, is for the young to attempt to influence the elderly and to involve them in the changes. Attempting to bypass them is much the same as attempting to bypass religious leaders.

Another significant difference in the two projects was the choice of projects. In the village described by Sibley the teachers had little interest in finding out what the villagers wanted, but rather attempted to impose the general goals of their agency. Unfortunately, they placed the heaviest emphasis on the most difficult projects that could be chosen: sanitation and public health. We have noted in other case histories that the idea of sanitary privies is very difficult to transfer, mainly because their benefits are not clear to anyone who lacks Western ideas of disease transmission. Many public health innovations have this quality. It is not that peasants cannot learn such concepts, but they cannot do so on the basis of a few months of casual contact. Therefore, to begin with sanitary innovations involves considerable risk of failure when other possibilities might succeed with much less effort. The resulting confidence can later be used for introducing the more complicated ideas of sanitation.

The project in the Orata village was different in this regard. All the innovations were based on problems which the villagers already recognized and for which there existed positive motivations to begin work. One project even provided a sanitary advantage—the irrigation–drainage canal—though to the villagers this was probably secondary to the benefits of fire prevention, greater food production, and making the road more passable. The stagnant pools were taken out incidentally, but nevertheless effectively.

Perhaps the over-all significant difference was in the fact that Orata understood the ways of the village people and took them seriously, whereas the well-meaning teachers in the other village thought that the old had to be replaced immediately and that the villagers could be manipulated in the desired direction. Orata adapted to local conditions instead of ignoring them. He involved all the local leaders, he used the need for individual status as a means of social control in the pigpen project, and he even adapted to the local land tenure system with its vested interests. His decision to make a crooked road that would satisfy the power interests instead of fighting for a straight one and alienating them was a masterly stroke of adaptation to local conditions, as well as good flexibility. His decision was based on the social realities of the village community, rather than on what was more desirable technically. Such a decision often has meant the difference between a goal at least partially achieved and a goal completely abandoned.

SOCIAL STRUCTURE AND PLANNED CHANGE: A CASE STUDY FROM THE PHILIPPINES *

WILLIS E. SIBLEY

This article reports a case in which governmentally planned changes in activities related to economic life and sanitation in a Philippine peasant agricultural village failed to meet the expectations of the initiators of the village improvement program. The failure of the initiators of change to recognize the internal structure and culture of the village seemed to contribute to the program's collapse.

Established by the Philippine Department of Education after the second World War, the Community School program of adult education and community development was designed to ameliorate levels of living in the thousands of small, rural Philippine villages. The program was instituted in response to a rural population steadily increasing in size, the serious effects of inflation in the period following the second World War, and declining agricultural productivity, all of which had, by the mid-1950's, intensified forces already leading to noticeably lowered levels of living even before the second World War. Field data utilized in this article were gathered in a village in southwestern Negros Island, central Philippines, during 1954 and 1955. The village shall be called Ma-ayo.

THE VILLAGE

Ma-ayo, a village of about 400 persons, is the principal village in a *barrio* bearing the same name. Culturally, the village is placed in the Bisayan zone of the Philippines. The population of Ma-ayo is quite homogeneous, nearly all nominally Catholic, and it subsists mainly upon piece-work wage labor in neighboring absentee-owned sugar fields and in tenant rice farming in nearby rainfall-watered paddies.

Kinship is reckoned bilaterally. In work teams, and in power groupings associated with community affairs, kin-based structures with some continuity in time are observable. Village endogamy is

* Reprinted from *Human Organization,* Winter, 1960, Vol. 19, No. 4, pp. 209-211, by permission of the publisher. Dr. Sibley, who spent several years studying village life in the Philippines, is Associate Professor of Anthropology at Washington State University.

marked. A 1954 census showed that in fifty percent of all marriages, both partners claimed Ma-ayo as their natal village. The necessity for approval by a large number of kinsmen of spouses brought in from other villages in cases of exogamous unions tends strongly to preserve basic beliefs and values shared in the community. Residence patterns tend toward bilocality at marriage, with neolocality as an ultimate goal. Initial residence choices for newly married couples are influenced strongly by the locus of available living space, and by the fact that most newly married couples cannot afford to fulfill the ideal neolocal pattern by building a house.

As in many nucleated Philippine villages in areas characterized by absentee land ownership and high tenancy rates, the raised bamboo and thatch houses in Ma-ayo are crowded cheek-by-jowl in the limited space which can be kept from agricultural use. Immediately around the houses are small groves of banana and coconut trees which provide important dietary supplements to the daily fare of fish and rice, but which are not important as cash crops. A few families possess small kitchen gardens. The village is neatly quartered by a village street running north and south, and by a narrow-gauge railway (connecting the village with the sugar milling center twenty miles distant) running east and west. This undoubtedly fortuitous, unplanned geographical subdividing of the village by the street and the railway assumes considerable significance in later sections of this report.

ESTABLISHMENT OF THE COMMUNITY SCHOOL PROGRAM

During 1953, the year immediately preceding my fieldwork in Ma-ayo, the six teachers of the elementary school established Community School development sections, or zones. These zones, called by the Tagalog term *purok,* or "little hamlet," were established not only in the main village of Ma-ayo, but also in the satellite hamlets or *sitios* within the geographical area of the *barrio.* Emphasis was placed upon the cleaning of paths and yards, the building of sanitary privies, and a reduction in the use of surface water for drinking and cooking purposes. The 1953 attempt at village improvement appears to have been a total failure, with the teachers suggesting that their efforts had been spread too thinly over too large an area to achieve satisfactory results.

In the latter months of 1954, the Community School program was reinstituted, this time only in the village of Ma-ayo itself. Apparently at the behest of higher officials of the program (I have been unable to find documentary evidence to prove the preceding surmise), an attempt was made to encourage competition in village improvement activities through the setting up of four named zones, or *puroks,* each with an elected President, Vice President, and Secretary-Treasurer.

These zone officers were promptly elected under the supervision of the teachers although, significantly, none of the officers chosen were of the established, observable leadership group in the village. In general, those chosen for zone officers were younger, had had more formal education, and were closer to the teachers socially than were the older established leaders in the village. A majority of the twelve zone officers were, in fact, unmarried, in a village in which marriage clearly is a mark of sociological maturity and a necessary condition for consideration as a fully adult member of the group. They may well be persons who will ultimately assume leadership roles in the community, but they had not gained such status in 1954.

Following the pattern of quadrangles already established by the existence of the village street and the sugar-mill railway mentioned above, the teachers designated these areas as the named zones for village improvement.

As in 1953, but limiting the scope of their activities to the village of Ma-ayo itself, the teachers initiated programs of street cleaning, yard maintenance and fence building, privy construction, well digging, house repair, animal inoculation, kitchen gardening, and agricultural improvement. Almost daily, the elementary school children could be seen pulling weeds from the street, carefully aligning rocks as street borders, and informing their parents that their yards should look neater. Periodic inspections of residences were conducted by the teachers, to count new water and privy facilities which were supposedly under construction, but which actually were rarely completed.

Despite a lack of noticeable progress on projects which might ultimately improve levels of living (such as better gardening or the inoculation of animals, vaccines for which were provided free of charge by the government), certain changes could be observed during the weeks immediately following the initiation of Community School programs. The village street was handsome indeed, with its neat borders and lack of weeds. Some houses were repaired, and their tiny yards put in order. Rarely, however, could substantial activity be observed in the absence of a teacher supervisor. Perhaps it was partly because of local disappointment at the failure of a widely heralded official inspection committee from the provincial capital to arrive for an evaluation inspection which led to the rapid loss of interest in community improvement, and to its virtual abandonment within about two months after the initial designation of improvement zones. Yet still more important reasons for the failure seem to exist, and attention is turned next to these.

THE STATUS AND ROLES OF TEACHERS

How do we account for the failure of the Community School program? Let us consider first the status and roles of the teacher group in this peasant village, since the teachers were the primary initiators of change.

Teachers are assigned a high status position in the village by virtue, at least in part, of their education and *relatively* high, steady incomes. They are accorded respect and deference behavior. The villagers do not, however, consider the teachers able to render competent advice concerning agriculture and animal husbandry because they do not plant rice or gardens, nor do they raise pigs and chickens. To some extent, the teachers behave as if they do not know the mechanics of rice planting or pig feeding. This "not knowing" role appears to be a part of their perception of themselves as teachers; for, with the acquisition of formal education and a college degree in this culture, very frequently manual labor is felt to be inappropriate, both by the formally educated person and by his associates and manual laboring acquaintances. Yet most of the teachers in Ma-ayo come from agricultural village backgrounds in which husbandry and planting techniques are learned by all growing youngsters. The villagers' perception that the teachers know nothing about agriculture or animal husbandry is an important part of their contribution to the maintenance of the role of teacher. It should be added here that reinforcing the villagers' reluctance to alter techniques of animal husbandry and rice planting are the facts of scarcity and risk. An ensured, although inadequate, rice crop, or a slender pig, are more highly valued than an uncertain but potentially larger harvest or product.

Socially, the teachers do not participate in gossip and joking sessions at the coconut wine stands after the day's work is finished.

Thus, the teachers stand apart. It is not unlikely that the teachers' relatively more frequent interaction with the younger members of the community at least indirectly influenced the election of younger persons rather than established village leaders as improvement zone officers.

More important even than the role of the agents of change in the outcome of this experiment are social structural considerations of a different nature. Work in Ma-ayo is often accomplished in parties of two or more persons, this pattern being strongly marked in the traditional practice of rice culture. Through actual counting and tabulation, it was found that the leaders of such parties for work in the paddies, in the sugar fields, in house building, and in other operations, tend strongly to choose kinsmen in preference to non-kinsmen as work partners. It has already been noted that residence in Ma-ayo is either bilocal or neolocal, with the choice of locale dependent largely upon the availability of space in or near the household of either the bride's or groom's parents. The net result of the juxtaposition of desire for working together, along with contemporary residence patterns, is that groups of persons (kinsmen) accustomed to working together often do not reside in contiguous living sites, or even in sites within the same sector of the village as marked by the street and the railway. By designating as operational zones the quarters of the village neatly arranged by the position of the street and railway, the teachers unknowingly ignored a more important principle of organization, namely, accustomed working partnerships.

The fact that the teachers did not tap the internal leadership group provides another possible reason for the failure of the program. Positions of leadership in Ma-ayo traditionally are not actively sought, but are rather imposed upon persons with qualifications, including pleasing personality characteristics, the existence in the village of a sizable kin group of potential followers, relative economic well-being, and seniority in age. In addition, the prospective leader must make at least a nominal show of religious participation, preferably Catholic. The latter statements express the general proposition that the leader must know and conform to existing systems of values and tradition. During 1954-55, there existed about six such leaders, each of whom had a consistent following in local affairs. The teachers did not succeed in convincing these men of the merits of the Community School program. The role of the "follower" is well developed in Ma-ayo, and in our stay in the village few instances could be recorded of collective action not preceded by the approval of one or more of these leaders. Those actually selected as officers in the improvement zones had the further serious disadvantage of youth, for the population of Ma-ayo forms a sub-society in which the principle of age respect provides a key to the understanding of many habitual patterns of behavior, authority, and decision making.

In closing this brief analysis, certain relevant features of the local culture are to be stressed. In the rural Philippines, and in Ma-ayo, there is a general lack of awareness of the relationships between sanitation and health. Thus, the sanitary privy and safe water programs seemed to many informants to be additional burdens involving extra work, the value of the projects not being clearly perceived. Similarly, there was little acceptance of the need for improvements in the traditional modes of agricultural practice and animal husbandry, despite patent and recognized inadequacies in the food supply. It should be added in defense of the rational powers of residents of Ma-ayo that drastic changes in rice grow-ing were avoided because of the potential risk as they saw it. One lost crop is to them far more disastrous than the insufficiency of an inadequate but sure crop. To be advised on rice growing and animal husbandry by teachers, who did not themselves partici-pate in such activities, was clearly laughable to a sizable proportion of the adult population. To be directed in village improvement by juniors in age, the elected zone officers, was improper and often insulting, for such direction necessarily ignored or seriously modi-fied traditional beliefs concerning age respect. The importance of age respect cannot safely be ignored in such cases, and it is not uncommon to find young people trained in government agricultural schools who are subsequently deeply discouraged when they return to their natal villages and are prevented from putting their new knowledge into practice. The young people are diffident in putting their new knowledge forward, and their elders are reluctant to accept their advice. It might be possible in such a situation for a young person to convince an elder leader of the value of his new skills and techniques, thus gaining the backing necessary for the initiation of changes. Such behavior was not, however, observed in Ma-ayo.

CONCLUSION

This case provides an example from a non-Western area to demonstrate the proposition that, for planned changes to be successful, they must be congruous with existing cultural beliefs (or at least not be in direct conflict with them) and must be presented in a manner which makes full use of existing social structural arrangements. It might have been better for the Community School authorities to initiate their programs by working on problems which were perceived as problems by the villagers themselves, even if they were of little interest to the initiators. That the villagers in Ma-ayo could, on occasion, organize themselves for collective action was amply demonstrated late in 1955 when several local leaders organized a large group of men who labored mightily for several weeks to rebuild the village street so that it would not be muddy during the rainy season and at fiesta time.

Since 1956, the Philippine government has developed a new program for rural community development, separate from the school system, which may eliminate some of the problems reflected in this paper. An attempt is being made to recruit, select, and train as local agents of change high status individuals who, after a period of training in a national center on Luzon Island, will return to their natal villages to initiate changes of various kinds. While it seems clear that structural features of local village organization are being given much more attention in the new program of training, the problem of age may remain a serious one. High status in the village ordinarily means that a man must be adult, preferably married, and reasonably well-to-do, at least in comparison with his village mates. Such men, of course, have the least motivation and interest in taking the risks involved in engaging in a new and little-tried venture. It is, however, still too early to assess the result of the new community development program.

COMMUNITY EDUCATION IN
RURAL PHILIPPINES *

PEDRO T. ORATA

Coming home to the Philippines on leave two and a half months ago, I found the country in a state of profound disturbance over a report on the conditions of living in the rural areas of the Philippines. As it turned out, there was nothing new at all in the report. Everyone knew that the rural folks were a neglected and exploited lot; that they bore the greatest burden in feeding the nation but were not getting a fair price for their crops; that they paid usurious interests to loan sharks who lived in towns and cities, that they were living in want, disease and ignorance; that everybody was talking about them but did nothing to help them; that their living conditions have remained practically the same while everything else, including the schools, have improved, and so on *ad infinitum*.

It is most gratifying that the village people are awakening to the fact that they, and they alone, can improve their lot. In my home town, Urdaneta, in Pangasinan, many villages are cleaner and more prosperous than the *poblacion,* thanks to the community school movement which has caught the imagination of the people of this province as no other movement has ever done before. In this article it is my purpose to describe a number of projects and activities, especially in the villages and on behalf of the village people, by the village people themselves, designed to improve the living conditions among themselves.

THE MENACE OF SELF-SUPPORTING PIGS

It is commonplace that no food production campaign can be successful if pigs and goats, not to mention other self-supporting animals, are let loose to destroy crops, to scatter waste, to make filth, and to spread disease. In our town, as in most places, the municipal council from time immemorial has passed ordinances carrying penalties for those who let their animals go astray. These ordinance in due course become a dead letter, for reasons known to everybody. What happens usually is this. The mayor and the mem-

* Excerpts from *Oversea Education*, April, 1954, pp. 3-10, by permission of the Controller of Her Britannic Majesty's Stationery Office. Dr. Orata has worked in education for over 30 years in the Philippines and in the United States. He is now an educational consultant of Dagupan Colleges.

bers of the council, as human beings, are influenced by human motives and incentives. They naturally do not want to offend the sensibilities of influential people who, regardless of ordinances, choose to let loose their pigs and use the town plaza and even school yards to pasture their goats, horses and buffaloes. One exception made invalidates the ordinance, the result being that nobody cares whether the ordinance exists at all.

In the villages, this is what happens. The rural policemen, who are supposed to enforce municipal ordinances, do not receive salaries from the government. At the end of each harvest season they go from house to house to ask for "donations" in rice and similar produce. If they are strict with law enforcement, most particularly the enforcement of the ordinance against loose pigs, the chances are that, since nearly everybody has one or more pigs, they be told "No mercy on pigs, no rice." So they, too, have to be "diplomatic," and as before, one exception is enough to break the whole scheme of regulating the ownership of pigs, goats, horses, chickens and other domestic pets.

What are we doing in regard to this problem?

First we tried this in Bactad, which we have since found successful. The Bactad elementary school appointed two squads of "special catchers of stray animals" among the larger boys, each squad being under a male teacher. I am myself a member of one of the squads. Mr. Segundino Obra, one of the teachers, is a member of the other squad. We receive our official appointment from the mayor of Urdaneta as "special catcher of stray animals," with the instruction to report to him from time to time "the results of operations."

Second, all the pupils of the schools, from the first grade up, are "informants," and have to report stray animals to the particular squad assigned to the zone. When the squad receives the information from any of the 400 pupils who act as "intelligence observers" for the whole village that a pig, goat, buffalo, or horse is found loose outside their own yard, they go to the spot—day or night— to catch the animal.

Third, the purpose of the project is educational more than to enforce law. When the offender appears to claim his animal, he is asked to read the ordinance, or the ordinance is read to him. He learns of the provisions of the ordinance, and he therefore begs to be given back his animal with the promise not to let it loose again. Before the squad allow him to take back his pig or goat, an enquiry is made as to why the animal was let loose in the first place. If it is found that the family cannot construct a pig pen because it lacks either the manpower or the material, or both, to do so, the squad volunteer to help them make the pig pen. The construction of the pig pen is then made a community project, to which the pupils and adults who wish to do so may contribute material and labour, in the sensible belief that it is more economical in the long run so to contribute than to suffer the consequences of loose animals. So far, there has been no second offence, and the response has been most successful. Parents no longer resist the operation of the ordinance because their own children enforce it, and they are themselves assisted in keeping their animals in suitable pig pens, the making of which has in some cases been made the concern of the whole community.

Fourth, the problem of loose pigs and other animals is presented to all the grades. The pupils are made to see evidences of destruction of plants and property, of fences, fishponds, and similar establishments, and to calculate the approximate amount, in pesos and centavos, of the damage caused by stray animals. They are made aware of the impossibility of raising good home gardens if animals are allowed to destroy them. They are led to become indignant and to report the presence of loose animals anywhere in the vicinity.

Fifth, the owners of pigs, goats and other animals, are being educated to see the value of the waste from such animals through the making of compost fertilisers. This is yet a new idea which may take time to penetrate the minds of the people, but it has positive possibilities which cannot be gainsaid. If and when the people begin to appreciate the value of waste products for their own vegetables and fruit trees, they will naturally want to keep their own animals at home so that they can put their waste to the compost pit in the backyard.

We have far to go in this, but it is reassuring to see other communities in Urdaneta following the lead of Bactad. The central school has already appointed eight squads, under male teachers, of the intermediate pupils to catch stray animals in different parts of the district. Many pigs have already been caught. The menace to themselves and to the community of stray animals is rubbed into the schoolchildren from the first grade up, through observation outside and discussion inside the classroom in connexion with social studies, arithmetic, reading and language, character education, health education and even geography and spelling, and of course, the national language. The children now do not hesitate to report to the special catchers the presence of loose animals in their neighbourhoods.

Going still further, the Urdaneta high school, a community high school, in a special project that will be described in another section, includes the making of pig pens by the high-school boys, who accept private orders for the construction of the same at a fixed wage plus the cost of material to build the pig pens. Also, from this year on, no student will be given his diploma who cannot show proof of having an adequate and well-built pig pen for pigs and corrals for other animals. Also, the district supervisor and principals and head teachers of elementary schools and the teachers themselves have adopted the Bactad plan of dealing with the problem of loose pigs and other stray animals. Furthermore, encouraged by the Bactad plan, the municipal council and the mayor have recently passed an ordinance requiring specifically that pens be constructed for pigs, which is a supplement to the existing ordinance requiring the tying-up of animals. The schools, both elementary and high, will help in the positive implementation of this ordinance by actually helping the home owners, with or without pay, in the construction of their pig pens.

We believe that ordinances are important, but they become dead letters unless they are positively implemented—unless the people are aided to carry them out through education and other means. When they see the value of controlling pigs and other animals, are assisted in the control, and realise what a good thing it is to be free from the menace, they will want to follow such ordinances and build pig pens and corrals for their animals. Only in this way, we believe, will the problems of loose pigs and other stray animals be solved, as it is indeed gradually being solved in Bactad and the district of Urdaneta. Positive practice at implementing an ordinance is worth more than a million ordinances themselves. Prevention is better than cure or enforcement, as the case may be.

FLOWING WATER: SANITATION, FIRE PREVENTION, FOOD PRODUCTION

For the first time water, clean and fresh water, flows through the road canals of Bactad, not only on one side but on both sides, in one section of the village. And what a joy to see the faces of men, women and children who expressed delight, happiness and relief when they saw the water flow. The first time everyone took to sprinkling the dusty street, and since then the large clouds of dust stirred up by the traffic no longer settle on the faces and hair and lungs of the people, or on plants and trees along the road. Also, the vegetables and fruit trees have become more vigorous as a result of being watered daily. The stagnant pools that used to disfigure the street sides are no more, and significantly indeed mosquitoes and flies are much fewer, fewer indeed than in the rest of the district and in other villages. If any fire starts in any house, there will be water ready to put it out, whereas before the people would have had to depend upon wells which are few and far between. In fact, the day before we left Bactad to go to Manila, a fire started in a lot in front of my sister's house, which was promptly put out with water from the canal.

Better sanitation, more effective fire protection and prevention, and greater food production—these are the results of the flowing water in Bactad, which has since been the subject of admiration and envy by people, including teachers, from other towns and villages who passed through or visited Bactad. Last week I visited the village of Bantug, in Asingan in this province, and there too was flowing water in a part of the village. As I passed through the street, the principal who took me round said to the persons we encountered: "This is Dr. Orata whom we have been expecting for many weeks and who was responsible for the flowing water in Bactad and, indirectly, our own flowing water." It was indeed a joy to see the people watch with pride their flowing water.

Inspired by this example, the students of the Urdaneta High School resolved to bring water to the high-school ground and farm. On Saturday morning, at seven o'clock, on 28 February, 105 seniors and junior (boys) and seven male teachers and I went to San Vicente, about one kilometre from the high school, to build a reversion dam, to raise the dykes on both sides of the canal to prevent the water from overflowing and destroying the bean crop in the adjoining fields, and to clear and deepen the irrigation canal to the high-school grounds. We worked for four hours, barefooted and in shorts and shirtsleeves. It was indeed refreshing to see the boys work joyfully and hard, no doubt partly because their teachers worked with them. I, myself, enjoyed using my own shovel from beginning to end. It was a real vacation from paper work!

Within the hour after the dam was constructed the water, in gushes, flowed through the canal to flood the high-school ground, thus disproving what was generally claimed, that the ground was too high to be irrigated. Once more, the stagnant water in the canal originating from the nearby artesian well was swept away and in place of it flowed clear, fresh water. As soon as the water started to flow the people along the road—men, women and children, all very happy—began to sprinkle the road. Fire—dare it come now!

Less than a week later, there was a move started to bring water into the district of Urdaneta. If it is possible to have water flow into Bactad and into the high-school ground, why cannot water from somewhere be made to flow into the canals in the district? Why not? Indeed it was possible, as was shortly afterwards shown when Mayor Sison, the district supervisor of Urdaneta, a few others and I went to make a survey on the spot where the water could be reverted by a dam in a nearby brook. When the news was known, without being asked to volunteer, three hundred students in the high school, central school, and Badipa elementary school raised their hands, saying: "I want to work, sir." The mayor promised to have the dam constructed in a short time, as there is pressure from the people to bring the water to the canals in the district to sweep away filthy and stagnant pools, to provide water to sprinkle the streets or put out fire, and to water vegetables and fruit trees.

The reader might think that bringing the water into Bactad and into the Urdaneta High School grounds was a simple, dictated activity, which it was not at all. As a matter of fact, there were certain steps to follow and considerations to take, as for instance:

1. Each project was educational through and through, as well as practical and economic. The importance of flowing water was brought out through observation, reading and discussion, before a survey was made of the possible source of water. The high-school students were led to realize the danger to the bean crops in the adjoining fields should the water overflow the dykes, and to accept the responsibility of raising the dyke on both sides of the canal to a requisite height, of seeing to it that holes in the dyke were filled, and of taking further steps to follow up their initial work continuously from then on.

2. The students were made to feel the responsibility of using the water to irrigate, to sprinkle the streets, and to put out fires, and the teachers, once again, saw to it that their resolutions were carried over into appropriate action. There have to be constant reminders,

but even in arithmetic there have to be frequent drills with flash cards and on the blackboard. They were also made to realize that the water is public property and no one, even students, can have a monopoly of it.

3. The participation of adults was secured in each case, since it was clear that it was the joint concern of all the people that water should flow freely into the community.

4. The project was related functionally with lessons in science, in arithmetic, in geography, in physics (water seeks its own level), in economics, in art and literature (the beauty and freshness of flowing water), in horticulture, in piggery and poultry raising, in home economics, not to name the other subjects, including health and character education.

Once again it has been proved that students in elementary and high schools are alert and responsive to the call of duty to serve their community if they see the urgent need of their acting so to serve. We had read rumours allegedly emanating from private school students making fun of the public school pupils and students, calling them "the road gang," but we paid no attention at all, and indeed, we went right ahead. We did not, however, compel the students to work. We asked for volunteers in every case, and the response, while not unanimous, was greater than we had expected. I believe private school staffs and students will soon realise the value of running water and come to accept their personal responsibility to help bring it to the road borders.

VILLAGE PEOPLE BUILD A FEEDER ROAD

Every year, from time immemorial, there has been a proposal to build a road from the hamlets of Sogcong, Portugal and Timbogan to the main (provincial) road in Bactad. In these hamlets reside 68 families and 40 schoolchildren who attend the Bactad elementary school. During the rainy season it is most difficult to come to Bactad over rice paddies, and even during the dry season the people have to carry on their heads heavy loads of vegetables or fish to sell in Bactad or in the town market. Many school-children are forced to be absent during the rainy months, and it is not infrequent that pupils who get wet before reaching the school have to be advised to go home in order to put on dry clothes. When rice is planted and until after harvest it is impossible to get animals into or out of Bactad as all ways are closed. This and similar difficulties are suffered by the people of Bactad as well for lack of a feeder road.

When I arrived in December, the first thing I was asked to do was to help secure the right of way from the owners of lots that might be crossed by a road from Bactad to the hamlets named above. It was explained to me that the year before a road had been started, but it could not be continued because one of the owners of the lots that were affected said: "The road will be built over my dead body." One other owner objected also, on the ground that his lot was to be divided and that he would be forced to give up quite a bit of land, besides having to incur expenses for a new survey to be made after the road was constructed, and for the purchase of two new titles.

We then started on a new site. All went well, and in fact we started to mark the places where the ground was to be broken. All of a sudden the very leader who wanted the road to pass through his zone objected because his land was affected. He also tried, successfully, to influence others who had already agreed verbally to withdraw their approval. Once again, one of the persons affected threatened: "Over my dead body." We could have gone through this by using the method of expropriation, but it would take time, whereas we aimed to have the road completed by the first of June before the rainy season starts. Besides, the Mayor of Urdaneta had promised us sand and gravel for the road provided it could be completed in that time.

That was three weeks ago. We were about to give up when a new thought occurred to us. We had always aimed at a straight road, and always there were lots that had to be cut through at the middle. We decided to avoid this by making the road pass along the boundaries between two or more lots. This would avoid crossing any lot at the middle, and it would also mean that no owner would be forced to give more than half the road space, namely three metres. We made a new plan, but this time it meant a very crooked road. However, we figured out that a crooked road was better than no road. We then went ahead to get the right of way for the new proposed road. We did succeed in every case except one. Again, our perennial objector set out to obstruct our activities. This time, since he was not affected, he tried to influence the people from Sogcong, Portugal and Timbogan who had promised to build the road, to object to the proposed road on the ground that it was "too crooked."

I then learnt that there were politics in the whole thing. Our perennial objector belonged to the party opposed to that of the Mayor, and so he and others in his party decided to do everything they could to obstruct the project on the ground that if successful it would be credited to the Mayor. Right there and then I gave up and said nothing more for a few days, and did not even talk to anyone interested in the road. Whereupon the principal of the Bactad elementary school, Mr. Isidro Bravo, thought of verifying the rumour that the ones building the road objected, by sending a letter requesting each one to say "Yes" or "No" to the question: "Would you be willing to work on the road as proposed at present even though it be crooked?" This manoeuvre proved to be a device to save everybody's face. It gave a chance for the people to vote. Mr. Bravo very wisely started with persons who were certain to vote in favour of the new plan. As it turned out, to the surprise of everybody, there was not a single "No" in the replies to the questionnaire. Before the questionnaire was circulated it was known that I was no longer interested, and as everyone believed, including the Mayor, who had tried in the last five years to get the road constructed, that if we failed this time, as one leader put it: "This will be the last."

The road was actually started one Monday morning, and the workers have been at it, three times a week, on Mondays, Wednesdays and Fridays. As it looks now, the road will be built. The people are enthusiastic and they work hard at it. I was there helping them yesterday, and they were in very good spirits and we exchanged jokes. I worked for three hours doing what they were doing—shovelling and breaking the earth—and they seemed pleased to see that I had not forgotten how to use the shovel.

Again, the procedure was not all that it might seem, namely to talk people into agreeing to give us the right of way. Following are some of the steps that were taken.

1. All zone chiefs (six altogether) agreed on the proposal in our first conference just after my arrival. The matter of road building, its importance to the people and to the pupils themselves,

was the subject of discussion in the different classes in the Bactad school. This was to get the pupils to influence their parents to help in the construction of the road.

2. We had a meeting with the people of Sogcong, Portugal and Timbogan one evening at which we told them that we would be willing to work for the construction of the road provided that they would agree, not only to build it, but also to install in their yards the following—which most of them did not have: sanitary latrines, dry *pagbabasaan* (blind drainage under the kitchen), compost pits, and pig pens. We reasoned out that the purpose of the road was to enable them to market their products, to improve standards of living, to enable doctors and nurses to visit them when they got sick, and to make it easier for the children to come to school. But unless they also helped themselves by putting their pigs in corrals, providing sanitary facilities, conserving waste for fertilizers, and seeing that the children did not get sick often, the road would be of little help to them. This was our chance to explain the value of the health and security measures that was uppermost in our minds in order to help them most, and we decided to match the privileges that they asked for with the corresponding responsibilities which we believed it was to their own interest to accept and do something about. They agreed, after a long discussion, and a date was set aside to visit them in order to check on what they did in implementation of their promise. The visit was made, and even though the result was far from 100 per cent, the committee was satisfied that they had made a significant effort to carry out their agreement. We suggested that they continue improving, and we saw they were in earnest. I might say that at the time of the visit many of them were still at work threshing their rice, and we thought this was sufficient reason for a number of them not doing all that they had agreed to.

3. The schoolchildren were asked if they were willing to help in the construction of the road according to their physical ability to do so. Even first-grade pupils could carry half a pound or kilo of earth to place on the "roadbed," and nearly 400 pupils could do a great deal if they did nothing but this. The point is that we wanted them to have a part in the making of the road so that they will later appreciate and take good care of it, and not do anything to damage it. Of course every little thing would help, and one or two hours a week in lieu of physical education at an appropriate hour

—not too hot—would not be detrimental to their health, and it would certainly add to their moral character. This turned out to be a good thing to do, following the example of Indian schools.

RETROSPECT AND PROSPECTS

I shall confine myself here to a few principles basic to our work.

1. The only way to start is to start, and the place to start is right here with what little we have and with even a minus quantity. In every case we did not wait for experts to come, or for money to be appropriated, or for certain things to be done. Had we waited, we would still be waiting. Our only capital was ourselves, our health, our determination to succeed, and of course our own resources—land, artesian well, canals, some shovels, and good humour. We did not have any budget. We studied our needs, made plans, and went ahead the best we could to achieve our objectives.

2. There was sufficient local talent to guide us. Our Mayor was easily the best-resource person who, most fortunately, was interested in the same things as we, namely, in the improvement of Urdaneta and its many barrios. His pet projects are peace and order, food production, road construction, and irrigation. Then, there is Mr. Isidro Bravo, principal of the Bactad elementary school, whose knowledge about food production is tremendous and varied and who exemplifies his theories in his own yard. Mr. Isidro Fabia, principal of the Urdaneta high school, never wavered in his determination to give his 1,000 boys and girls a chance to work and earn money. The teachers of Bactad, of the high school, and in the central school of Urdaneta co-operated with us whole-heartedly in both word and deed. This does not mean that we did not utilise outside help such, for instance, as the three instructors from the Central Luzon Agricultural College.

3. Schoolchildren and high-school students may be relied upon to render community service, be it digging ditches, constructing latrines and compost pits, or catching pigs. They know that their communities leave many things to be desired in sanitation, in food, in leadership, and given a chance they would, as did those in the elementary and high schools on many occasions. Some of us were afraid of criticism emanating, it was claimed, from the private schools, but the words of encouragement from officials, parents, and the schoolchildren and students themselves were more than we

could have anticipated. There need be no fear so long as one was rendering useful service, and we saw nothing trite or dangerous in causing water to flow over stagnant pools, irrigating a dry farm, building a road, making fish-ponds to take the place of open toilets, giving students a chance to earn their tuition fees, constructing sanitary latrines, blind drainage, compost pits, and pig pens, or even catching stray animals and later helping the owners to build corrals for them. There has been no adverse criticism of any kind that has come to my attention directly or indirectly.

4. We found the educational and positive approach most effective and satisfactory. Heretofore, the only approach to the problem of hygiene and sanitation has been through ordinances and community lectures. The head of the sanitary division of Urdaneta has been here twenty-six years, and he has long given up in despair. We found the district and the villages filthy—they still are—but at last sanitary latrines are being constructed, stagnant pools being drained or swept away by flowing water, and drainage systems under the kitchens being installed. We heard this remark from one private citizen: "The happiest person among us is the president of the sanitary division. The things which he has been advocating in his last twenty-six years that he has been in Urdaneta are being done at last." No one chooses to be without a latrine or to get along with one that smells bad if he can help it. We provided a service to build such latrines, and people are making use of the service. One person told me this: "I could have done these things before, but whom could I have relied upon to do them? I do not know myself how to construct a latrine or to drain our *pagbabasaan,* and I do not have the time even if I knew how, but now that the high-school boys can do them for me at so cheap a price, why I would indeed be a fool if I did not ask for the service."

5. Community health is everybody's business. If the people in the next lot use the open spaces near the fence as their latrine, that is the business of the people in the neighbourhood if not in the whole community to take notice and do something helpful about it. Or, if there are loose pigs roaming around, we must not wait for the policeman to catch them. Again, if a family cannot dig the canal in front of their house, we could not fold our hands and wait until they do if we want the water to flow freely. We have adopted the policy that we should, as a community, or as groups of individuals, do something to help construct latrines, to catch pigs, to

dig canals, or build dams with or without pay. We would even contribute material and labour, as indeed we did, to do these things for persons who need our assistance, in the belief that it would be far more expensive in the long run to let well enough alone.

6. We have proved once more that the longest way round is the shortest way to the goal. Year after year Bactad has wanted a straight road which it did not get, now it is finally going to get a crooked one which is nevertheless going to be a road. In other ways we have applied this principle and found it sound. For instance, we chose a round-about way to bring the water to the high-school ground. We could have chosen another way which would have required one-tenth the time and effort spent upon it. But, the shorter way would have given us only water—whereas the longer way— because it passed through a road with houses on the sides—gave us water to sprinkle the road and plants and put out a fire, and further-more, it swept away the ugly and filthy stagnant water that resulted from the use of the artesian well near the high-school building.

7. We tried, in every situation, to live by the principle that a good leader must be a good follower. There is not a single activity in which we, the leaders, acted in the capacity of overseers. When there was digging to do, we had our own shovels and used them. The leader must be willing and able to do what he asks his follow-ers to do. He must live among them and with the problems. I stayed in the village most of the time, going to town only when I needed to work in the high school. In the same way, our Mayor, our prin-cipals and teachers and adult leaders—they all tried to exemplify in what they did and the way they did it this kind of leadership.

8. We believe that the surest and most effective way to kill a project is premature publicity. We declined requests to be visited. Individuals, groups, even whole schools or classes wanted to come to "see your wonderful project." We replied saying that there was nothing wonderful about it. "We are just beginning," we told them. We shunned picture-taking as a rule, and did not invite newspaper men. Truthfully, there is nothing unusual, much less spectacular, in Bactad or the high school. We have far to go.

21

A Literacy Campaign
in Sarawak

Although it is inevitable that the great majority of induced change efforts for the nonindustrialized world will begin in the offices and planning rooms of "experts," such a procedure does create a major difficulty. No people will undertake an unaccustomed task of their own volition unless they are positively motivated to do so, and this will occur only when they obtain some advantage for their efforts. The difficulty which arises with planning specialists is that they frequently do not understand the motivations that they themselves would have if approached with such new ideas. It has often seemed to us that if by some magic one could include a day in the training period of the development adviser in which he not only lived the life of a peasant but also had his thoughts, ninety per cent of the development problems would disappear. Unfortunately, this cannot be done. The most that can be done is to impress upon the innovator the need to try to understand how the peasant would consider the new idea.

What we are trying to point out here is that if strong positive motivations exist for a new idea, almost all other problems become insignificant. This is clearly indicated in the following case history, where the desire for literacy was so strong that once the initial idea was planted the innovator could not satisfy the recipients fast enough. They took matters into their own hands to learn to read and write more quickly. Of course, it should be mentioned that literacy is widely recognized in the non-Western world as a skill of great value and a "hard-sell" job is rarely needed. It is particularly significant that this is true even with tribal people, like the Dyak in this instance. But what is most important to recognize from the this case history is the considerable effort made by the change agent to be sure that the local people really did have such a positive motivation, even if he may have known that literacy in general is desired. Too often, change agents consider the problem of motivation much too lightly, once they have decided that a particular kind of innovation will benefit the local people. That the local people may not see such a benefit is given little thought.

It is worth noting, also, that this change agent saw the tribal recipients as eminently rational people who could see an advantage clearly when offered. The so-called "irrational" behavior which less successful innovators attribute to potential recipients of new ideas when co-operation does not occur is usually a result of a lack of understanding the frame of reference of the local people. Many new ideas proposed by Westerners or their local counterparts are not clearly advantageous to the individual recipients. Family planning is not a perceived advantage to parents who have lost half their children in infancy and can expect to lose more.

This change agent believed so much in the necessity of full participation and involvement of the recipients that he offered no rewards of any kind. The participants paid for their own teachers and their own books. This was self help of the most pristine kind. It is obviously the most desirable kind, although it must be freely admitted that it works only when a very high level of motivation exists. Rewards in the form of material assistance and subsidies are, of course, more common in government-sponsored programs. Though they maye be needed to fill the motivation gap which more normally exists, there is always the danger that the participants will cease their efforts once the rewards stop.

The one significant negative note in this effort is frequently found in literacy campaigns: a great shortage of books. As we have indicated before, no new idea can truly be considered as transferred to another people unless patterns for maintaining it have been established. Lack of providing reading material is a common difficulty in literacy campaigns. The knowledge of reading fades rapidly if there is no way to keep up the practice.

PILOT LITERACY SCHEME
IN THE ULU PAKU, SARAWAK *

ROBERT NICHOLL

THE GENESIS OF THE SCHEME

In February 1949 the committee which had been set up to advise the Government on adult education submitted a scheme for a pilot literacy scheme to be carried out in the Ulu Paku during the first half of 1950.

THE CHOICE OF THE AREA

Several factors combined to suggest the Ulu Paku as a fruitful field for experiment in adult literacy. In the first place, there was already a positive demand for some form of adult literacy campaign. This had been encountered by the registrar of co-operative societies in the course of his work in the river, and whilst it came principally from members of the rapidly growing co-operatives, it was symptomatic of an attitude more widely adopted.

The Sea Dayaks of the Saribas have for long been regarded as the most progressive members of their race, and the rapid development of co-operative societies in their midst during the past year is an example of their receptivity to new ideas. Such a community stands most to benefit from a literacy campaign, for literacy is but one means to the broader end of community development.

Finally, the Saribas possess a certain strategic importance in the Dayak world, for from here emigrants have gone out to colonise various other rivers in Sarawak. The links between these colonies and the "mother country" are strong, so that developments in the latter might be expected to produce reactions in the former, and the effects of a literacy campaign here might well be felt over a wider area.

* Excerpts reprinted from *Oversea Education*, July, 1951, pp. 141-152, by permission of the Controller of Her Britannic Majesty's Stationery Office. Mr. Nicholl served as an administrative and education officer in Sarawak for about 19 years, with particular responsibility for the organization of adult literacy campaigns, youth clubs, and adult classes in community services.

THE APPROACH

In planning this literacy campaign the basic principle was that of self-help. To carry out such an operation is possible only if the people themselves desire it, and are prepared to co-operate actively. As a preliminary, therefore, we made two visits to the area in order to gauge as far as possible how effective the demand for literacy was likely to be.

With this end in view we held discussions in most of the houses, in which the matter was debated at length. We did not urge the need for literacy, but discussed the subject in general terms, leaving it to the people themselves to say whether they really thought it desirable or not. Although we knew that there was much interest in literacy for adults, we were not prepared to undertake anything except at the express invitation of the people themselves. This principle was observed throughout the operation; we taught only in houses to which the people had offered their help.

This was a matter of major importance. We had to make it clear from the outset that the campaign was not a form of mass government schooling; there was no question of Government providing teachers or equipment: indeed, it was not a government undertaking at all. We pointed out that there were only two of us, my assistant, Mr. Charles Ensir, and I; and if the people cared to tackle the problem of adult literacy themselves, we were ready to advise and assist, but could not do more. From first to last the operation was one of self-help springing spontaneously from the people and not a movement foisted on them from without.

In order to ensure this essential element of spontaneity our initial approach was exceedingly cautious. All emotional appeals and all forms of revivalism were rigorously avoided. Such approaches have been used with success elsewhere, but here they were completely out of place. It is my impression that the Sea Dayak are a hard-headed people, rather akin in temperament to the Lowlands Scot. With such people an emotional appeal achieves little; the rational approach stands more chance of success, for once they are convinced that a thing is to their advantage, more especially for their economic advantage, they can be exceedingly tenacious in its pursuit. This was, indeed, admirably verified by the course of events.

In some campaigns certificates of literacy and badges of proficiency have been issued. All these, however, we eschewed. The argument for literacy was, that it was the normal accomplishment of the progressive adult, and as such would bring its own reward, thus rendering these things superfluous. Further, there is the danger that the credulous may attach to such certificates a value which they do not possess, and by trying to use them, for instance as a substitute for school certificates, bring them into ridicule and disrepute.

A literacy campaign demands enthusiasm, but enthusiasm of a persevering sort, such as will carry people through the toils of learning, which cannot but be discouraging in the beginner. But a heady emotionalism will not prove a sufficient dynamic for so serious an undertaking.

THE SEASON OF OPERATIONS

One of the postulates of a literacy campaign is that the greater part of the population should be living at home whilst it is in progress. In consequence the timing of such a venture will be governed by the farming season, whenever this involves a migration away from the long-house.

In some Dayak areas, of which the Ulu Layar may be cited as an example, the farm lies close at hand, and agricultural operations entail no disruption of community life; people go out to farm during the day and return at night to the long-house. But the people of the Ulu Paku, with an eye to economic possibilities, had long since planted all the land adjacent to their houses with rubber, and are for the most part compelled to farm at a distance, in some cases, of a day's journey and more. In consequence they live away from the long-house on their farms for varying periods from approximately August to March.

A literacy campaign to be successful needs a clear two months, during which people will be continuously at home. But from the time when they first clear the land about August to the harvest, approximately in March, the Paku people are ever being called away to their farms, now for planting, now for weeding, now for the harrowing task of bird-scaring. At no time during this period are they at home continuously for two months.

On this account the period between March and August was the only possible season for the operation. It was in fact planned to begin in April, but we could not begin until May because the primers were not ready in time.

PRELIMINARY STEPS

In order to appraise the situation, I made a visit to the Ulu Paku in company with the registrar of co-operative societies in December 1949. He had arranged a series of meetings at different houses for the purpose of discussing co-operation. These meetings provided good opportunities for assessing opinion, as they were attended by people from practically all the houses in the upper part of the river.

When the problems of co-operation had been discussed, I raised the question of adult literacy, inquiring whether they considered it desirable. On this all were agreed, but they thought it exceedingly onerous to go to school late in life, more especially as learning to read was a lengthy and toilsome matter. I then enlarged on the idea of a literacy campaign in which adults could, by following modern methods, learn to read in a matter of weeks. This evoked approval, and I was requested to organise such a campaign. I made no promises, however, but said that I would see what could be done after harvest. The whole question was discussed at length and several interesting points were raised; for instance, "Should women be literate?" This provoked debate in a vein of broad humour on the merits of literate as against illiterate wives, but the final conclusion was that they were better literate.

These discussions proved to be of a much greater importance than at the time appeared. They were carried on in a sober and unemotional fashion, and events proved that, by causing the whole question of literacy to be talked over, they gave an impetus to the starting for adult classes by the people themselves. Beyond expressing a general willingness to help, I made no promises of any sort, so that the initiative was left with the people, but what I had seen convinced me that there was a demand, and an effective demand for a literacy campaign. I therefore returned to Kuching and set about preparing the requisite primers and other necessary materials.

In March 1950 I paid another visit to the Ulu Paku, this time escorting Miss Gwilliam of the Colonial Office. I had arranged for my assistant, Mr. Ensir, to travel the area at the same time, and between the two of us, all the houses in the upper portion of the river were visited. The object of these visits was to inquire definitely whether or not the people wish to join in a literacy campaign. The response was truly astounding. The discussion of the previous visit had roused interest in the whole question, and many illiterates had set about learning, some by private tuition, some in classes, with the final result that now very few of the men were illiterate and the demand for the campaign was coming almost entirely from the women. Requests for a start to be made came from almost every house in the upper portion of the river, some indeed expressed a measure of impatience, but to suit out work to the demands of agriculture, we decided to put it off till after the harvest, and promised to make a beginning in mid-April. In fact, this was unavoidably delayed until May 8th.

THE PLAN OF OPERATION

The area of operations had been broadly defined as the Ulu Paku. The preliminary survey in March had enabled us to plan exactly for the ten houses to which we had been invited; these lay in the main river from Tanjong upwards, and its tributary the Anyut. They averaged some thirteen doors apiece.

There was no staff apart from my assistant and myself, and to cover the area we planned three tours. The first would allow us approximately three nights in each house; the second, a fortnight later, would allow only a one-night visit; and the third, a month later, would likewise give only one night in each. As explained earlier, our role was that of advisers and organisers; the actual work of teaching would have to be done by volunteers from among the existing literates.

On our first tour we planned to spend three nights teaching, and then to hand over to a local teacher chosen by the pupils themselves. This teacher would have to be selected on the first night, so that he could follow the demonstration of our method, but we calculated that he would have ample time to accustom himself to it; meanwhile the pupils would have overcome the initial and most difficult stage of learning.

During the day most people would be away from the house, and would not normally return till between three and four in the afternoon. We, therefore, planned to begin our classes between four and five o'clock and teach for about two hours, then after a break for the evening meal, to resume until bedtime. This was in practice realised, and classes normally terminated with coffee some time after eleven. The more zealous pupils, however, continued to solicit individual attention long after that, and even the bed was no escape from their importunities, for they would continue to make the approved syllabic sounds until we went to sleep.

Teaching would be done in *ruai*, which combines the characteristic of market-place, tavern, and crêche. This also proved a sound choice, for whilst there was much distraction, and a tendency for dogs, fowls, infants, and irrelevant persons to become confounded with the pupils, it allowed the more bashful and undecided to join the class unobtrusively.

THE METHOD OF TEACHING

The method of teaching was largely based upon that popularised by Dr. Laubach. The first step in devising the course was to make a list of the more common Dayak words, amounting to some nine hundred in all. These were then divided into two groups, one of words containing only open syllables, the other of words using both open and closed. A syllable count was made of each, and the lessons were worked out to introduce the syllables according to the frequency of their occurrence in these counts. One series of twenty-four lessons covered the open syllable words, a subsequent one of twenty-five dealt with the closed syllables. The spelling followed was that of the Howell and Bailey Dictionary, and in the choice of words the Saribas usage was adopted against other alternatives.

The initial stage was to teach the five vowels and two diphthongs (it was found more convenient to treat *oi* as two separate sounds); in each case the letter was accompanied by a mnemonic picture, which gave the pupil a clue to the sound. Having thus learned *a, e, i, o, u, ai, au,* the pupil was introduced to *ka, ke, ki, ko, ku, kai, kau,* and this permitted the building of eight words with simple phrases. In this case only the sound *ka* had a mnemonic picture, the others being deducible from it. The second lesson introduced *ba, be, bi, bo, bu, bai, bau,* and enabled simple sentences to be constructed. Other consonants were added in order of the syllable count. Throughout the first twenty-four lessons, i.e. those dealing with open syllables, all words were printed in capital letters. It is a theory of mine that, in the earlier stages of learning to read, adults can more readily distinguish and memorise capital than small letters, and our experience tended to support this.

The second stage of twenty-five lessons covered the closed syllables. Lesson one dealt with *n* in the forms *an, en, in, on, un, ain, aun,* and *ban, ben, bin, bon, bun, bain, baun.* In these lessons mnemonic pictures were used only for the first syllable in each set, e.g. *an* and *ban.* This series of lessons covered all the closed syllables which actually occur in the language. In the script capital and small letters were used in the normal way, and in the construction of sentences the sottises so painfully common in school readers were avoided; the sentences all dealt with the realities of adult life, e.g. "My wife's mother is mad."

In devising this course it was my intention to teach people to read, but I never envisaged that more than a handful of pupils would learn to write; at least within the compass of the literacy campaign. Experience showed that an enthuiastic adult would acquire a certain competence in reading in a matter of days, but to acquire a similar command of writing would necessitate weeks of hard practice; the hand of the adult is more apt for the *parang* than the pen, and a rare enthusiasm is required to sustain it through the drudgery of learning to write.

Although the whole course was embodied in two small primers, the actual teaching during the first few lessons was almost entirely by syllable cards. These greatly facilitate the task, for one of the difficulties the adult encounters is that of breaking words into syllables. In this the cards are of great assistance, if a pupil is given a card *ka* whose sound he knows, and another similarly familiar, *ki,* he can put them side by side and form the word *kaki,* "a foot." In this way he quickly acquires the syllabic method. The difference between teaching with cards and teaching with a book only in the early lessons proved astonishing, but the value of the cards diminished rapidly after the fifth lesson, for by then the pupils had mastered the method.

THE PRODUCTION OF PRIMERS

The course of instruction was embodied in two primes: *Pengrak Ati* ("The Awakening Mind"), covering the open syllables of the language in twenty-four lessons, and *Pun Penemu* ("The Beginning of Knowledge"), covering the closed syllables in twenty-five lessons. The selling price was thirty and fifty cents respectively. These primers were of octave size and were produced by Gesteprint process.

The matter of each page was drawn out in Indian ink on tracing paper. This allowed not merely for the production of mnemonic pictures, but also for the use of a large script, so bold indeed as to be legible by the veriest glow-worm lamp. These drawings were photo-printed on Geste-film, which were processed, and then put through the Gestetner in the normal fashion. Each primer was produced in an edition of 490 copies.

The Gesteprint process is admirably suited to this type of work, as it gives endless scope for illustrations and does not limit the script to any set forms of type. Lack of experience on our part, however, led to the production of work which did not do the process full justice; and some of the script was unduly heavy, whilst some of the illustrations were a trifle obscure.

The work of drawing the facsimiles of the pages was done by a Chinese artist of much skill and endless patience. Being completely ignorant of Roman script, he made many errors in his treatment of the text, and the need to amend these before the books could be printed delayed production considerably.

In addition to the primers, a foolscap chart showing all the open syllables of the language, together with mnemonic pictures, was also produced. This proved to be of considerable help in the early stages.

The syllable cards contained letters two and a half inches high, which were hand-drawn. Each card had a small hook at the back, so that it could be suspended from a string stretched across a blackboard or along a wall. This proved a great convenience when demonstrating word-building to a class. Smaller cards with letters one inch high were also produced for use by the students individually; these likewise were hand-drawn.

Two folding blackboards of singularly ingenious design were made, but they were of such weight as to be ill-suited to conveyance in the smaller type of *prahu*. They were abandoned in the early stages of the operation and shift was made with wooden walls, partitions, and other suitable surfaces.

THE BACKGROUND

To be fully appreciated, the work of the literacy campaign must be seen against the background of contemporary events in the Paku. The period covered—May, June, and July—coincided with a rubber boom without precedent. Practically the entire population was out tapping from early morning till late afternoon. All the Paku houses possess extensive plantations, and some of these contain comparatively high-yielding trees; at one house I was informed that a man and wife in a normally good day's tapping could get rubber worth twelve dollars.

Even so, it was complained that a considerable portion of the trees were untapped for lack of coolies. Before the war the Dayaks had employed Chinese, but these were no longer obtainable, and they had now to make shift with a limited number of Malays. Such coolies work on a share-cropping basis.

This intense tapping made it practically impossible to travel by *prahu* except in the evenings, for paddlers could not be procured at any other time. On this account we decided to go by land on the second and third tours, and whilst we were in consequence limited to the barest minimum of luggage which we could ourselves carry, we were independent of local assistance in moving about.

In consequence of the rubber boom, there was more money available in the river than before, and this led to a spate of commercial development, of which the co-operative societies were the most important manifestations. Apart from this larger concern, there were many smaller ones, such as shops, and a host of minor partnerships for the marketing of rubber. Some of these commercial ventures were of a novel character, such as the outboard service running regularly between Beduru and Spach.

Saving and investment are also taking place on a large scale. As an example of the latter I would cite the case of two men from the Ulu Layar, who were seeking to invest three hundred dollars in a *tajau*, or ancient jar. This appeared to the Paku people a heaven-sent opportunity for getting rid of their own *tajau*, because they lost all economic significance.

All this activity bore directly on the literacy campaign; it accounted for that demand for arithmetic which everywhere confronted us. It had earlier been suggested that to teach adults arithmetic would merely encourage them in a futile pursuit of "white collar" jobs. This might be true of other places, but it certainly did not hold good of the Ulu Paku. Here the demand for arithmetic sprang directly from the wave of prosperity that was passing over the area; arithmetic was wanted not as a means of escape to professional life; as was frequently said: "If we cannot do sums, we shall certainly be cheated of our money."

Despite the rubber boom, people were under no illusions that a golden age had commenced. They have in the past suffered much from fluctuations of the market, and when, owing to speculation in high financial circles, there was a momentary slump, during which the Spaoh *tawkays* even ceased buying altogether for one morning, the general reaction was: "Of course the boom will not last, that is why we must make the most of its whilst we can." This sound economic common sense has led to an interest in alternative cash crops to rubber, and there were many requests for information on the subject. Not, of course, that people are prepared to abandon their rubber in favour of something else, so long as it is profitable, but when the slump does come they want to be able to plant some alternative crop without delay. This interest in cash crops is at the moment academic; it is a quest for information, but it is a very useful line in the production of follow-up literature.

REACTIONS

Any operation such as a literacy campaign can be expected to call forth interesting reactions from people of various types. The following are generalisations based on our experience:

(a) Literates were very helpful. There was no trace of opposition on their part to an extension of literacy, as has been found in some other literacy campaigns.

(b) Children did not come within the scope of the campaign. Any that attended the initial classes were either sent away by the parents or soon lost interest and withdrew. In some cases the older boys (aged eighteen to twenty) helped as teachers, but this was always on the invitation of the adults.

(c) Old men were either literate or too decayed in senility to learn.

(d) Husbands were by the time of our arrival practically all literate, and were interested almost entirely in arithmetic. So far from offering any opposition to their wives becoming literate, all gave encouragement, and some were assiduous in helping them to learn.

(e) Old women provided one of the major surprises. An astonishing number joined the classes, and they became some of the most eager pupils, indeed the enthusiasm of some importunate grandmothers was most exhausting.

(f) Wives provided the majority of the pupils and were most assiduous. The exact motives behind their desire for literacy were difficult to define; basically, I imagine, it was a wish to keep up with their husbands, for women in Dayak society have always enjoyed a practical equality with men, indeed Dayak husbands seem more henpecked than most.

(*g*) Opposition came from only one quarter down-river and was then largely due to existing jealousies between rival communities. It was formulated in the phrase: "What good will it (literacy) do you?"

THE LESSONS LEARNED

(*a*) The extent of spontaneous activity that can result from even slight encouragement. One of the most remarkable features of the operation was the impetus given by the preliminary visits and discussions to spontaneous activity by the people themselves. The fact that so many of the men learned to read, and that small classes and groups started up without any external help, is an index of what even a slight impetus can achieve in a really progressive community.

(*b*) The danger of under-estimating women. Throughout the preliminary visits there was little indication of any outstanding interest in literacy on the part of the women. The statistics of girls' school attendance would suggest a lack of enthusiasm, whereas in fact there was an exceedingly active interest on their part, as was shown when we commenced to teach.

(*c*) The weakness of relying on existing literates as helpers, when there is a question of using a new method of teaching. Although we had given them three evenings of intensive demonstration, none of our helpers proved capable of teaching by the phonetic method. They themselves had been taught in school by a purely alphabetic method. They would spell out each word, letter by letter, using the English names for these letters, which bore no relation whatsoever to the Dayak sounds. With this method it is quite possible for a pupil to spell a word without giving any idea of what its sound is; indeed, it treats all words as if there were Chinese ideographs, which have to be memorised individually. By following our phonetic course a pupil could learn to read with both ease and speed, but in the hands of our helpers all these advantages were thrown to the winds, and progress became a slow and toilsome grind. It speaks volumes for the enthusiasm of our pupils that, even despite this, they persevered and became literate.

In dealing with a community that is already partially literate it is difficult to see how one can avoid using helpers, who have themselves been trained in obsolete ways, and will certainly not use the phonetic or any other progressive method. In such circumstances there is little to be done beyond trying to minimise the evils. When, however, there is a question of dealing with a totally illiterate community the problem is much simpler, for the helpers themselves will have to be trained first, and they can then be depended upon to use the phonetic correctly. Such a procedure could not be followed where there were already literates, as these latter would invariably be selected as teachers by the pupils, who would always have more confidence in them than in somebody who had newly learned to read.

(d) The type of organisation needed for an area in which there are no literates. Here the first step would be select one person of promise from each house as a teacher. These teachers would then all be assembled at a centre and themselves given an intensive course in phonetic teaching lasting about a fortnight. This should be sufficient for an intelligent man to absorb all the forty-nine lessons in reading. He would not, of course, be able to write; certainly not to write on a blackboard for teaching purposes; hence he would have to be provided with a large supply of syllable cards as a substitute. No doubt in time he would learn to write, as would some of his pupils; but for the time being he would have to rely entirely on the cards and primers for teaching reading. Provided there were an occasional visit from a supervisor, this would, I think, be a satisfactory way of tackling illiteracy in the more backward areas.

(e) A larger number of the syllable cards is needed. Those that we used were hand-drawn and there were not enough of them. A large supply of both sizes of card is desirable.

(f) The supply of vernacular literature needs to be much augmented. There is a pathetic lack of reading matter in the language, and the most urgent need at the moment is for books that are entertaining or interesting, but not necessarily improving.

When the subject of literacy campaign was first discussed by the adult education committee, I suggested that before such an operation were undertaken, it would be better to spend a year or so concentrating on the production of vernacular literature, and I am still of opinion that this would have been a wiser course. The lack of reading matter everywhere confronted us; indeed, it was astonishing to find so much enthusiasm to learn, when there was so little to read. Further, the extent to which the results of the campaign will prove permanent must largely depend on the rate on which books can now be produced, for there are many examples elsewhere of literacy campaigns being followed by relapse back into illiteracy for lack of anything to read. In this case we had the advantage of a monthly journal and some half-dozen books already printed in the language, which provided a bare nucleus of reading matter, but from our experience I would most strongly urge that no further literacy campaign be undertaken in local vernaculars until a substantial number of books have been produced.

Index

ACAR, 79
acceptance rate, 264
adopter, 11
adultery, 131
adult education, 271
affiliations, organizational, 14
age, respect for, 276, 277
agriculture, 8, 166
Americans, 2
American Friends, 165, 194
Anchau Scheme, 109
Andes, 60
anomie, 135
anthropology, 61, 67, 87, 193
anti-Americanism, 241
apathy, peasant, 164
APRA, 74
Arab refugees, 165
arithmetic, learning of, 301
Asia, 34
attitude toward change, 58, 164, 184
authoritarianism 87, 108, 236
Ayacucho, 75
Aymara, 46, 54, 56

Ba-Ila, 126
Barpali, 194
beadwork, 149
behavioral science, 67
beliefs, 3, 37
    medical, 38
    supernatural, 37, 200, 218
Berelson, Bernard, 256
birth rate, 126, 258
Blanchard, William, 65
Bolivia, 42-57
bone-meal, 207
Brahmin caste, 228
Brazil, 77-90
bridges, building of, 4, 6
British Africa, 107, 118
Buddhism, 233-245

canals, 281
case history method, 5

cash crops, 302
caste-class, 34, 192, 199, 209
Catholicism, 73
cattle, 157, 162
central authority, 36
Chamar caste, 206, 209
change agents, 8, 11, 13, 17, 18, 20, 86
change, constancy of, 1
    economic, 3
    process, 10, 12
    projects, 7, 8
    technical, 3
chiefs, 127
children, love of, 134
Christianity, 233
circulation effect, 261
cities, 135, 246
civic organizations, 33
civil servants, 32
climate, 122
coercion, 108, 116, 118, 125
colonial period, 107, 118
Comilla Academy, 177, 189
commercial development, 301
committees, 102
communal labor, 115, 239
communication, audio-visual, 16, 17, 85, 100, 101, 102, 254, 260, 261, 299
    channels of, 13, 15, 56, 59, 77, 88, 92, 108, 119, 125, 156, 164, 246, 256
    demonstration, 17
    feed back, 18, 121
    formal, 15, 100, 197, 260, 294
    personal, 16, 18, 168, 189, 260
    among recipients, 24
Communist party, 73
community center, 80, 137
community development, 20, 42-57, 58-76, 77-90, 135-154, 186, 191-216, 237, 246-254, 268-290, 271, 293
Community Development Bulletin, 248

307

Community Development Review, 157
community disorganization, 64
community education, 278
community rivalry, 303
community selection, 91, 95
competition, 29, 225
compost pits, 287
concepts of disease, 112, 116, 124, 130, 191, 276
conflict, 230
constitution, 250
consumption patterns, 39
continuity, of projects, 19, 22
contraception, 259, 262, 265
contractors, 183
contribution, public, 186
convenience, motivation of, 28, 198
Cooper, B. K., 120
co-operation, 225, 246, 295
co-operatives, 42, 50, 93, 94, 98, 164-174, 192, 206, 293
Cornell University, 60, 67
Costa Rica, 91-106
coup d'état, 241
court action, 230
crafts, traditional, 136, 149
credit, 83, 104
crisis, 21, 59
cultural change, 115, 140
cultural linkage, 198, 212
cultural patterns, 22, 108, 212
cultural resistances, 153, 148
culture, 1
    integration of, 21
    local, 21
    traditional, 11, 30
    utilization of local, 21
culture contact, 109
curses, 151
customs, 3, 22, 39, 148
    sexual, 125, 133
Cuzco, 75

dam, 282
debts, 171, 208
decision making, 165, 167, 172, 193, 210, 237
defecation, 198
Delhi, 227
democracy, 60
democratic method, 99
demonstration, 17, 22, 27, 124, 152, 164, 197, 202
diesel plant, 103
diet, 176, 187, 203
diffusion, of ideas, 2, 261
discussions, 294
disputes, 185, 237

Dobyns, Henry F., 67
doctrine, religious, 235
drainage, 178
Dyak, 291
dyes, 207

economic benefits, 27, 165, 203
economic system, 36, 42, 160
economics, agricultural, 96
education, 28, 43, 52, 53, 57, 82, 85, 99, 161
    agricultural, 167
egalitarianism, 35
elders, 114, 269, 276
electric plant, 98
élite, 36, 107
Emir, 111, 114
employee relations, 211
engineer, sociocultural, 4
engineering, 183
English learning, 240
Entokozweni, 137
environment, adaptation to, 1, 199
epidemic, 110
ethnic groups, 35
Europe, 3
Evans, A. J., 126
experimentation, social science, 256, 260
expert, 14

factionalism, 213, 225-232
family, 34, 302
family planning, 255-267
fatalism, realistic, 38
felt need, 25-26, 92, 96, 98, 116, 118, 197, 255, 270
fertilizer, 167, 169, 207
films, 101
fines, 129
fire prevention, 282
flexibility of implementation, 22, 119, 122, 180, 285
folk dances, 150
food, consumption of, 3-4, 187
Foster, George M., 225
Fraser, Thomas M., 193
Freedman, Ronald, 256
Fulani, 111
funerals, 133

Galilee, 166
galvanized roofing, 240
gambling, 239
germ theory, 108, 124, 200
Gesteprint process, 299
goddess, 219
gonorrhoea, 128
gossip, 24, 77, 256

graft, 185
government, national, 75
group behavior, 15, 226, 246
Gujjar caste, 228

Hausa, 109
Harijans, 199, 204, 228
headmen, 32, 111, 115, 127, 237, 244
healer, traditional, 55
health, 8
health center, 139
health education, 85, 217-224
health projects, 25, 55, 82
hierarchy, 16, 18, 108, 111
Hinduism, 3, 218, 235
Hirakud Dam, 195
Holmberg, Allan R., 60
home visits, 168, 260
Hong Kong, 246-254
housing, 118, 120
humanitarianism, 107
Human Organization, 109, 137, 193, 271

Ibadan, 120
illness, 38
illustration, 17
International Labor Organization, 45, 47
income, 170
India, 39, 191-216, 217-224, 225-232
Indians, American, 2, 3, 35, 42, 58
indirect rule, 111, 114
induced needs, 152
infant mortality, 259
innovation, adaptive, 21, 31, 56, 77, 155, 218, 226, 247, 270
  continuity of, 22
  flexibility in, 22
  maintenance of, 23, 176, 199, 234, 243, 292
  replacement, 21, 270
  techniques of, 23
  timing of, 21
innovator characteristics, 11, 13
insecticides, 169
Institute of Indian Affairs, 63, 65, 67, 79
institution building, 20
International Co-operation Administration, 157
International Development Review, 177
intra-uterine devices, 265
irrigation, 178
Islam, 3, 235
Israel, 164-174

Johannesburg, 137
Junod, Violaine, 137

Kaifong, 248
Keen, K., 248
Khadi, 210
Khan, A. H., 177
kinship, 34, 275
Kong Le, 241
Koran, 113
Kotwali Thana, 177

language, 1
  use of local, 13, 42, 148
language learning, 240, 303
Lake Titicaca, 45
land expropriation, 53
land reform, 42-57
land tenure, 42, 96, 160, 285
landlords, 69, 72
Laos, 40, 233-245
La Paz, 45
latrines, 17, 59, 84, 89, 191, 196, 269, 287, 289
Laubach method, 298
law enforcement, 279
leadership, administrative, 31, 237, 244, 283, 288
  eduators, 32, 54, 244, 268, 273, 279, 288
  local, 21, 31, 50, 77, 89, 98, 167, 177, 185, 211, 247, 273, 275
  religious, 6, 24, 32, 73, 218, 219, 233
Lear, John, 60
leather workers, 206
Leghorns, 204
Link, Eugene P., 219, 227
literacy, 28, 29, 32, 291-305
livestock, 51
loans, 71

machinery, 51, 53, 166, 168, 170
magic, 150
Mahony, Frank, 157
mail campaign, 260
maintenance of innovations, 23
malaria eradication, 20
Mali caste, 201
manual labor, attitude toward, 274
marketing, 202, 209
Marshall Plan, 3
mass media, 17
McDouall, J. C., 248
medicine, 27, 221
Mehta, Sushila, 219, 227
merchants, 70
merit making, 238, 244
Mestizos, 69, 70

migration, 68, 295
  to city, 135
migratory labor, 133
milk, powdered, 4
milk consumption, 24, 39
Minas Gerais, 78
Miner, Horace, 109
model village, 120
Mohsen, A. K., 177
Monge, Carlos, 63, 65, 67
morality, 131
motivation, for change, 24, 257, 291
  convenience, 28, 198
  economic, 27
  educational, 28
  felt need, 25
  medical, 27
  novelty, 30
  practical benefit, 26
  reward, 29

Nash, T. A., 110
nation state, 175
National Bank of Costa Rica, 93
negativism, project, 38
Negros Island, 271
neighborhood, 248
nervous system, 112
newspapers, 74, 252, 254
Nicholl, Robert, 293
Niehoff, Arthur, 234
Nigeria, 107-117, 118-123
nomads, 159, 160
norms, 212
nutritional standard, 203

Oberg, Kalervo, 78
officials, 16, 59
Orata, Pedro T., 278
ordinances, 289
Organization of American States, 93
organizations, civic, 86
Orissa, 194, 219
over-grazing, 160
over-population, 120
Oversea Education, 278, 293

pagoda, 238, 244
Pakistan, East, 175-190
Pakse, 241
pamphlets, 102
Pan American Union, 93
panchayat, 229
participation, labor and time, 19,
    115, 176
  material contribution, 19, 186
  organizational, 20
  passive, 20

on projects, 18, 20, 92, 119, 165,
    171, 193, 243, 292
passive resistance, 108, 112
patron, 63
Pax Britannica, 110, 119
Peace Corps, 182
penicillin, 38, 129
personality, change agent, 13
Peru, 58-76
Philippines, 268-290
pigs, 278, 287
Pillapi estate, 45
pilot project, 91, 137, 157, 177, 293
ploughing, 168
police, 159, 279
politeness, 111, 148
politics, 35, 77, 87, 111, 229, 240,
    286
Population Council 257
population explosion, 255
pork, consumption of, 3
position of women, 296, 302
positivism, 39
posters, 101, 260
potatoes, 65
poultry, 201
practical benefit, 203
practices, local, 39 /
prestige emulation, 29
primers, 299
project, agricultural, 166
project administration, 146, 180
project co-ordination, 80, 86
project planning, 8, 77, 107, 118,
    120, 179, 214, 215, 291
projects, health, 20, 25, 84, 107-117,
    124, 172, 269, 287
  vegetable gardening, 144, 201
proprietary rights, 155
psychoanalysis, 60
Public Law, 177, 480
public service, 249
Puno-Tambopata Project, 75

quality control, 208
Quechua, 63
questionnaire, 97

race relations, 145, 152
racism, 135
rainy season, 284
range management, 155-163
rapport, 13
"rationalism," 108, 151
rationalizations, 234
rational behavior, 292
reaction, recipient, 23
reading matter, 304
recreation patterns, 39, 200

religions, world, 37
religious expenditures, 236
resettlement, 118-123
resources, limitations of, 225
responsibility, delegation of, 247
revolution, 44, 60
reward-punishment, 29, 119, 176, 292, 294
Rhodes-Livingstone Journal, 126
risk taking, 210
ritual purity, 200, 213
road construction, 172, 188, 284
role behavior, 274
role of change agent, 13, 136, 141
rubber boom, 300
rumors, 24
rural development, 175-190

sanitary practices, 196, 281
Sanskritization, 205
Sarawak, 291-305
Saturday Review, 60, 67
school boys, 279, 287, 288
school, night, 144
  nursery, 143
schools, 52, 53, 68, 89
Schweng, Lorand D., 44
Scientific American, 256
seeds, improved, 170
self-help, 54, 77, 91-106, 237, 294
servicio, 78
Sharp, Lauriston, 61
shoemakers, 206
Sibley, Willis E., 271
slavery, 110
sleeping sickness, 107-117
smallpox, 219
Smithsonian Institute, 87
social environment, 135
social mobility, 205
social pressure, 119
social structure, 33, 58, 191, 227, 271
social survey, 139
social worker, 220, 230
sociocultural system, 5
sociology, rural, 96
South Africa, 135-154
South America, 60
Southeast Asia, 24, 35
Somalia, 155-163
Spanish, 54, 56
spirits, 113, 116, 200, 218
standard of living, 91, 258
status, 87, 274
status quo, 70
stereotype, 234
students, high school, 283
study club, 100

subsidies, 176
supernatural, 108, 113
superstition, 37
surveying, 184
survey, socioeconomic, 96
syllabic writing, 298
syllable cards, 300, 304
syphilis, 128

Taichung, 258
Taiwan, 255-267
teaching aids, 299
teaching methods, 303, 304
technical advice, 182
technical advisers, 4, 18, 234
technical competence, 13, 14
technical solutions, 155
terrorism, 241
test plots, 167
Thailand, 39, 237
Theravada Buddhism, 234
time sense, 148
timing of innovations, 21, 199, 295
tractors, 51, 171
tradition, 159
training, administrative, 189
  technical, 182, 184
tribalism, 158
Tsetse fly, 108, 131
Tur'an Project, 165

Union Councils, 179
United States, 3, 17
United States aid, 238
United States Embassy, 101
University of Michigan, 258
urban influence, 227

vaccination, 217, 220
Vasquez, Mario C., 65, 67
vegetarianism, 204
venereal disease, 124-134
vested interests, 31, 33, 42, 59, 77, 89, 185, 285
veterans, 68
Vicos, 58-76
Vietnam, 233
village pride, 122
village rivalry, 123
vocational training, 53, 75
voting, 286

Washington, D.C., 61
water boiling, 26, 38
water control, 177
water resources, 156, 196, 281
weavers, 206, 207

welfare association, 248
wells, 28, 196, 234, 241
Westernization, 140, 149
wheat consumption, 4, 187
witchcraft, 150
work patterns, 275, 295
work program, 177
writing skills, 299

yields, agricultural, 170
Yoruba, 120
younger generation, 269, 276
youth club, 231
youth training, 172

Zambia, 124-134
Zulu, 141